CU00839292

The Daily Telegraph

AIRMEN'S
OBITUARIES
BOOK THREE

The Daily Telegraph

AIRMEN'S OBITUARIES

BOOK THREE

Compiled and Edited by

AIR COMMODORE GRAHAM PITCHFORK MBE, BA, FRAeS

Foreword by Air Chief Marshal
Sir Richard Johns GCB, KCVO, CBE, FRAeS

GRUB STREET • LONDON

Published by
Grub Street
4 Rainham Close
London SW11 6SS

A CIP record for this title is available from the British library

ISBN-13: 978-1-911621-92-8

Design by Lucy Thorne

Printed and bound by Finidr in the Czech Republic

DRAMATIS PERSONAE
(in order of appearance)

FOREWORD

Since retiring from the Royal Air Force in 1995 Air Commodore Graham Pitchfork has established an enviable reputation as a chronicler of RAF history. He is the author of 14 books, most notably *The Royal Air Force Day by Day*, which was specially commissioned by the Chief of the Air Staff to record the RAF's first 100 years of service to the nation.

As an extension of his authorship Graham Pitchfork has been the aviation obituary writer for the *Daily Telegraph*. Since 2003, 610 of his obituaries have been published from which he has selected 91 for publication in this third book of airmen's obituaries; they cover the period from 2007 to the end of 2017.

The obits paint vivid pictures of the men and women who contributed so much to the development and employment of our national air power during times of war and peace. As may be expected the majority served with professional distinction and great courage during the Second World War and subsequent conflicts. While fighter and bomber pilots are in the majority, others involved in less dazzling activities such as maritime and transport operations, including the ladies of the Air Transport Auxiliary, receive public recognition so richly deserved.

But this is not to the omission of other specialists such as those involved in aviation medicine whose work was vital to ensure air crews could accommodate ever-increasing physical demands of rapidly advancing aircraft performance – particularly the challenge of 'G' loading and high altitude flying.

The rank and file of the RAF was truly cosmopolitan as evidenced by the vengeful young men from the occupied countries of Europe who continued their fight from the UK. And there they were joined by many others from the dominions and North America who enlisted in the RAF long before the United States entered the global conflict. The obituaries in this volume pay fulsome tribute to the heroic scale of their contributions to eventual victory.

Today, common knowledge of RAF history in the Second World War goes no further than the Battle of Britain and the bomber offensive with occasional acknowledgement of Coastal Command's activities during the Battle of the Atlantic. The obituaries in this volume thus merit detailed study to inform understanding of the sheer scale and imaginative variety of RAF operations conducted from the ground as well as from the air. Moreover while pilots enjoy the lion's share of plaudits, it is pleasing to read about the honing of navigational skills by some quite exceptional airmen who relied principally on the accuracy of their dead reckoning and exceptional map-reading skills; and all of this long before technology was to guarantee the accuracy that today we take for granted.

It was my good fortune to serve under command of some of those whose deeds of valour are recorded in this book. By far the majority were the products of grammar schools and technical colleges who were to thrive within a service that was, and remains, a true meritocracy. Not surprising perhaps that so many were to enjoy successful second careers in a wide variety of employment that took them comfortably into old age and eventual retirement.

I have resisted the temptation to try to name names in this foreword with attribution of aeronautical achievements to individuals. It's simply impossible to judge objectively their comparative value and it is for this reason that the book offers the reader many surprises that merit consideration and admiration in equal measure. Graham Pitchfork's industry in compiling each and every one of the obituaries most certainly merits our congratulations and thanks.

Air Chief Marshal Sir Richard Johns
GCB, KCVO, CBE, FRAeS

INTRODUCTION

Since the publication of Book Two in 2007 of *The Daily Tele-graph Book of Airmen's Obituaries*, a further 476 airmen's obitu-aries have been published in the newspaper. This presented me with an extremely difficult task to select about 90 for inclu-sion in this volume. To ease the task slightly, I decided to limit the choice to those published before the end of 2017. Never-theless, this left me with a very wide choice and many that I would dearly loved to have included have had to be left out.

It was important to have variety and to include as many as-pects of the aviation world as possible. As might be expected, the majority outline the remarkable lives of those involved in the Second World War including those of our Common-wealth and Allies who answered the call. As that patriotic generation fades away, inevitably there is an increasing num-ber of those who took part in later conflicts. As a former RAF officer, I am very conscious of the crucial roles played by men and women of the non-flying branches, and of those in other sectors of aviation, and a selection of them deserve their place in this collection.

In preparing the obituaries I have received a great deal of assistance from many people. Without the help of Sebastian Cox and his superb staff at the Air Historical Branch, of Susan Dransfield and Tim Pierce at the RAF College Cranwell, and friends from the RAF Historical Society, my task would have been immensely difficult.

The staff of the *Daily Telegraph* obituaries desk have been patient, have given me wise advice and encouragement – they have also become great friends and I want particularly to thank the current team of Andrew Brown, Katharine Ramsay and Chris Maume. Amongst their predecessors, Harry de Quette-ville, Jay Iliff and David Twiston-Davies guided me through the early days of my time. I also want to thank Michael Stenz for paving the way for this edition to be published.

Relatives of those included have provided the majority of the photographs that appear in the text. Where I struggled, Lee

Barton of the RAF Air Historical Branch came to my rescue. I am also grateful to the British Airways Heritage Collection for the photograph of Barbara Harmer and to the United States Air Force Historical Research Agency for the photograph of Lieutenant Colonel Archer.

Finally, my thanks goes to Air Chief Marshal Sir Richard Johns, whose dynamic leadership of the RAF I witnessed at first hand, for his eloquent foreword and to John Davies and his superb staff at Grub Street.

Air Commodore Graham Pitchfork
MBE, BA, FRAeS

GROUP CAPTAIN PETER NORTON-SMITH

Group Captain Peter Norton-Smith (who died on May 18, 2007 aged 91) carried out a spectacular air evacuation of British families during riots in Burma in 1949.

In March that year Norton-Smith was the senior flying training advisor to the Burmese government when insurgents captured the town of Maymyo, a hill station in Upper Burma where a British Army Staff College was located. All road communications were cut off and the evacuation of the British community had to be planned by air. Norton-Smith took charge of the situation and elected to land a twin-engine Anson transport aircraft on a makeshift strip on the nearby racecourse to rescue the British wives and children.

The weight of the aircraft had to be reduced to an absolute minimum; every piece of loose equipment was stripped out and a barely sufficient amount of fuel was taken on board (Norton-Smith even declined his breakfast).

The cleared strip was only 450 yards long and a belt of high trees seriously hindered the aircraft's approach; a landing was made even more dangerous by a strong crosswind. Despite these major difficulties, Norton-Smith made a perfect landing and took off with his passengers. Two RAF pilots who observed the operation said it was one of the finest feats of flying they had ever seen.

Norton-Smith was subsequently awarded the AFC and the citation concluded, "he appeared completely unconcerned and his calm manner did as much to hearten the beleaguered British community as did the superb handling of his aircraft".

Peter Norton-Smith was born on May 18, 1915 and educated at Brighton College. He joined the RAF Volunteer Reserve in 1939, completing his initial training as a pilot with the de Havilland School of Flying at Hatfield.

He was commissioned in November 1940 and posted to No. 50 Squadron to fly the Hampden bomber, a pre-war design. The lightly armed Hampden was used for bombing targets in the Ruhr and for minelaying operations off the Dutch coast and in the Kattegat. Losses were high, but Norton-Smith completed 32 operations and was awarded the DFC.

After attending a course at the Central Flying School, he became an instructor at a bomber training unit equipped with the Wellington. For the 1,000-Bomber Raids mounted in May and June 1942, the main bomber force had to be supplemented by aircraft from the training units flown by instructor crews. Norton-Smith took a war-weary Wellington to Essen and a few weeks later flew three more bomber operations before he was sent to Palestine to train RAF and South African bomber crews destined for the squadrons based in the Middle East.

Early in 1944, Norton-Smith was appointed a flight commander with No. 104 Squadron, which had recently arrived at Foggia in Italy, flying Wellingtons. As well as bombing ports and marshalling yards in the north of Italy, he flew re-supply missions in support of the Yugoslav partisans. In January he was promoted to wing commander and took command of another Italy-based Wellington squadron, No. 40. After the loss of its previous commanding officer (CO), morale was low, but under Norton-Smith's quiet, unassuming leadership, this was soon changed.

The squadron flew a mix of supply drops to the partisans and bombing operations, the latter including nerve-wracking sorties bombing enemy troops a few hundred yards ahead of the Eighth Army lines.

In March, No. 40 started to receive the four-engine Liberator heavy bomber. As a previous bomber instructor, Norton-Smith took on the majority of sorties to train the new pilots. He also continued flying operations, which included longer-range sorties to southern Germany and Austria. By the end of the war he had flown a further 23 operations and was twice mentioned in despatches.

With the end of the war in Europe, No. 40 was employed in

the transport role, including the repatriation of POWs from Italy. Landing at an airfield in Hampshire, Norton-Smith ensured that there was always a 36-gallon barrel of beer for his squadron on his returning aircraft – a gesture that further enhanced his reputation with his ground crew. When his own airmen were repatriated to England, some after five years on the squadron, he paid handsome tribute to their service and loyalty.

Norton-Smith took No. 40 to Egypt in October 1945 and left for a staff appointment four months later. His adjutant commented: "He had done a first-class job restoring the vigour and enthusiasm with his quiet authority and willingness to lead from the front."

Norton-Smith was instructing at an advanced flying school when he learned of a vacancy in Burma. Knowing that the job offered variety, and that the area was endowed with excellent fishing and guinea fowl shooting, he decided to apply. For the next two years he trained the aspiring pilots of the young Burmese Air Force. At the end of his appointment, the Burmese government awarded him the Burmese Air Force Flying Wings.

After attending the RAF Flying College, Norton-Smith was given command of No. 269 Squadron flying the Shackleton in the maritime-reconnaissance role. He took a detachment to Darwin to fly support operations during the testing of the British atom bomb at Monte Bello Islands off the coast of Western Australia in May 1956.

After promotion to group captain in 1959 and an appointment as the senior air staff officer at HQ No. 18 (Coastal) Group in Scotland, his last appointment was as the commanding officer of RAF North Front, Gibraltar. He retired in June 1965 when he was appointed CBE.

He and his wife Teresa moved to Devon to fish the rivers of the south-west. They were instrumental in the rejuvenation of the River Torridge that was, at the time, heavily polluted with farm effluent. The Torridge once again became one of the best salmon pool wild fishing rivers in Devon. They also established a fishery at their house for the replenishment and conservation of stocks. Norton-Smith was the chairman of the Torridge Fishing Association, a post his wife held later.

A hair-wing salmon fly was created in his honour, and the Norton-Smiths were the subject of a poem, *Torridge Salmon*, by Ted Hughes.

Peter Norton-Smith married Teresa Tapper in 1948 with whom he had a son and daughter.

BRIGADIER GENERAL ROBIN OLDS

Brigadier General Robin Olds (who died on June 14, 2007 aged 84) was one of the USAF's most charismatic fighter pilots, achieving 'ace' status during the Second World War before implementing innovative tactics during the Vietnam War, when he was widely recognised as the outstanding fighter leader during the campaign in South East Asia.

Olds had just been promoted to colonel when he was sent in October 1966 to command the 8th Tactical Fighter Wing (TFW) – the 'Wolfpack' – based at Ubon in Thailand. He was 44 years old and a highly experienced fighter pilot. His views on tactics did not always accord with accepted practices and current fighter-pilot training and he immediately set about introducing a new approach to combating the North Vietnamese MiG fighters.

He set the tone for his period in command by immediately placing himself on the flight schedule as a rookie pilot under officers junior to himself, then challenging them to train him properly because he would soon be leading them.

In January 1967 he led his wing over North Vietnam against the enemy's new aggressive MiG-21s on Operation Bolo, later recognised as the most successful air battle of the Vietnam War. His detailed plan was to simulate a bomber formation using their tactics, radio call signs and electronic countermeasures. He timed the attack to arrive in the area where the MiGs would be flying a standing patrol, and catch them as they returned to their airfields short of fuel.

The weather was poor when Olds and his formation of Phantom F-4Cs arrived over Hanoi, but he soon caught some enemy fighters and launched two air-to-air missiles against one of them: the MiG-21 exploded.

The pilots of the 8th TFW gained the advantage and they shot down seven of the enemy and suffered no losses. Olds' tactics, and the aggressive spirit he had given to his crews, gave them a psychological advantage over the North Vietnamese Air Force, which became very wary of the Americans' superior fighters after their severe losses.

In May, Olds destroyed another MiG and two weeks later

he was flying during one of the USAF's biggest raids north of Hanoi when he shot down two more, making him the most successful fighter pilot during the early years of the Vietnam War. He was awarded the Air Force Cross, one of America's highest decorations, and the Vietnam Distinguished Service Order.

When Olds left Vietnam in October 1967, he had flown 152 combat missions; his predecessor had flown 12 over a similar period of time. His wing had accounted for 24 aerial victories, a total unsurpassed by any other during the war in Vietnam.

The son of a US Army Air Corps brigadier general, Robin Olds was born on July 14, 1922 in Honolulu and spent his younger years in Virginia, where he was educated at Hampton High School, before attending the United States Military Academy at West Point. He was a member of the academy football team and was selected as an All-American tackle in 1942. He completed his pilot training in 1943.

Olds joined the 434th Fighter Squadron and sailed for England in May 1944. Flying the P-38 Lightning fighter he became an 'ace' (five aerial victories) after his first two combat missions. On August 14, he shot down two Focke-Wulf Fw 190s over northern France. Eleven days later, flying on a long-range escort sortie to Rostock, he accounted for three Messerschmitt Bf 109s.

In September his squadron converted to the P-51 Mustang and he achieved his next success on October 6. He did not score again until February 9 when he downed a Bf 109 over Magdeburg. Over Berlin five days later he shot down two fighters and a month later he destroyed two more.

Promoted to major when he was 22, he took command of the 434th nine months after being the junior pilot. On April 7 he was escorting bombers deep over Germany when he shot down a Bf 109, his last success of the war. During 107 combat sorties, Olds was also credited with destroying 11 aircraft on the ground during strafing attacks in addition to his 13 air-to-air successes.

To add to his US Silver Star, Legion of Merit and Distinguished Flying Cross, he was awarded the British DFC, for "his great skill, bravery and aggressive leadership". He was also awarded the French Croix de Guerre.

On his return to America, Olds was assigned to the first jet squadron and was a member of the USAF's first jet aerobatic team. In October 1948 he returned to England under a USAF-RAF exchange programme and joined the RAF's No. 1 Squadron flying Meteor jet fighters from Tangmere in Sussex. Six months later, Olds took command of No. 1, the first USAF exchange officer to command an RAF squadron.

He later served as the commander of a Sabre fighter wing based in Germany before assuming a staff appointment in Washington. In September 1963, Olds was given command of the 81st Tactical Fighter Wing at Bentwaters in Suffolk flying the F-101 Voodoo fighter-bomber.

On completion of his one-year tour of duty in Vietnam, Olds was promoted to brigadier general and became the commandant of cadets at the US Air Force Academy at Colorado Springs. In February 1971 he became the director of Aerospace Safety but was restless to return to flying operations. He offered to drop a rank to take command of a fighter wing in Vietnam, but when this was refused he retired to the ski slopes of Colorado in June 1973.

Olds was the epitome of the aggressive fighter pilot who led from the front. He was a flamboyant and courageous leader and one of his senior pilots in Vietnam commented: "Quite simply, he was a leader of men to an extent that few have become, and the finest USAF fighter pilots of the day worked their way to Ubon to follow this icon into combat."

During his time in Vietnam he grew an extravagant waxed handlebar moustache as a mark of his individuality. On his return home he soon discovered that not everyone appreciated his maverick behaviour. When he reported to the Air Force Chief in Washington, he stood to attention and saluted. The chief walked up to him, stuck a finger under his nose and said: "Get it off." Olds replied: "Yes sir."

Olds was inducted into the US National Aviation Hall of

Fame in 2001 when he became the only person to be enshrined in the Aviation Hall and the College Football Hall of Fame.

Until a few months before his death he remained in great demand as a speaker and lecturer for his inspirational and motivational talks.

Robin Olds married the Hollywood actress Ella Raines in 1947 with whom he had two daughters. They separated in 1975 and after her death in 1988, he married his second wife Morgan; they were later divorced.

WING COMMANDER 'TUBBY' BAKER

Wing Commander 'Tubby' Baker (who died on July 28, 2007 aged 88) was among Bomber Command's most experienced Pathfinder master bombers and one of the RAF's most highly decorated pilots.

It was Bomber Command policy to 'screen' aircrew after they had completed two tours of operations and post them to non-operational jobs. But as soon as Baker reached the end of his second tour in September 1944, he immediately volunteered to start a third.

His bombing career started in March 1943 when he joined No. 7 Squadron, equipped with the four-engine Stirling bomber at RAF Oakington near Cambridge. On March 27 he attacked Berlin and, as he commenced his target run, his aircraft was 'coned' by searchlights and hit several times by anti-aircraft fire; one destroyed an engine and seriously damaged another. In attempting to evade the searchlights and flak, he lost a great deal of height; the damaged bomber was unable to climb and he was forced to take a longer route home than planned.

Baker's aircraft had suffered other damage as well and was difficult to control. After five exhausting hours he arrived back at Oakington after being airborne for eight hours. The flak had damaged a wheel and his undercarriage collapsed on landing, causing the aircraft to slew across the airfield; the Stirling was a write-off.

Over the next few months Baker attacked all the major targets, including Bremen, Munich, Magdeburg and Kiel. He flew on all four of the raids in what became known as the Battle of Hamburg and, returning from one of them, his gunners shot down an enemy night-fighter. A few days later he was awarded the DFC.

On August 17, 1943 Baker attacked the secret weapons testing establishment at Peenemünde. Rather than make a steady bombing run, his tactic was to approach the target in a curve, and weave before levelling out for the last 15 seconds to release his bombs. His bomb aimer commented: "That's how I survived so many trips with pilots like Baker."

Due to the heavy losses in the Stirling force, Baker was appointed a flight commander a few months after his arrival. He attacked Berlin again and bombed targets in the Ruhr. On raids to Turin and Milan he was airborne for over 10 hours. After 40 operations he was rested and awarded the DSO.

Sidney Baker was born in Bristol on November 19, 1918. After attending St George's School, Bristol, he spent three years as a clerk with the London, Midland and Scottish Railway. He joined the RAF in March 1940 and trained as a pilot.

He was identified as an above-average pilot and immediately after gaining his wings he became a pilot instructor for a year. During his training to fly bombers in December 1942, his Wellington flew into high ground in the Pennines and burnt out. All his crew survived but he later described it as "that ghastly night in the Peak District". In March 1943 he joined No. 7 Squadron.

After his first tour Baker was an instructor at a bomber training unit before returning in May 1944 to No. 7, which had been re-equipped with the Lancaster and was then part of the Pathfinder Force. Bomber Command had begun concentrated operations in support of the D-Day landings, and Baker attacked many targets in northern France, including the V-1 launching sites in the Pas de Calais.

He was appointed a master bomber in July, a role given only to the best bomber captains. Arriving over the target first, he had to orbit overhead for 30 or 40 minutes to direct the Pathfinder crews dropping flares and markers; at the same time he was controlling the main bomber force by giving instructions on the precise aiming points and any necessary corrections as the raid developed. Many master bombers were lost in the process.

In September 1944, Baker was promoted to wing commander and took command of another Pathfinder Lancaster squadron, No. 635. During the German offensive in the Ardennes in December, some bomber airfields were covered in fog on Boxing Day, but it became imperative to attack a large build-up of enemy armour at St Vith. Baker was appointed as master bomber, and with the aid of FIDO (a fog dispersing aid), a force of 294 bombers took off and attacked in daylight. The bombing was described as "accurate" but Baker and his crews had to return to land at the fog-bound airfields. He was awarded a Bar to his DFC.

On March 13, 1945 Baker attacked Wuppertal in daylight, and on landing was informed that he had been grounded having completed his 100th operation at a time when the average life of a bomber pilot was some 10 sorties.

Baker's achievement was particularly impressive since he completed all his bombing operations during the height of the strategic bombing war when enemy defences were at their most effective. He was awarded a Bar to his DSO for "pressing home his attacks despite any opposition…when his cool courage and unfailing devotion to duty inspired the utmost confidence and have won high praise".

Baker remained in the RAF and later commanded a Lancaster squadron before spending three years with the Royal Auxiliary Air Force. Later he commanded a pilot training school before returning to the bomber world. In November 1957 he took command of No. 138 Squadron equipped with the RAF's first V-bomber, the Valiant.

After appointments in Germany and at Headquarters Training Command, Baker retired from the RAF in June 1966. He worked as the personnel manager for a large Bristol-based building firm until 1985.

Baker's bomber crews revered him. One described him as "the ideal commander" and added: "When we were on operations, everyone was behind him, but when the squadron was stood down [from operations], Tubby made sure it was really stood down with no unnecessary work to give an appearance of being busy." Baker was an unassuming and modest man. A close colleague of 20 years was unaware that he had served in the RAF during the war.

Baker was a countryman but his greatest love was horse racing and he rarely missed a visit to the Cheltenham Festival.

'Tubby' Baker married his wife Freda, a WAAF officer, in January 1947. They had two sons, one pre-deceasing him.

GROUP CAPTAIN WILLIE 'TIRPITZ' TAIT

Group Captain Willie 'Tirpitz' Tait, (who died on August 31, 2007 aged 90) had a brilliant career as a bomber commander; he attacked some of the most demanding and difficult targets, the majority as the leader or master bomber and will long be remembered for his three attacks against the German battleship, the *Tirpitz*. By the end of the war he had flown over 100 operations, in respect of which he had been awarded, uniquely, four DSOs and two DFCs.

The spectre of the *Tirpitz* emerging into the Atlantic to

cause havoc amongst convoys carrying vital supplies and troops, particularly the crucial convoys to Russia, dominated naval strategy in the European theatre. During 1942, RAF and Fleet Air Arm bombers had made several attempts to destroy the battleship in German ports and Norwegian fjords, but they had managed to immobilise her only temporarily. Although the battleship made few forays to sea, its latent menace frequently caused major political difficulties with the Russians, while the prime minister, Winston Churchill, pressed incessantly for her destruction.

By 1944 the *Tirpitz* had been moved to northern Norway, and out of range of RAF bombers operating from British airfields. Carrier-borne Fleet Air Arm aircraft made a number of daring attacks as the battleship was moored in Kaa Fjord, but no decisive damage was inflicted. In September 1944 an ambitious plan for a force of Bomber Command Lancasters, striking from Russian airfields on the Kola Peninsula, was devised. Tait, who had recently taken over No. 617 Squadron from Leonard Cheshire VC, was appointed to lead the force.

By mid-June 1944, No. 617 had demonstrated the devastating effect of the new weapon designed by Barnes Wallis, the 12,000-lb Tallboy bomb and it was decided that they were the most likely weapons to put *Tirpitz* out of action. On the night of September 11, Tait led a force of 37 Lancasters to the Russian airfield at Yagodnik near Murmansk. During the first night, asleep in rudimentary bedding, all his crews were bitten by a plague of red fleas, but Tait escaped. One of his crew commented: "Even communist bugs have respect for rank."

On September 15, 27 of the Lancasters took off for Kaa

Fjord. As they approached, the ship's smoke screen hindered the attack, but Tait's bomb aimer sighted the ship before it was fully obscured and released the Tallboy claiming to have seen a hit. One Tallboy did indeed hit the battleship's bow and the Germans were forced to move *Tirpitz* further south to Tromsø for repairs. Bomber Command staffs were not aware of the extent of the damage and a further attack was planned.

With the move south, the battleship came within range of RAF Lossiemouth in the north of Scotland and on October 29, Tait led 37 Lancasters of Nos. 9 and 617 Squadrons on a second attack. Cloud appeared at the last minute and, although all the Tallboys were dropped, no hits were recorded.

Under intense political pressure to dispose of *Tirpitz*, and allow much-needed naval forces to reinforce the Pacific Fleet, Tait and his crews were ordered to make a final effort. On November 12, 28 Lancasters of the two squadrons took off for Tromsø. The weather was clear and the German fighters tasked to protect the battleship failed to appear. Tait attacked first and his Tallboy hit the ship; in the first four minutes, 18 more were released achieving another direct hit and several near misses. There was a violent internal explosion and the huge battleship capsized and rested bottom up with great loss of life.

Tait earned the nickname 'Tirpitz' Tait and there was great relief in political and naval circles that 'The Beast', as Churchill had dubbed *Tirpitz*, had finally ceased to be a threat after more than two years' effort to neutralise her.

James Brian Tait, known to bomber crews as Willie, was born on December 9, 1916 at Manchester and he attended Wellingborough School. In 1928 his father took him to see the Schneider Trophy events, which made him determined to fly. He was awarded a cadetship at the RAF College Cranwell graduating in 1936 as a pilot.

He joined a bomber squadron but, due to an injury, did not fly his first operation with No. 51 Squadron until April 1940 when he bombed Oslo Aerodrome in a Whitley. He attacked targets in Germany and flew on the first raid on Italy when a force of Whitleys crossed the Alps in a thunderstorm to bomb Turin. On August 25, he flew on the first raid on Berlin, mounted as a reprisal for the German bombing of London. Before the end of the year, he had attacked Berlin on three more occasions at a time when navigation and bombing aids were rudimentary. He was awarded the DFC.

Tait was made the CO of No. 51 and at the end of January 1941 he led a small force of Whitleys to Malta where he was given command of Operation Colossus – the first British Army parachute operation. On February 10, his eight aircraft took off to drop paratroops on the Tragino Aqueduct, in southern Italy. Tait dropped the first stick and then orbited the area until all the troops were on the ground. It was his last operation with No. 51 and he was awarded the DSO.

Tait joined the RAF's first Halifax bomber squadron, No. 35, and on June 30, he led a daring daylight raid on Kiel by three aircraft. Despite intense anti-aircraft fire, bombs were dropped on the target. He was awarded a Bar to his DSO for "his magnificent courage and leadership".

During a 'rest' in command of a bomber training unit he flew on all three of the 1,000-Bomber Raids in the spring of 1942. On the first, one of the four engines of his Halifax failed on the outbound route, but he pressed on and bombed the target.

In July he returned to operations in command of another Halifax squadron No. 78, and though squadron commanders were limited to one operation per month because of the casualties and shortage of competent commanders, Tait managed many more. He was mentioned in despatches.

In March 1944, he was appointed to RAF Waddington as the base operations officer. Although the post did not require him to fly on operations, in the first six weeks he flew nine with the junior crews of two Australian Lancaster squadrons.

In May he returned to operations and was appointed a master bomber in No. 5 Group. On the night before D-Day he circled Cherbourg and controlled a force of 200 Lancasters attacking the coastal gun battery at St Pierre du Mont, which posed a serious threat to the American landings on Utah Beach. The gun emplacement was eliminated. He was awarded a second Bar to his DSO.

Tait assumed command of No. 617 in July. The squadron specialised in low-level target marking and precision attacks. Shortly before the final raid on the *Tirpitz*, he led six Lancasters on a daylight attack on the Kembs dam on the Rhine just north of Switzerland. As he approached the target, his aircraft was hit and damaged but he pressed on. Attacking at 600 feet against fierce opposition, the bombers dropped their Tallboys with delay fuses against the lock gates of the dam, which were destroyed for the loss of two Lancasters. He was awarded a Bar to his DFC.

After the successful *Tirpitz* attack, Tait flew two more operations and on December 15 he was grounded having flown 101 bombing operations.

His air officer commanding recommended him for the Victoria Cross for his "sustained gallantry" over almost five years of constant operations; instead he was awarded a third Bar to his DSO for his "conspicuous bravery and extreme devotion to duty in the face of the enemy", making him the only airman during the Second World War to be awarded the DSO four times.

Tait remained in the RAF after the war and served in South East Asia, India, the Middle East and Singapore before taking command of the bomber base at Coningsby in Lincolnshire. After serving at the Headquarters Air Cadets, he retired as a group captain in 1964.

A very determined man and an inspiring leader and pilot, Tait was described by Leonard Cheshire's biographer, Andrew Boyle, as "a tall thoughtful man with light brown eyes that look through and beyond one. A man of few words, but words that count".

A squadron member recalled him looking like a hawk that had landed for a drink as he stood in the bar, slightly aside from a group, with a tankard in hand, listening, without speaking. If he did open his mouth it was to puff on his pipe, or occasionally to make a dry, but perceptive and meaningful comment.

A strict disciplinarian and consummate professional, he was a very reserved, almost shy man who shunned publicity and was reticent to speak of his achievements. His family knew little of his wartime exploits.

After leaving the RAF he returned to college and was trained as a computer programmer before working for ICL and Scottish Widows.

Throughout his service and domestic life, Tait was a meticulous planner and organiser, once taking over a run-down haulage firm and putting it back on its feet within two years before he moved on to other projects. In final retirement, he greatly enjoyed his allotment and the company of his dog. When the local council told him that dogs were forbidden, he took it to court but lost. He immediately abandoned his allotment.

Tait was the president of No. 617 (Dambuster) Squadron. In later years, he read widely and was passionate about the music of Schubert, particularly his *Lieder*, researching in great detail the background to more than 400 of them.

Willie Tait married a WAAF officer, Betty Plummer, on January 16, 1945. She died in 1990 and they had a son and two daughters.

AIR VICE-MARSHAL PETER HOWARD

Air Vice-Marshal Peter Howard (who died on October 21, 2007 aged 81) was one of a small group of RAF doctors specialising in aviation medicine with the task of testing and analysing human tolerances of flight.

The experiments carried out by Howard and others led to a greater understanding of the effects of stress on the body and thus to the development of a range of equipment used by aircrew subjected to the extremes of climate, atmosphere and aircraft performance.

The advent of high-speed jets had led to a need for assisted escape from a stricken aircraft. The Martin–Baker Company was at the forefront of the development and production of the cartridge-fired ejector seat; and, as aircraft performance increased even further, the company developed and manufactured a rocket-fired ejector seat. Following a series of tests with dummies, the next phase involved carrying out an airborne test with a human subject. Howard, a squadron leader with a fear of heights, and little liking for flying volunteered.

On March 13, 1962, Howard fired himself from the rear seat of a modified Meteor jet fighter. The aircraft was flying at 250 ft and 290 mph. The rocket pack strapped to the seat generated 3,600 lbs of thrust over less than a fifth of a second, giving a peak force of 16 G (16 times the pull of gravity), propelling the seat from the aircraft at a velocity of 80 ft per second.

This, the world's first rocket-assisted ejection from an aircraft in flight, was completely successful, and Howard landed with nothing more than a stiff neck – although he noticed that the flames had burnt the heels off his flying boots.

As he ejected, the company's chairman, James Martin, raced across the airfield at high speed in pursuit in his Rolls-Royce. When asked to describe his thoughts during the brief time he was descending in his parachute, Howard commented laconically: "The greatest hazard of the whole venture was the risk of landing on top of Mr Martin's car." Jimmy Martin (later Sir James Martin) vowed never again to conduct trials with live subjects.

Peter Howard was born on December 15, 1925, and was educated at Farnborough Grammar School and St Thomas's Hospital medical school. After a brief period as a house physician and research registrar at St Thomas's, he joined the RAF medical branch in August 1951.

Almost the whole of Howard's career as a medical officer was spent at the Institute of Aviation Medicine (IAM) at Farnborough. First he joined the altitude section and investigated the effects of decompression sickness. Often he acted as a guinea pig in tests conducted in a specialised chamber, being subjected to explosive decompressions.

Such work led to the development of pressure suits and breathing apparatus for aircrew and to demand oxygen equipment be fitted into aircraft systems. He later became head of the biodynamics division, helping to develop the newly built human centrifuge. He conducted experiments to explore and measure the effects of sustained acceleration on the body – in particular on lung function, cardiac output, mental performance and the circulation of blood. He was instrumental in the development and testing of the anti-G protective suits developed for aircrew flying high-performance jets.

Despite his fear of heights and dislike for flying, Howard chose to take a brief parachute course to prepare for the rocket-seat test. He recalled many years later that he was terrified as he stood in the door of the balloon cage waiting to drop (the first two jumps were from a cage suspended below a barrage balloon at 800 ft). It was a fear he never overcame, despite making more jumps, and his determination and courage was greatly admired by his colleagues.

Howard also undertook many tests on an ejector-seat rig, which allowed physiological and clinical measurements to be taken; these were used for improving the design of the seats and aircrew survival equipment. Over many years he subjected himself to the extreme boundaries of human endurance. A senior RAF doctor described him as "one of the medical heroes of the RAF".

In 1964 he was appointed a consultant in aviation physiology, and three years later played a major role in the establishment and accreditation of the Diploma in Aviation Medicine, which was authorised by a conjoint board of the Royal College of Surgeons and the Royal College of Physicians.

The availability of the six-month course, which led to the award of the diploma, gave added impetus to the application of aviation medicine in the civil aviation field. Medical officers from foreign and Commonwealth air forces, as well as civilian aviation medicine doctors from international airlines, attended the course.

In 1973 Howard was appointed director of research at IAM, and two years later he became commandant, a post he held until he retired in 1988. In 1978 he led a delegation of aviation medicine specialists on one of the first military visits to China after the Cultural Revolution.

Howard's knowledge and skills were also in demand in the arena of manned space exploration. During the American Apollo programme the BBC sought his expertise as a commentator and analyst.

He was the medical director to the panel selecting the British applicant for the Juno programme, funded by the Russian space agency and a consortium of British companies, which resulted in Helen Sharman becoming Britain's first astronaut in 1991.

Howard was always aware that his work was for the benefit and the efficiency of aircrew flying high performance aircraft and of others who travelled by air. He had a very positive attitude to unusual requests made to IAM, such as aviation record attempts and space candidate selection. He once commented: "A scientific organisation that loses its taste for the unusual and the freedom to indulge it will slowly desiccate."

Howard was also a formidable administrator, skilfully guiding IAM in a climate of increasing financial pressure; despite the enforced need to reduce personnel, by his force of personality he was able to maintain the dedication and enthusiasm of his staff.

He was the chairman of the Defence Medical Services postgraduate council in 1986, and on his retirement became the registrar of the faculty of occupational medicine at the Royal College of Physicians.

He was appointed OBE (1957) and CB (1989). From 1982

to 1988 he was an honorary physician to the Queen. Amongst many other prestigious awards he received the Lady Cade Medal in 1955, an annual award given by the Royal College of Surgeons to an RAF medical officer for "outstanding contributions to aviation medicine". He was elected a Fellow of the Royal Aeronautical Society and the Royal College of Physicians. He wrote widely on aviation physiology, medicine and occupational medicine.

Howard's great love was fly-fishing, and he shared a beat on the River South Esk in Scotland. He also had a passion for music, particularly that of Haydn and Mozart.

Peter Howard married Norma Fletcher in 1950 and they had a son and a daughter.

BRIGADIER GENERAL PAUL TIBBETS

Brigadier General Paul Tibbets (who died on November 2, 2007 aged 92) commanded the US-AAF bomber Enola Gay, which dropped the atom bomb on Hiroshima on August 6, 1945.

In September 1944, Tibbets, who had completed a tour of bombing operations in Europe, was briefed on the Manhattan Project, the code name for the development of the atom bomb. He was ordered to form a special squadron of B-29 Super Fortress bombers, the 393rd Bombardment Squadron, and train it to deliver these weapons in combat operations. He requisitioned 15 new B-29s and supervised the modifications necessary to make them capable of delivering the weapons. This included fitting fuel-injected engines, a re-configured bomb bay and changes to the aircraft's armour plating.

Flying from an airfield on the Utah/Nevada border, he and his crews trained over the remote New Mexico desert, and in December his squadron became part of the 509th Composite Group. Over the next few months the group moved to Tinian Island near Guam. On August 5, 1945, President Harry Truman sanctioned the use of the weapons against Japan. Tibbets was selected to fly the operation and that afternoon he named his B-29 (serial number 44-86292) the Enola Gay – his mother had been christened Enola after the heroine of a novel.

The bomb to be used was code named 'Little Boy'. The uranium-235 needed for the explosion was scarce and, since the weapon design was conceptually simple, it was only deemed necessary to do laboratory tests. Thus, the bomb had not been fully tested before the operation.

At 2.45 a.m. the following morning, Tibbets and his 12-man crew took off from North Field on Tinian and headed for Hiroshima with two observation aircraft in company. No opposition was encountered and, with the aircraft flying at 26,000 feet, the bomb was dropped at 8.15 a.m. local time.

The detonation occurred at an altitude of 1,900 feet with a power of 13 to 16 kilotons (estimates vary). Tibbets considered it to be a normal bombing operation until he turned to see the effect, which he described as "unbelievable". It was estimated that 70,000 died in the blast but many more died over the following days from radiation.

Tibbets landed back at North Field after a 24-hour flight to be greeted by General Carl Spaatz, who immediately decorated him with the Distinguished Service Cross. Japan did not surrender immediately and a second bomb was dropped on Nagasaki three days later. On August 10, the Japanese finally surrendered.

The son of a prosperous businessman, Paul Warfield Tibbets was born in Quincy, Illinois on February 23, 1915. His parents moved to Florida when he was 12 and he attended Western Military Academy before going to the universities of Florida and Cincinnati to study medicine. His determination to fly overcame his parents' wish that he should be a doctor, and in February 1937 he enlisted as a flight cadet in the Army Air Corps at Fort Thomas, Kentucky. A year later he was awarded his pilot's wings and commissioned as second lieutenant. In February 1942, Tibbets was appointed to command the 340th Bomb Squadron, 97th Bombardment Group, and left for England. His squadron of B-17 Flying Fortresses was based at Polebrook near Oundle. On August 17, 1942, the USAAF mounted the first B-17 raid, and Tibbets took off at the head of 12 bombers to attack the marshalling yards at Rouen. Altogether he flew 25 missions in B-17s, including some in Algeria where he led the first bombing operations in support of the North African invasion.

In March 1943, he returned to the USA to test the combat capability of Boeing's new Super Fortress, the B-29, an aircraft plagued with problems. He taught himself to fly the bomber and subsequently flew it for 400 hours in tests. This eventually gave him more experience of the capabilities and limitations of the aircraft than any other pilot at that time.

After the Hiroshima mission, Tibbets was amongst a group of senior officers who met with President Truman. The discussion was about the end of the war, and Truman turned to Tibbets and asked: "What do you think?" Tibbets responded: "Mr President, I think I did what I was told." Truman slapped his hand on the table and said: "You're damn right you did, and I'm the guy that sent you. If anybody gives you a hard time about it, refer them to me."

Tibbets remained in the USAF after the war. In 1946 he participated in the Bikini bomb tests as a technical advisor to the commander of the air task force. Later, he was responsible for the USAF's purchase of the B-47 six-engine jet-bomber and its service tests at the Boeing factory in Wichita, Kansas. He went on to command two of the Strategic Air Command's bomber organisations, before completing a tour with NATO in France. He was also responsible for establishing the National Military Command Centre in the Pentagon.

During the 1960s Tibbets was appointed military attaché in India, but the appointment was revoked after protests from all of India's political parties. He retired in the rank of brigadier general in August 1966.

Tibbets became a successful businessman. After a spell in Switzerland operating Learjet executive aircraft he returned to Ohio in 1970 to join Executive Jet Aviation, an all-jet air taxi service. He became chairman of the board in 1982 and retired three years later.

Tibbets was often in demand to comment on his wartime experiences. He had no regrets, regarding the dropping of the bomb as necessary, and would say: "Why be bashful? That's what it took to end the war." In 1976 he caused controversy by re-enacting the bombing of Hiroshima at an air show in Texas, flying over the show in a B-29 Super Fortress as a 'mushroom cloud' was released; the stunt caused outrage in Japan, and the White House apologised.

In 1952, the film *Above and Beyond* depicted the wartime events involving Tibbets, with Robert Taylor starring as Tibbets and Eleanor Parker as his first wife Lucy.

Paul Tibbets was awarded the DFC and the Air Medal and he is enshrined in the National Aviation Hall of Fame.

He was twice married and had two sons.

AIR COMMODORE RICKY WRIGHT

Air Commodore Ricky Wright (who died on November 5, 2007 aged 88) had an RAF career of many contrasts. As a sergeant he flew Hurricane fighters over south-east England during the most intense period of the Battle of Britain. In early 1942, he was captured in Java and spent over three years in Japanese prison camps. After the war he flew one of the first group of jet fighters to cross the Atlantic from

England to North America and later commanded two V-bomber bases.

Wright joined No. 605 (County of Warwick) Squadron in July 1940 a few days before it left its Scottish base for Croydon. He saw a great deal of action during the summer of 1940 and in the early days of September he shared in the destruction of a Messerschmitt Bf 110 fighter and a Dornier 17 bomber. On September 15, the climax of the battle, and a day commemorated as Battle of Britain Day, Wright shot down a Dornier 17 over Maidstone.

No. 605 was one of the most successful squadrons during the latter phase of the battle and remained in the front line for an unusually long time. Wright had further successes and by the end of the year, he had accounted for six enemy aircraft, probably destroyed three more and damaged a further six. At the end of November, he was awarded an immediate DFM (the first to his squadron) for his "fine qualities of leadership, outstanding skill and personal courage"; at the same time he was commissioned.

Eric William Wright was born at Cherry Hinton, Cambridge on September 21, 1919 and educated at Cambridge County School and the Technical College. He joined the RAF Volunteer Reserve in June 1939 and was called up at the outbreak of war when he completed his training as a pilot.

After the Battle of Britain, Wright remained with No. 605 until he left for India in 1941 when he was made a flight commander of No. 232 Squadron. After the Japanese attacks on Malaya, the squadron embarked on the aircraft carrier *Indomitable,* flying off to Java at the end of January 1942 en route to reinforce the beleaguered squadrons at Singapore. Within a week his CO had been killed and Wright was promoted to squadron leader to take command. He damaged a Japanese bomber off the west coast of Singapore but the squadron was soon forced to evacuate to Sumatra.

Within days a further withdrawal to Java had to be undertaken and Wright was made CO of a composite squadron made up of the remaining Hurricanes. They were hopelessly outnumbered and losses mounted. With only a few aircraft left, on March 1 Wright was ordered to pass his remaining Hurricanes to a group selected to stay behind and take his remaining pilots to Tjilatjap on the south coast from where they were to board a boat for Australia. Two Ford V-8s were commandeered and the party drove through the jungle at night, only to find that the last boat had been sunk. In vain they searched along the coast for other craft. A few days later the island fell to the Japanese and Wright and his pilots soon found themselves in the native jail of Boei Glodok.

After a period at Batavia filling bomb holes on the airfield, Wright and his party were shipped to Japan via Taiwan in the hold of a ship carrying iron ore. For a time they worked as farm labourers before Wright was sent to Habu on Innoshima Island to work in the shipbuilding yards. Late in the war he was moved to a camp holding Dutch prisoners, where conditions were more primitive and brutal. After the second atom bomb was dropped on Nagasaki the POWs awoke to find that the Japanese had left.

In September, Wright was taken to Guam and returned to England via the United States and Canada completing the final leg of his journey in the *Queen Mary*. Once the details of his work in Java became known, he was awarded the DFC "in recognition of gallant and distinguished services against the Japanese in the Netherlands East Indies".

Wright resumed his career as a fighter pilot flying the early jets and was a member of the RAF's official aerobatic team, No. 247 Squadron, flying Vampires. In April 1948 he flew one of the six Vampire F3s of No. 54 Squadron, which made the first Atlantic crossing by jet aircraft. Taking off from RAF Odiham, and flying via Stornoway, Iceland and Greenland to Goose Bay in Labrador, the distance of 2,202 miles was completed in a flight time of eight hours 18 minutes. They continued to the United States, where they were feted by their USAF hosts and the press, and undertook a number of air show appearances including the grand opening of Idlewild Airport. On his return, Wright was appointed to command No. 54.

After spending a year at the Central Fighter Establishment, Wright was appointed the wing leader at Linton-on-Ouse with command of three fighter squadrons. In late 1956 he converted to the Hunter and took the Tangmere Wing to Cyprus for the Suez operations. He was then given command of the RAF's first Bloodhound ground-to-air missile squadron. In 1960 he was promoted to group captain and spent three years at Headquarters Fighter Command where he was heavily involved in the introduction into service of the supersonic Lightning fighter.

In 1963, Wright moved into an entirely new flying environment when he was appointed to command the Vulcan bomber base at Coningsby in Lincolnshire, before moving to another Vulcan base, at Cottesmore, a year later. The V-force provided the country's strategic nuclear deterrent and was at the height of its capabilities. On promotion to air commodore in November 1965 he was appointed director of Flight Safety. Four years later he left for South Africa as the defence attaché before taking early retirement in 1973.

Wright was appointed CBE in 1964. He also received a King's Commendation for Valuable Service in the Air and the Air Efficiency Award.

Always a keen golfer, Wright was secretary and chief executive of Moor Park Golf Club until he retired to Somerset where he was club captain at Sherborne. A kindly man with a great sense of humour, he was an accomplished handyman and spent two years restoring an old property and its gardens, which became the family home.

Ricky Wright married Katherine Skingley in February 1946 with whom he had a son and daughter.

WING COMMANDER 'DAL' RUSSEL

Wing Commander 'Dal' Russel (who died on November 20, 2007 aged 89) was a highly decorated wartime Canadian fighter pilot whose logbook recorded kills in the Battle of Britain and the Normandy invasion; he later led attacks on enemy rail and road transport as the Allies entered the Netherlands and Germany.

Russel arrived in England in June 1940 with No. 1 (RCAF) Squadron, the first Canadian squadron to see action. Flying Hurricanes, the squadron was declared operational in mid-August and within 10 days, Russel shared in the destruction of a Dornier bomber over Gravesend. Flying from Northolt, he was involved in some of the fiercest fighting of the Battle and over the next few weeks he accounted for another five enemy aircraft, including two downed and one shared on the same day – September 27 – and he probably destroyed two others and damaged three more.

His ground crew nicknamed him 'Deadeye Dick' and painted the ace of spades on his Hurricane for luck. In October, he was awarded the DFC, one of three to No. 401 Squadron (as No. 1 became) and the first to be awarded to the RCAF in the war.

Russel sent telegrams home regularly and in mid-September wrote: "Cigarettes and food arrived. Many thanks. Got my third Hun yesterday. Heinkel bomber. Love to all." While almost every telegram asked for food and cigarettes, a later letter revealed the less cheery reality: "In the thick of a fight you haven't time to think much. Your mouth is dry as cotton and the palms of your hands are dripping wet as you try to get the enemy within reach of your eight guns and keep another fellow off your tail."

Blair Dalzell Russel was born in Toronto on December 9, 1917 but his family moved to Montreal shortly afterwards. He was educated at Trinity College School at Port Hope, Ontario where he was better at sport than his studies. He learned to fly at the Montreal Flying Club and by the end of the first week of the war, he and most of his colleagues from the club had joined the RCAF.

After the Battle of Britain, Russel was sent back to Canada to assist with recruiting, but he soon returned to flying being promoted to command a fighter squadron equipped with Kittyhawks. Disappointed not to be sent to the Aleutian Islands to fight the Japanese, he returned to England to fly Spitfires in December 1942.

Given command of No. 411 (RCAF) Squadron at Redhill, with the primary role of providing escort for bombers attacking targets in France, he was then promoted, at 25, to command No. 126 Wing, equipped with three Canadian Spitfire squadrons.

Russel's wing carried out 64 sorties as close escort in which over 500 bombers were taken to targets from Rotterdam to Cherbourg without a single bomber being lost to enemy fighters. Russel led many of these sorties himself, attracting high praise from the commanders of the bomber force. At the end of his tour in November 1943 he was awarded a Bar to his DFC. He then spent six months developing tactics at HQ 83 Group but by the spring of 1944 he was anxious to return to operational flying.

Following the loss of a Canadian squadron commander, he approached Johnnie Johnson, the RAF's highest-scoring fighter pilot and wing leader of the Canadian Spitfire Wing, and asked to take command of No. 442 (RCAF) Squadron. Johnson had a very high regard for the blond, curly-haired and handsome Russel, who he considered to have "all the attributes of the popular conception of a fighter pilot", adding that he was "a great favourite with the ladies". But Russel had to drop a rank to take command immediately.

Johnson's Canadian Spitfire Wing was at the centre of

operations leading up to the invasion of Normandy. On June 10, just four days after the Allied landings began, army and RAF airfield construction engineers had completed the first landing strip at Sainte-Croix-sur-Mer (B 6) in Normandy. Johnson sent Russel and his wingman to check the airstrip, making them one of the first to land in France. Two days later Johnson led his three squadrons to B 6 and operations deeper into France commenced. Russel shared in the destruction of a Focke-Wulf fighter and damaged a second fighter, but most of his sorties were against ground targets. During this hectic period, he learned that his younger brother Hugh had been shot down and killed nearby flying with another Canadian Spitfire squadron.

In July, Russel was once again promoted to wing commander and took command of the four Spitfire squadrons of No. 126 Wing. He led them during the devastating attacks in the Falaise pocket and then in support of the advancing Allied armies as they pushed forward through France and Belgium, reaching Brussels in September, and on to the Netherlands. His squadrons attacked transport targets and tank concentrations, destroying over 700 of them. On October 4, one of his pilots shot down a Messerschmitt Me 262 fighter, the first jet to be downed by a fighter.

Shortly afterwards it was announced that Russel had been awarded the DSO for his "masterly leadership and fine fighting qualities when his example had inspired all". Six days later he was summoned to Buckingham Palace, where King George VI decorated him with his DSO, DFC and Bar.

Russel continued to lead his wing in intensive operations as it advanced into the Netherlands. Based at the former German airfield at Volkel, his squadrons flew into Germany attacking road and rail targets.

After completing 256 operational sorties in three tours of duty, one of the few Canadians to do so, he was finally grounded at the end of January 1945. He had never been shot down, although a stricken German fighter that plunged to the ground after being shot down by Johnnie Johnson almost hit his Spitfire.

Russel, who was also awarded the French Croix de Guerre with Silver Star, the Order of Orange-Nassau with Swords and the Czechoslovak War Cross, was released from the RCAF in July 1945.

Russel held positions in Canada Wire and Cable, Canadair Aircraft Company and Sperry Gyroscopes before he and his wife bought a linen store in Montreal. In retirement he enjoyed salmon fishing but, although invited to hunt by friends, he never liked shooting after the war.

'Dal' Russel and his wife had two sons and a daughter.

FLIGHT LIEUTENANT MICK SHAND

Flight Lieutenant Mick Shand (who died on December 20, 2007 aged 92) was a New Zealand fighter pilot interned at Stalag Luft III at Sagan and survived the Great Escape – the last to emerge from the tunnel before it was discovered, he was recaptured after four days on the run.

Shand and his partner, fellow New Zealander, Squadron Leader Len Trent VC, planned to "hard arse" it on foot to Czechoslovakia in the hope of getting to Switzerland. They had no great expectation of reaching England and felt it would be impossible to make it across the frozen countryside undetected but they felt they "had to do something".

The two men moved down the 100-metre tunnel, code-named 'Harry', after midnight on the night of March 24/25, 1944. Delays meant that it was almost 5 a.m. when they reached the exit, which came out in the open a few yards from the intended spot in the cover of woods.

Shand was the 76th prisoner to emerge from the tunnel and

was running across the dead ground to the woods when a patrolling guard spotted Trent emerging. Shand threw himself to
the snow-covered ground. In later years he observed: "I knew
we had been rumbled. I don't think the goon knew what was
going on either as we all froze. The minute he looked away, I
made a run for the woods. That was it, I was out." The startled
guard fired his rifle, but the bullet passed over Shand's head as
he dived into the woods.

Finding himself alone, Shand began to walk and was on the
run for almost four days, travelling at night and resting by day.
The weather conditions were harsh, and two railway workers
finally caught him while he was waiting to jump on a freight
train. He was taken to Görlitz prison where he found himself
amongst a group of fellow escapers.

Over the next two days the Gestapo took most of the recaptured RAF prisoners away. Shand was amongst a group
of four who were collected by the Luftwaffe and returned
to Sagan, where he was horrified to learn that most of his
colleagues had been shot by the Gestapo. The final total of
those murdered was 50. Sometime later the POWs learned
that three men – two Norwegians and a Dutchman – had
successfully made it back to the United Kingdom.

Michael Moray Shand was born in Wellington on February
20, 1915 and educated at Nelson College. He was working
in the fruit industry when, in early 1939, he applied for a
short-service commission in the RNZAF, starting his pilot
training later in the year. After gaining his wings, he sailed for
England in June 1940.

The RAF was desperately short of fighter pilots and Shand
was rushed through training. After just 20 hours flying on the
Spitfire, during which time he never fired its guns, he was posted to No. 54 Squadron. The squadron was based at Hornchurch
in Essex and when he arrived in late August, the fighting during
the Battle of Britain was reaching a climax. He flew his first sortie as wingman to the outstanding New Zealand ace, Al Deere,
who told him to stay close and watch what was going on.

Three days after his arrival Shand was on an evening patrol over Dover when a Messerschmitt Bf 109 attacked him, damaging his aircraft. He managed to crash-land on the airfield at Manston, but had been badly wounded in the arm. He spent several months in hospital.

He returned to operations in October 1941 with No. 485 (RNZAF) Squadron, flying from Kenley in Surrey. The squadron was heavily involved in operations over northern France escorting bomber formations and attacking road transports.

Shand was appointed a flight commander in May 1942, and he and his pilots provided withdrawal cover during Operation Jubilee, the raid on Dieppe. By September he had flown 60 operations over France and was awarded the DFC, the citation describing him as "a skilful pilot and fearless leader".

On November 28, Shand led a formation of six Spitfires on a low-level sweep off the Dutch coast seeking targets of opportunity. They successfully attacked a tanker-barge on a canal and as they returned, Shand and his wingman went down to shoot up a train. Two Focke-Wulf Fw 190s attacked them and Shand was shot down and quickly captured. Within a few weeks he arrived at Stalag Luft III, 100 miles south-east of Berlin. It was Göring's 'show camp' administered and guarded by the Luftwaffe.

After the Great Escape, Shand remained at Stalag Luft III until the camp was evacuated in January 1945, when the POWs were forced to march westwards in the harshest winter for many years. In May he was liberated. He returned to England before going home to New Zealand in September.

Shand always considered himself extremely fortunate to be one of the few survivors of the Great Escape, in which three of his fellow New Zealanders were murdered. In later years he said he thought the venture was worth it, explaining: "We had to do something to hit back at the Germans. We did it to cause chaos behind enemy lines and that's exactly what we did."

Mick Shand farmed at Wairarapa in the south-east of North Island until he retired in 1978. His wife died in 2000 and they had a son and a daughter.

GROUP CAPTAIN DUDLEY HONOR

Group Captain Dudley Honor (who died on December 26, 2007 aged 94) flew during the Battle of France and as a fighter pilot in the Battle of Britain before going to the Middle East; shot down in the latter stages of the German invasion of Crete, he spent six days in the mountains before reaching the coast where he was picked up by an RAF flying boat.

Honor was the flight commander of No. 274 Squadron flying Hurricanes when his unit was sent to Crete in the middle of May 1941 in an endeavour to stem the German landings. On May 25, he and another aircraft were tasked to attack the German-held airfield at Maleme. As he approached he saw many Italian and German transport aircraft preparing to land. Ignoring the dense flak, he attacked and within a few minutes he had shot down two of the transports laden with troop reinforcements to the island.

As he broke away from the enemy airfield German fighters chased him. His aircraft was badly damaged and became difficult to control. He managed to evade further attacks before his engine stopped when he was forced to ditch into the sea. His Hurricane sank to 40 feet before he was able to escape from the cockpit. His German lifejacket – obtained during his service in France – inflated immediately and he surfaced.

The sea was rough but he managed to swim to the shore half-a-mile away. He had great difficulty climbing on to the rocks and his hands were badly torn before he was able to scramble ashore and head for the hills where the local peasants sheltered him. He travelled through the mountains to the coast on the south side of the island where he waited. On the sixth day he saw a Sunderland flying boat land close by – it had come to evacuate senior army officers and other survivors.

Honor flashed an SOS, which was detected and a single-seat dinghy was rowed ashore. He scrambled down the steep rocks to the shoreline and managed to squeeze into the dinghy and was taken to the waiting Sunderland. After collecting some Greek army survivors, the aircraft took off and flew back to Alexandria.

Honor soon recovered from his ordeal and rejoined his squadron, which had returned to the Western Desert after the fall of Crete. Shortly afterwards, he was awarded a Bar to the DFC he had received in 1940. The citation recorded his "great skill" and noted that he had destroyed nine enemy aircraft.

Dudley Sandry Garton Honor was born of British parents on September 5, 1913, in Quilmes, Buenos Aires, Argentina where he was educated. He was brought up speaking better Spanish than English. He joined the RAF on a short-service commission in July 1937 and after training as a pilot he was sent to No. 88 Squadron at Boscombe Down.

No. 88 was equipped with the Battle light bomber and went to France at the outbreak of the war with the Advanced Air Striking Force. In May 1940, the outdated and inferior Battle squadrons were thrown against the German blitzkrieg when the RAF suffered appalling losses. Honor flew reconnaissance and attack sorties against the advancing German columns and dive-bombed the bridges over the River Meuse. He was one of the few pilots of his squadron to survive and escape back to England. He was later awarded the DFC for his services in France.

As the Battle of Britain opened in July 1940, Fighter Command was short of pilots and Honor volunteered to fly Hurricanes. With no previous experience as a fighter pilot, he was sent to No. 145 Squadron. Off Scotland he shared in the destruction of an Arado floatplane but after his squadron was transferred to the south he was forced to crash land in Sussex after a running battle with a Messerschmitt Bf 109. His Hurricane was a write-off. After a spell on night-fighting duties, he was sent to the Middle East.

In January 1941 he sailed in the aircraft carrier *Furious* and a few days later he took off in a Hurricane for Takoradi in the Gold Coast (now Ghana). He then ferried his single-engine aircraft across the desert over Nigeria, Chad and the Sudan to Egypt where he joined No. 274 as a flight commander in the Western Desert.

Honor soon opened his account when he shot down a Bf 109 over Tobruk, shortly after the German fighters had made their debut in North Africa. On May 15, 1941, the British forces launched Operation Battleaxe and Honor and his pilots were in constant action. He shot down a Bf 109 and damaged three others. However, most of his actions were in attacking enemy motor transports and fuel and ammunition dumps. With the German parachute landings in Crete, his squadron was sent to reinforce the depleted RAF squadrons and he soon shot down a German fighter and destroyed a large transport aircraft on the ground. The fighting was fierce until he was shot down.

Shortly after his return from Crete, his photograph appeared on the front cover of a topical magazine under the title "What our boys are doing for us". This was the work of Mary Bentley who was employed as a broadcaster with the Egyptian State Radio and was also on the editorial staff of the magazine. Two weeks later Honor walked into her office and she recognised him as her 'pin-up boy'. They spent the rest of their lives together.

Honor took command of No. 274 in August and four months later he was promoted to wing commander to lead No. 258 Wing in operations over the desert. He achieved his final success in December when he shot down an Italian fighter near Tobruk. Honor served on the fighter operations staff in Malta before landing in Sicily and then in Italy.

He returned to England in 1944 before leaving as the air

attaché in South America covering Colombia, Venezuela and Ecuador. He was promoted to group captain in 1946 but resigned his commission a year later to become 1st UK civil air attaché accredited to Argentina, Uruguay, Chile, Bolivia and Brazil.

In 1951, Honor became director, Latin America, of Bristol Aeroplane Company. In 1960 he became Canadair's director in the region before becoming the manager of Air Canada, South America. His companies provided him with a Dove transport aircraft and he and his wife flew together over most of South America.

In retirement the Honors moved initially to Canada, where they were given Canadian citizenship, but in 1973 they left for Spain where they started to grow lettuces. Honor introduced new varieties to the region and was dubbed the 'Lettuce King of Andalusia'. In 1990 they moved to England settling in Devon. Honor was an avid golfer and his wife walked virtually every course with him.

Dudley Honor and his wife had no children.

SQUADRON LEADER B.A. 'JIMMY' JAMES

Squadron Leader B.A. 'Jimmy' James (who died on January 18, 2008 aged 92) was an inveterate escaper during his five years in captivity in the Second World War.

James was one of the few to escape execution after the Great Escape, and joined two others at the notorious death camp at Sachsenhausen, from where he made another daring escape by tunnel, only to be recaptured 10 days later.

He had already made a number of unsuccessful escape attempts by the time he arrived at Stalag Luft III in the spring of 1943. Plans were being made to dig three tunnels, and he was soon recruited to the organisation and appointed to the security team. After the discovery of one of the tunnels, work was temporarily suspended. When work resumed in January 1944

James was put in charge of dispersing the sand excavated from the tunnel 'Harry'. More than 40 tons was deposited under the camp theatre built earlier by the prisoners.

On the night of March 24, 1944, the tunnel was ready. James was to be the 39th to travel along the 365-foot long tunnel, which surfaced in the open a few yards short of the intended spot on the edge of woods, and the escape from the tunnel suffered long delays.

Eventually James and his travelling companion, a Greek fighter pilot, emerged into the open at 1.30 a.m. and made their way to the local station to catch the 5 a.m. train for the Czech border. They travelled south, and after leaving the train, headed for the mountains. The cold was intense and after two days, the two men were recaptured and taken to a Gestapo headquarters north of Berlin.

Fifty of the 76 escapers were shot and James and two others, including 'Wings' Day, the senior RAF officer to escape, were sent to Sachsenhausen. On meeting James, Day commented sardonically: "The only way out of here is up the chimney." The men were housed in a special camp (a Sonderlager) near the perimeter with a few other British officers. James was horrified at the evil he witnessed, the daily executions and privation. Undaunted, the team immediately started a tunnel. Using a table knife with a serrated edge, James and a colleague did the digging. By the middle of September, the 120-ft tunnel was ready, and on the night of September 23, six men broke out.

Travelling with Jack Churchill, James headed north hoping to reach a Baltic port and board a ship to Sweden. They walked for three days before jumping a goods train to

Neustrelitz where they took to the woods again. After 14 days of freedom they had travelled 100 miles, but were captured whilst sleeping and returned to Sachsenhausen. Himmler ordered their execution, but they were reprieved and spent the next five months in solitary confinement.

The son of a tea-planter, Bertram Arthur James (he would always be known in the RAF as Jimmy) was born in India on April 17, 1915. After the King's School, Canterbury he sought work in British Columbia; but the prospect of war brought him back to England, where he was granted a short-service commission in the RAF. After training as a pilot, he was posted to No. 9 Squadron based in Suffolk.

On the night of June 5, 1940 James was the second pilot of a Wellington bomber sent to attack Duisburg. The aircraft was shot down south of Rotterdam on the outbound flight and James parachuted to safety. He was captured after 24 hours, and was one of the first to arrive at the new camp at Stalag Luft I on the Baltic.

He was soon involved in tunnelling his way to freedom but, as he was about to escape, the plan was discovered. Undeterred, James started another beneath an incinerator. On the night of the attempted escape, he was trapped as he moved in the dark from his hut to the tunnel entrance and was captured – but his colleague, John Shore, already in the tunnel, managed to escape and return to England.

For the next two years, James was constantly attempting to tunnel his way to freedom, but each effort was thwarted before he could break out. One night, when the security lights failed, he made an attempt to walk out of the camp in disguise, but the lights came on just as he approached the main gate. On another occasion he started a tunnel whilst still in solitary confinement.

In February 1945, as an increasingly paranoid German high command ordered the execution of many prisoners, James and his colleagues were moved to Flossenberg, where the conditions were particularly harsh. James was with a group of prominent individuals – the Prominenten – who were being held as possible hostages as the German Reich collapsed.

With the Allied armies advancing, the party was moved to Dachau before being segregated and taken by road to the Austrian Tyrol, where there was a tense stand-off as fanatical guards considered executing them. Eventually, an American army column liberated the party and James arrived back in England on May 13.

Throughout his time as a POW James could think of nothing but escaping from his German captors and returning home. He utterly refused to accept incarceration, even when recapture carried the prospect of summary execution. He once said: "It was our contribution to the war effort." When the full extent of his exploits came to light, he was awarded the MC and mentioned in despatches. James elected to remain in the RAF and for three years he worked in Germany.

During his captivity, and when not attempting to escape, he had learnt Russian, which he developed further on a language course at London University before returning to Germany for intelligence duties. In 1953 he transferred to the RAF Regiment and retired in 1958.

For 20 years, James worked for the Diplomatic Service holding posts in Africa, Western and Eastern Europe and in London before retiring finally in 1975. For a period he was the general secretary of the Foreign and Commonwealth Office-sponsored Great Britain-USSR Association.

James was an intensely modest man who described his experiences in a laconic style that almost belittled his extraordinary adventures – one noted historian considered him to be the greatest escaper of the war.

Although reluctant to return to Sagan, in 2004 he joined other survivors on the 60th anniversary of the event and to lay a wreath. He observed: "Having lost 50 of my comrades, the ghosts of the past will inevitably rise up and one feels a great loss in that respect. I never thought 60 years ago when I crawled out of the hole in the snow that there would be a ceremony to commemorate the event."

During the ceremony soldiers of the Polish Army stood guard as candles were lit along the length of the tunnel in memory of the 50 murdered airmen.

In 1983 he published *Moonless Night*, an account of his wartime experiences.

Jimmy James married Madge Tughan in July 1946. Their only son predeceased them.

WING COMMANDER PAT GIBBS

Wing Commander Pat Gibbs (who died on March 8, 2008 aged 92) was awarded a DSO, DFC and Bar during the Second World War, then served as the *Daily Telegraph's* fiercely independent film critic for more than 25 years.

Gibbs specialised in torpedo attacks against shipping; the tactics he developed in the Mediterranean against fearsome opposition were subsequently developed for the highly successful Strike Wings that operated from airfields in Britain later in the Second World War.

A highly experienced and decorated maritime attack pilot, Gibbs arrived in Egypt in late 1941. He was utterly dedicated to the airborne torpedo as a weapon against shipping. Assigned to a headquarters staff job in Cairo, he fought an uphill battle against the powers that be to convince them of his beliefs. In due course, he not only changed tactics but also influenced strategic policy for attacks against convoys. Gibbs found his desk job immensely frustrating and constantly badgered his superior officers to allow him to return to operations. In April 1942, the only Beaufort anti-shipping squadron in the theatre suffered devastating losses during an attack on an Italian convoy and Gibbs was sent to No. 39 Squadron as a replacement flight commander.

He led his first attack on June 4 when his was the only aircraft in the formation to reach the target successfully. Against heavy anti-aircraft fire he released his torpedo from

50 feet and hit the 6,847-ton Italian merchantman *Reginaldo Trieste*, which sank after the destroyer escorts made a fruitless attempt to tow her to Benghazi. This first attack was only a prelude to the action ahead for Gibbs and his navigator, John Cresswell, and demonstrated his single-minded and determined approach to attacking the crucially important Axis convoys re-supplying Rommel's armies in North Africa.

Ten days later, Gibbs led 12 Beauforts to attack two 35,000-ton Italian battleships. Enemy fighters attacked his formation but Gibbs pressed on with the survivors. As he released his torpedo, his aircraft was badly damaged by fire from an escorting destroyer but he made for Malta where he crash-landed.

Gibbs remained on Malta with a detachment from No. 39, where he combined his force with the resident, but depleted, squadron. Within days, he led the combined squadron to attack an important convoy of oil tankers heading along the Greek coast towards Libya. Gibbs released his torpedo, despite being hit by anti-aircraft fire, and his target limped into an Italian port.

On July 3, this same convoy made another attempt to re-supply Rommel's army. Gibbs took off at the head of 12 Beauforts to intercept it but returned after a fruitless six-hour search. The following day he led eight of the tired crews on another attempt. Four were forced to turn back and two were lost over the target. Gibbs' aircraft was extensively damaged but he managed to struggle back to Malta to make a crash-landing. A few days later it was announced that he had been awarded a Bar to an earlier DFC.

Losses amongst the Beaufort crews were severe and the strain on the survivors was immense, but Gibbs had a determination and professionalism that frightened some of the less experienced crews but was greatly admired by others. If a target was missed on one attack, he insisted on another attempt the following day. On August 20 he led a large formation to attack a vital oil tanker. The torpedoes missed but the resolute Gibbs returned the next day with nine Beauforts and an escort of Beaufighters. Destroyers had joined the convoy but Gibbs led his torpedo-carrying aircraft into the attack and the convoy was demolished.

Gibbs drove himself harder than anyone else. More of his crews were lost but he managed to survive despite his aircraft constantly being damaged by the intense anti-aircraft fire he encountered on every attack. On August 30, the tanker *San Andrea* set sail from Taranto. Gibbs, at the head of his well-drilled formation, headed to intercept it. Enemy fighters appeared but he led in three aircraft and delivered an accurate torpedo attack. Once again his aircraft was hit, but as he ordered in the second group of Beauforts, the oil tanker blew up and sank. It was the last attack he made. Mentally and physically exhausted, he was rested and in September it was announced that he had been awarded the DSO for "his exceptional skill and courage".

One of the RAF's finest operational leaders on Malta, Laddie Lucas, wrote: "There is not the least doubt that the success of his strike operations had a material effect upon the fortunes of our Eighth Army in the desert and the outcome at Alamein; there were few operational efforts in World War Two to compare with it."

The son of a Cardiff shipowner, Reginald Patrick Mahoney Gibbs was born at Penarth on April 2, 1915. He was educated at Oundle and in August 1934 won a prize cadetship to the RAF College Cranwell. He trained as a pilot and excelled at sport winning his colours for rugby, squash and tennis.

Gibbs specialised in maritime strike and reconnaissance

operations and was seconded to the Fleet Air Arm for two years operating from aircraft carriers flying Swordfish and Sharks. He became an instructor at the Torpedo Training School at Gosport before joining No. 22 Squadron in 1940 as a flight commander flying the new Beaufort torpedo bomber. For the next year he undertook many daylight attacks against shipping off the Dutch and Norwegian coasts in addition to bombing the Biscay ports. After a year he was promoted to squadron leader and awarded the DFC. He then spent six months as a very bored instructor before volunteering for flying duties in the Mediterranean.

After returning exhausted from Malta in late 1942, Gibbs worked in the Air Ministry but the strain of the intense flying told and he was medically discharged from the RAF in 1944. One of the squadron navigators described him as "a man of extraordinary dash and courage who inspired the utmost respect amongst other aircrew".

After leaving the RAF Gibbs had become interested in the theatre, after seeing and meeting the actress Muriel Pavlow; this led to his being introduced to W.A. Darlington, the drama critic of the *Daily Telegraph*, who invited him to review some of the less important productions. At first he received no byline, adding his initials RPMG to the bottom of notices rarely more than 150 or 250 words long.

In 1960 Gibbs became the paper's film critic and displayed independent opinions; he showed no interest in cultivating the acquaintance of directors, actors or moguls. The critic's task, he believed, was to strive for detachment. He was so reluctant to introduce a personal touch into his notices that, in his approving review of *Battle of Britain*, he had to be persuaded to mention at the end that he was a former RAF man.

He recorded his wartime experiences in two books, *Not Peace, But a Sword*, which was published to critical praise in 1943, and *Torpedo Leader*, which described his time on Malta. It ran to several editions.

He continued to enjoy the theatre and opera. Every Saturday he left his Holland Park house, where he had built all the shelves himself, to drive hard bargains for Staffordshire pottery, silver and furniture at Portobello market. To aid his pension he was a shrewd investor on the stock market and part-owner, with an old RAF friend, of a chain of launderettes.

Patrick Gibbs was married twice and had a son and a daughter.

WING COMMANDER JIMMY DELL

Wing Commander Jimmy Dell (who died on March 25, 2008 aged 83) was one of Britain's foremost test pilots who used his outstanding skills as a RAF fighter pilot to test the Lightning fighter, as well as the highly advanced TSR-2 bomber controversially cancelled by the Labour government in 1965.

After the first five flights of TSR-2, all flown by Roly Beaumont, Dell took over the main responsibility for testing the aircraft. Of the 24 flights made by the aircraft, Dell was the pilot on 12 occasions. The early flights indicated that it had great potential; its performance and possibilities for further development placed it well ahead of any contemporary aircraft.

Its cancellation dealt a massive blow to the British aircraft industry, and this great sense of anti-climax, and in some quarters anger, was intensified when the government ordered the destruction of all the airframes, plans and jigs. Dell always thought that the aircraft would be a world-beater, and considered it a great privilege to fly it.

James Leonard Dell was born in Liverpool on August 23, 1924. His enthusiasm for flying was fired when Alan Cobham's Flying Circus visited his local area. After serving in the Air Defence Cadet Corps he volunteered to fly in the RAF as soon as he was 18. He was trained in South Africa and after gaining his wings, was selected to be a flying instructor.

He returned to England at the end of the war and soon established himself as an excellent fighter pilot. After serving on No. 43 Squadron, he joined the staff of the Day Fighter Leaders School as an instructor. In 1954 he left for the USA where he flew the swept-wing Sabre fighter with the 60th Fighter Squadron. Returning from a gunnery exercise he was forced to eject when his aircraft ran out of fuel in bad weather.

The Sabres of his squadron were equipped with an air defence radar, and when he returned to the UK he was seconded to the English Electric company as the RAF project pilot for the P1 fighter (later called the Lightning), which became the RAF's first single-seat radar-equipped fighter.

Dell remained at English Electric for more than three years, during which time he was forced to eject for a second time when he had to abandon his Lightning over the Irish Sea. He returned to the RAF to form the Air Fighting Development Squadron where he was involved in carrying out the initial operational trials on the Lightning and introducing it into RAF service.

In October 1959, Dell was persuaded to leave the RAF to join English Electric at Warton, and within a year he was appointed the chief test pilot. He flew many test flights developing the Lightning before becoming involved in the TSR-2 programme. After the TSR-2's cancellation, much of his work was directed towards the Anglo-French project that led to the

Jaguar ground-attack aircraft.

In 1968 he was sent to perform an air display for the King of Saudi Arabia. Those who saw it remember it as one of the finest displays ever seen; shortly afterwards a substantial order for the Lightning was placed by the Royal Saudi Air Force. This proved to be the start of a long and very successful relationship between Saudi Arabia and the British aircraft industry.

In 1970 Dell became increasingly involved in the new tri-national MRCA project (Tornado) when the doctors discovered that he had a minor heart defect that was sufficient to ground him.

Though tempted to retire from aviation, he remained at Warton and took up the position as the manager flight operations for the MRCA flight test programme, initially in Britain and then in Munich, before becoming director of test programme. He retired in 1989.

Dell was appointed OBE in 1966 and was awarded the Derry and Richards Award by the Guild of Air Pilots and Navigators, and the Royal Aero Club Silver Medal for his services to test flying.

After he retired companies and organisations often sought Dell's help and advice, and he greatly enjoyed speaking to various groups about his career. He also liked golf, travel and walking. He gave great support to the Lightning Preservation Group at Bruntingthorpe.

A modest man, he once commented: "I was so very lucky, in the right place at the right time….and I got paid."

Jimmy Dell married his wife Marjorie in June 1946 and she died in 1993. They had two sons; one pre-deceased him.

AIR COMMODORE 'KIT' NORTH-LEWIS

Air Commodore 'Kit' North-Lewis, (who died on March 25, 2008 aged 90) led his squadrons of rocket-firing Typhoon fighters in the fierce fighting during the Normandy campaign

and the advance through the Netherlands to Germany.

North-Lewis had taken command of No. 181 Squadron in May 1944, and was heavily engaged in attacking road and rail targets in the days leading up to the Allied invasion of France a month later. He led his squadron in attacks against the coastal radar system – including the installation at Saint Peter Port on Guernsey – and in the first five days of June all but one of the important coastal radar sites had been put out of action.

Once the land forces were established in Normandy, the operational task of the Typhoon force was to provide close air support to the British Second Army. On June 7, North-Lewis led No. 181 on three operations to attack tanks and transports. He had a very narrow escape as he flew over Carpiquet airfield when a bullet shattered the canopy of his Typhoon, missing his head by inches. For the next few days, his squadron was constantly in action and in the 10-day period after D-Day, North-Lewis flew 20 close-support sorties. By the middle of June his squadron was operating from a temporary airstrip near Caen.

On August 7, a major German counter-attack, spearheaded by five Panzer divisions, was identified moving against just two US infantry divisions. The Panzers had already captured three key villages and were threatening to cut off the US Third Army as it began moving into Brittany. A shuttle service of Typhoons was established and by the end of the day they had flown more than 300 sorties, three of them led by North-Lewis.

The counter-attack was defeated and the 'Day of the Typhoon' (as it became known) was adequately summed up by an intercepted signal from the chief of staff of the German Seventh Army: he reported that the attack had come to a standstill at 1 p.m. owing to the "employment of fighter-bombers by the enemy and the absence of our own air support".

On August 15, North-Lewis was promoted to wing commander and took command of No. 124 Wing of three Typhoon squadrons. A few days later it was announced that he had been awarded a Bar to an earlier DFC. He then led his squadrons during the Battle of Falaise when the Typhoons wreaked havoc amongst the escaping German forces.

During the airborne landings in the Netherlands in September, North-Lewis and his pilots supported the Guards Armoured Division as it began its dash to link up with the forces at Eindhoven. The Typhoons put down a rolling barrage on either side of the road, allowing the tanks to drive forward. His wing was the first to arrive when, three days after the capture of Eindhoven, his Typhoons landed at the nearby, and badly damaged, airfield.

The comparative calm of the autumn months was broken on December 16 when the Germans mounted a major offensive through the Ardennes. The weather was atrocious, and the enemy advance made significant progress. By Boxing Day, when the weather had improved, No. 124 Wing was tasked to deal with a dangerous German thrust towards a bridge over the Meuse. North-Lewis and his squadrons attacked a large concentration with rockets and cannons. British forces were a few hundred yards away and were given a grandstand view of the attack. The German thrust was halted and within a few days the Battle of the Bulge was over.

On the morning of March 23, 1945, as the Allies mounted an airborne assault and amphibious crossing near Wesel on the River Rhine, North-Lewis led his squadrons against a strongpoint east of the town. His Typhoon was hit by anti-aircraft fire and the engine stopped. He managed to crash-land on a small island where he was taken prisoner; but the Germans' situation deteriorated overnight, whereupon his captors decided to surrender to him. He found an abandoned canoe and paddled to the Allied lines.

North-Lewis's AOC directed that he was not to fly again. In the previous 14 months he had flown 176 operational sorties at a time when the losses in his own wing had been 116 pilots killed or taken prisoner. A few days later he was awarded an immediate DSO.

Christopher David North-Lewis (always known as Kit) was born on March 13, 1918 into a family of Welsh colliery owners. He was educated at Marlborough, where he performed well in the Officers' Training Corps. Before the outbreak of war, he was commissioned into the 2nd Battalion of the Queen Victoria's Rifles.

Bored with the inactivity of army service in England, North-Lewis answered an RAF request for army volunteers to train as pilots. He began flying training in late 1940 then joined No. 13 Squadron. On the night of March 30, 1942, he was part of a small force of Blenheims tasked to bomb German night-fighter airfields in support of the first 1,000-Bomber Raid on Cologne.

He evaluated the American-built Tomahawk and Mustang fighters for army co-operation work and in late 1942 joined No. 26 Squadron as a flight commander, flying the Mustang. He completed many reconnaissance sorties along the length of the north coast of France photographing enemy defences. These operations, flown 200–300 yards offshore provided important information for the planning of the invasion of Normandy. He also flew many ground-attack operations against trains and transport columns in northern France. In March 1943 he was awarded a DFC.

Soon after returning to England in May 1945, it was announced that the Dutch government had awarded him the Bronze Lion (Dutch DSO) and the Dutch Flying Cross for his contribution to the liberation of the Netherlands.

North-Lewis remained in the RAF after the war and in the early 1950s much enjoyed a tour with the Rhodesian Air Training Group. His tour at the NATO headquarters at Fontainbleu was interrupted when he was summoned to London to join the planning staffs for Operation Musketeer, the seizure of the Suez Canal. Once it was decided to mount the operation in late 1956, he left for the headquarters in Cyprus where he remained until the withdrawal from Egypt in December.

In August North-Lewis assumed command of No. 7 Squadron flying Valiants. After just a year he was promoted to group captain and took command of RAF Wyton, where the strategic reconnaissance force was based with Valiants and Canberras. As an air commodore he commanded the RAF's large air base at Akrotiri in Cyprus when the Javelin squadron based there was despatched to Zambia following the Southern Rhodesian government's declaration of independence. During his time in Cyprus he raised a polo team and played in Jordan against King Hussein's team. After serving on the intelligence staff in the MoD, he retired from the RAF in February 1971.

North-Lewis became the director of the British Printing Ink Manufacturers, where one of his tasks was to maintain relations with NATSOPA, at the time one of the more militant print unions, and to help negotiate annual pay negotiations, an event he found both stimulating and enjoyable. He retired after 12 years in the job.

Once described by a friend as "a man from the old school", North-Lewis could be both impatient and irascible, but was known for his modesty, integrity and honesty. Throughout his life he enjoyed sport, and was a keen golfer at Liphook, in Hampshire where he served on the club's committee for a number of years, and continued playing until his late eighties.

He was a strong supporter of reunions of his wartime colleagues and was particularly touched when the French raised a memorial at Noyers-Bocage in memory of the 151 Typhoon pilots lost during the liberation of France.

Determined to make his 90th birthday, Kit North-Lewis died a few days after reaching this milestone. He married Virginia Lockhart in April 1948 and she died in September 1985. They had a son and a daughter. His second wife Susan survived him.

SYDNEY DOWSE

Sydney Dowse (who died on April 18, 2008 aged 89) was one of the principal constructors of the tunnel used in the Great Escape; he was among those that got away, and was at large for 14 days before being recaptured and sent to the death camp at Sachsenhausen, where he dug another tunnel to gain a few more days of freedom.

Dowse had been in captivity for just over a year when he arrived in May 1942 at Stalag Luft III, at Sagan – Hermann Göring's 'escape-proof' camp. He made two unsuccessful attempts to escape before further efforts by the prisoners were put on a more formal footing by the formation of an escape committee under the chairmanship of Roger Bushell, known as 'Big X'.

The committee decided to attempt a mass break out through three tunnels – known as Tom, Dick and Harry – dug from the north compound to the nearby woods. Dowse had dug tunnels at his previous camps, and was soon recruited to be one of the main diggers for Harry. The trapdoor to the tunnel in Block 104 was beneath one of the stoves that were in the corner of every room. A 25-ft shaft was dug down into

the sandy soil beneath the block before the tunnel headed for
the camp perimeter.

Although Dowse spent most of his time underground, he
also befriended a German corporal who worked in the cen-
sor's office of the camp headquarters. Through this contact he
obtained numerous authentic documents, which were passed
to the escape committee for copying, and much valuable military intelligence. He even managed to persuade the corporal
to provide him with a tailored suit, which he subsequently
wore for his escape.

On the night of March 24, 1944, Dowse was the 21st man
to exit the Harry tunnel along with his Polish friend 'Danny'
Krol. Due to delays in exiting the tunnel, the pair were unable
to catch their intended train. Their plan was to head for Poland, where they hoped to meet up with the Polish resistance.
The ever-resourceful Dowse had obtained a three-week supply of genuine food vouchers from the German corporal, so
the two men decided to set off on foot and follow the main
railway line eastwards.

Having walked for 14 days, they were close to the Polish border when a member of the Hitler Youth spotted them.
They were arrested, the last to be recaptured. While Dowse
was taken to Berlin for interrogation, Krol was handed over
to the Gestapo and was the last of the 50 prisoners executed
on the orders of Adolf Hitler. (Dowse was descended from a
distinguished German family and always assumed that this had
saved him from the Gestapo.)

Sydney Hastings Dowse was born on November 21, 1918 at
Hammersmith and was educated at Hurstpierpont College. In
July 1937 he joined the recently formed RAF Volunteer Reserve, learning to fly at weekends. At the outbreak of war he
was called up for regular service and completed his training.

Dowse initially flew Coastal Command Ansons on anti-submarine and convoy escort operations with No. 608 Squadron. At the end of 1940 he volunteered to join the expanding
reconnaissance force and, after converting to the Spitfire, he

joined No. 1 Photographic Reconnaissance Unit (PRU).

The high-flying Spitfires spent much of their time monitoring the movements of Germany's capital ships, and Dowse, who flew many such sorties, was mentioned in despatches. On September 20, 1941, he set off on the familiar route to the Brest Peninsula to photograph the *Scharnhorst* and *Gneisenau*, but his aircraft was shot down over the French coast and he was forced to bale out; he was suffering from a leg wound and was soon captured.

In December Dowse escaped from the hospital where he was being treated, but three days later a guard caught him as he crossed the German–Dutch border and he was sent to Stalag IXC at Bad Sulza. By mingling with a working party, Dowse soon managed to get away again. He travelled by train towards Belgium, and then continued on foot towards the German–Belgian frontier, where, suffering from extreme exhaustion, he was recaptured. After hospital treatment he was imprisoned at Oflag VIB, where he helped to build four tunnels, through one of which officers escaped in April 1942. A month later, Dowse was transferred to Sagan.

After his interrogation in Berlin following the Great Escape, Dowse was sent to the death camp at Sachsenhausen, where he found three others who had been spared, among them his friend Jimmy James. Within days of their arrival, the men were discussing how to get out.

Undeterred by the threat of execution if they escaped, the four, together with another prisoner, started a tunnel. Dowse and James were the two diggers using spoons and a kitchen knife. It was a massive undertaking, yet they made a 110-foot-long tunnel.

On the night of September 23, the five men broke out, an event which astonished the Germans who launched a widespread search and placed a high price on their heads. Dowse travelled with 'Wings' Day, and a few days later they were captured on the outskirts of Berlin. On their return to Sachsenhausen, they were chained to the floor of a death cell and cruelly interrogated. They did not expect to survive.

In the event, after five months of solitary confinement, they were released back into the main camp, where they witnessed daily executions.

From February 1945 they were transferred to other concentration camps with a group of prominent prisoners to be held as possible hostages. They were moved to Dachau and then to the Tyrol, where Allied forces liberated them in May 1945. On May 13, Dowse and his colleagues were flown back to Blackbushe for a period of convalescence. In due course, it was announced that Dowse had been awarded the MC for his conduct whilst a prisoner. He was released from the RAF as a flight lieutenant in January 1946.

Dowse served as an equerry at Buckingham Palace and had a long and successful career as a civil servant. For a number of years in the 1950s, at the time of the communist insurgency, he served in Malaya as assistant secretary to the Penang Settlement.

In 1966, Dowse and his colleagues sought compensation for those who had suffered in concentration camps. The Foreign Office claimed that the RAF men were "held under conditions which could not be equated to those of proper concentration camps". Airey Neave MP, who had escaped from Colditz, led the protests. After a very acrimonious debate in Parliament a lengthy enquiry was held and two years later the Ombudsman found in favour of 12 British servicemen who had been imprisoned in Sachsenhausen, including the RAF men.

To commemorate the 50th anniversary in March 1994 of the escape from Stalag Luft III, Dowse organised, and financed, a memorial service at the RAF church at St Clement Danes followed by a champagne reception at the RAF Club. Seventeen of the survivors were amongst those who attended and, 10 years later, some of them were reunited at the Imperial War Museum, where Dowse met the actor John Leyton, who played him in the film *The Great Escape*. Leyton commented: "It was an honour and a privilege. What you did was absolutely extraordinary."

Despite the loss of so many men, Dowse always believed

the Great Escape was worth it. In later years he observed: "We caused havoc to the Germans, we tied up thousands looking for us."

Dowse had an irrepressible enthusiasm and easy-going bonhomie. In Sagan he gained the nickname 'Laughing Boy', but this disguised a tough and determined resolve. His friend Jimmy James remarked: "His spirit was undimmed, even in Sachsenhausen he was as ebullient as ever."

In retirement Dowse divided his time between his elegant homes in Chelsea and Monte Carlo. Well known at the Savoy Hotel in London, he never needed to book for dinner always being shown to one of the best tables.

Throughout his life Dowse was passionate about rugby. Both before and after the war he turned out for Harlequins (whose tie remained his favourite neckwear), and at Stalag Luft III, during breaks from his tunnelling duties. Generous and smart, he continued to enjoy the fine things in life – including his Rolls-Royce and fast cars – into old age, and once remarked: "Once one escapes from that place [Sachsenhausen], life holds no difficulties."

It is thought that Sydney Dowse married three times, but at the time of his death he was single.

_____

WING COMMANDER PADDY BARTHROPP

Wing Commander Paddy Barthropp (who died on April 16, 2008 aged 87) was one of the RAF's most ebullient and colourful characters; he fought in the Battle of Britain, escaped twice from prisoner of war camps and later became a test pilot and a winning jockey in Hong Kong.

Aged 19, Barthropp joined No. 602 Squadron to fly Spitfires from an airfield on the south coast. His first day of action was September 15, 1940 the climax of the battle, when he was airborne four times. In his excitement he managed to fire off all his ammunition during each engagement and

readily acknowledged that he was "absolutely terrified". On September 27, he achieved his first success when he shot down a Heinkel bomber near Brighton. A few days later he shared in the destruction of a Junkers 88.

In February 1941 Barthropp joined another Spitfire squadron, No. 91, at Hawkinge in Kent; its role was to send pairs of aircraft across the Channel to shadow enemy shipping, seek out transport targets and attack aircraft on the ground.

Throughout that summer he was constantly in action and was credited with destroying two enemy fighters, probably destroying two others and damaging two more. On numerous occasions his Spitfire returned damaged by anti-aircraft fire. In August 1941, after completing 150 operations, he was awarded the DFC and sent to a fighter training unit as an instructor.

Patrick Peter Colum Barthropp (known throughout his life as Paddy) was born during a family visit to Dublin on November 9, 1920. His mother died in childbirth and Barthropp was brought up and educated in Shropshire before going to Ampleforth College where he won his colours in four sports. He later admitted: "My academic career was not as brilliant." As the son of a distinguished amateur steeplechase rider, he developed a great love of riding and was tutored by the champion jockey Steve Donaghue. On leaving school he took up an engineering apprenticeship at the Rover works in Coventry.

Barthropp joined the RAF on November 1, 1938 on a short-service commission and trained as a pilot. During some training flights, he would divert from the air exercise and trail the local hunt in his Tiger Moth. He was posted to No. 613

Squadron, flying Lysanders on army co-operation duties, and flew on operations in support of the British Expeditionary Force until the end of the evacuation from Dunkirk. In August 1940 he answered a call for volunteers to transfer to Fighter Command to help make up the heavy losses of pilots sustained during the fighting of the summer of 1940.

During his time flying on operations after the Battle of Britain, Barthropp did not neglect his social activities. He managed to acquire a two-litre Lagonda in exchange for 400 gallons of 100-octane aviation fuel. His ground crew fitted a 25-gallon tank under the car's back seat, which he later said, "gave me an extra supply of juice to keep me ahead of the game when I set off for pastures green".

One evening he wrote the car off after colliding with a London taxi. On another occasion he and a colleague were fined £1 for assaulting the proprietor of the Red Lion Hotel, Hounslow after they were refused entry to a dance. When Barthropp called the magistrate a "silly old bastard", the fine was doubled.

Barthropp's time as an instructor provided ample opportunity for low-flying, beat-ups and a hectic social life in Shropshire. Addicted as he was to fast cars and lively ladies, he saw himself as the sworn enemy of stuffed shirts and unsympathetic authority. Returning from a particularly uproarious party in Oswestry, he drove his latest car into a lake after missing a turn. This proved to be the last straw for his commanding officer, who decided he was not setting a good example to the students, and arranged for him to be sent back to an operational squadron. On May 12, 1942, he accordingly drove his newly acquired drophead Rover to Hornchurch to join No. 122 Squadron.

Five days later, Barthropp was escorting six Bostons bombing a factory near St Omer when Focke-Wulf Fw 190s attacked his formation. He shot one down, but then the controls of his Spitfire were hit and damaged and he was forced to bale out. He was soon captured, and later that evening met the pilot who had engaged him. Four weeks later, Barthropp arrived at Stalag Luft III at Sagan where he and a colleague attempted to escape by hiding in a drain covered by a manhole cover; they were soon apprehended.

Over a period of 18 months, he spent 100 days in solitary confinement for a series of misdemeanours before being transferred to a camp in Poland. Here he was involved in digging a tunnel. After six months it was ready and 32 men escaped. Barthropp was the third to break out and he headed for Warsaw with a companion. A few days later the Gestapo caught them.

On January 28, 1945, the prisoners were herded from their camp and marched westwards during an intensely cold winter. They eventually reached Lübeck where they were liberated in May. Barthropp managed to acquire a Mercedes fire engine and he and a friend drove it to Brussels via Hamburg where they met two ladies who were happy to spend the night with them for a tin of corned beef.

Barthropp remained in the RAF and worked in Norway locating the graves of missing airmen – he received the Order of King Haakon of Norway to add to an earlier Cross of Lorraine awarded by the French government. He was also mentioned in despatches.

To his astonishment, his application in 1946 to attend the Empire Test Pilot's School was successful and, after completing the course, he tested many fighter aircraft, including the first jets, at Boscombe Down. After a period in Khartoum responsible for hot weather trials of the Meteor jet fighter, he went to HQ Fighter Command.

He returned to operational flying in 1952 when he was appointed to command the Waterbeach fighter wing flying Meteors. During the flypast to celebrate the coronation of HM the Queen, he led a formation of 288 Meteors. As he left London he was forced to fly over an RAF airfield where the controller ordered him to change course to avoid overflying. Barthropp responded with a few expletives and suggested he move his airfield because there was no way he could turn away the tightly packed formation in time. At the end of his tour of duty at Waterbeach he was awarded the AFC.

Barthropp left for an administrative post at the Air Head-quarters in Hong Kong in March 1954, an appointment for which he had little enthusiasm. Claiming to be inadequately trained he felt able to delegate most of his responsibilities to a junior officer and a corporal. This allowed him to take up horse racing at which he was successful, winning a number of races at the Happy Valley racecourse, which provided him with sufficient winnings to enrich his social life.

After commanding RAF Honiley, the home of two Royal Auxiliary Air Force jet fighter squadrons, he was made the senior administration officer at RAF Coltishall in Norfolk.

Barthropp found administration dreary and he accepted his release under a 'golden bowler' scheme and left the RAF in 1957. He used the handsome gratuity and part of an inheritance to buy a Bentley and a Rolls-Royce Phantom VI. Dressed in an expensive chauffeur's outfit he started to drive the well-heeled around Britain. Over the next few years his luxury car-hire business became very successful and he soon owned a fleet of Rolls-Royces. One of his cars featured in the James Bond film *Casino Royale*.

Barthropp was a great raconteur and *bon vivant* with a huge sense of humour. According to a colleague, "he only obeyed those rules he agreed with". He was a great supporter of the Battle of Britain Fighter Association and for many years fought to get ex-POWs the back pay they were denied. He greatly enjoyed country life, shooting and fishing. He wrote an amusing autobiography, *Paddy* (1987), the proceeds going to the Douglas Bader Foundation.

His first marriage to Barbara Pal in 1948 was dissolved in 1958. He married his second wife Betty in 1962.

AIR CHIEF MARSHAL SIR JOHN BARRACLOUGH

Air Chief Marshal Sir John Barraclough (who died on May 10, 2008 aged 90) gave an exceptionally long period of devoted service to the Crown and to defence affairs; after serving in the RAF for 38 years, in retirement he conducted various studies for the Air Force Board and the chiefs of staff before becoming the Inspector-General of the Royal Auxiliary Air Force.

During the Second World War, Barraclough flew continuously on maritime air duties with Coastal Command and in the Indian Ocean. Before the war he flew Ansons with No. 269 Squadron from Abbotsinch near Glasgow, and with a taste of what might lie ahead, he was engaged in the air searches for the submarine *Thetis* when it failed to surface in Liverpool Bay in 1938.

On the outbreak of war, he converted to flying boats, and in 1940 he operated with No. 240 Squadron from the Shetland Islands. Flying over the northern North Sea he flew in support of the ill-fated British Expeditionary Force to Norway and on searches for German naval forces seeking to break out from the Baltic. After a period flying anti-submarine patrols and convoy escorts off the west coast of Scotland, he was made chief instructor of the flying boat conversion unit at Invergordon where he was awarded the AFC for developing innovative methods of operational training.

In February 1942 Barraclough reformed No. 209 Squadron, equipped with the Catalina flying boat, before leaving in June for the Indian Ocean to support the Eastern Fleet for the Madagascar campaign. Operating with the barest facilities from Comoro Island in the Mozambique Channel, and from other island bases, he flew intensive operations and was awarded the DFC. "This officer," the citation concluded, "has shown the greatest devotion to duty and is a born leader of men."

Barraclough continued to operate with No. 209 over the vast areas of the Indian Ocean providing convoy escorts and seeking out U-boats and their mother ship, *Elizabeth Schliemann*. Promoted to wing commander aged 24, he commanded the captured Italian airfield at Mogadishu in Somaliland where Wellingtons conducted anti-submarine operations. On his return to Britain in May 1944 he was the chief instructor at a flying boat training unit and was mentioned in despatches.

John Barraclough was born in Hounslow on May 2, 1918 and educated at Cranbrook School. After three years volunteer service with the Artists' Rifles while working in the City of London, he was granted a four-year commission in the RAF in 1938 to train as a pilot.

At the end of the war, Barraclough was negotiating his admission to the Middle Temple as a student when he was offered a permanent commission in the RAF, which he accepted. After completing a period of service in Egypt, he joined the Central Flying School and was appointed to its examining wing, first as a flight commander and then in command of the wing responsible for the flying instructional standards in the RAF and in many other national air forces where the RAF was held in great esteem. As a staff officer at the headquarters of Training Command, he wrote an imaginative paper on the pros and cons of using a basic jet aircraft for initial pilot training and this paved the way for the introduction into service of the long-serving Jet Provost aircraft.

Barraclough was always a restive staff officer who hankered after action – he flew more than 70 different types of aircraft – and he was able to persuade his commander-in-chief that he should take the first Vampire training aircraft on a trial flight to Southern Rhodesia. With little or no navigation aids for the venture, Barraclough and his fellow pilot completed the 10,000-mile round trip in the cramped cockpit of the short-range, single-engine jet without mishap. He was awarded a Queen's Commendation for Valuable Service in the Air.

After commanding the two fighter stations at Biggin Hill and Middleton St. George (now Durham Tees Valley Airport), he served in the Far East during the campaign against the Communist terrorists in Malaya. On promotion to air commodore in 1960 he took up the post of director of public relations at the Air Ministry, where he was deeply engaged in defending the philosophy and strategy of nuclear deterrence then exercised by Bomber Command; he also defended (in the event unavailingly) the emerging TSR-2 from its political opponents. His efforts on these sensitive issues were recognised with a CBE.

On completion of his time as AOC No. 19 Group in Coastal Command, Barraclough took a sabbatical and, at his own expense and on unpaid leave, enrolled on the advanced management course at the Harvard Business School. On his return in 1968, the RAF appointed him Air Officer (Administration) of Bomber Command to manage the imminent, and highly emotional, mergers of Bomber, Fighter, Coastal and Signals Commands. Such was his success that he was promoted and appointed CB.

He served as vice chief of the defence staff before becoming the air secretary, an appointment he did not relish. His final post before retiring from the RAF in 1978 was as the Commandant of the Royal College of Defence Studies. He was appointed KCB in 1970.

Barraclough had a sharp intellect, dry wit and a boundless energy and enthusiasm. He was an eloquent and persuasive writer, and after retirement from the RAF was much in demand. For 12 years he served as a commissioner and vice chairman of the Commonwealth War Graves Commission. In 1976 he had been appointed an honorary air commodore in the Royal Auxiliary Air Force and, with the force employed in the ground-defence role, he found himself very much at home as a former territorial rifleman.

For five years he was the Inspector-General of the force, during which time he was appointed a Gentleman Usher to the Sword of State with occasional ceremonial duties. He was able to take advantage of an informal opportunity after a State Opening of Parliament to seek the Queen's agreement to the award of a Colour. This was granted, and in June 1989 750 serving members of the Royal Auxiliary Air Force paraded at RAF Benson on the occasion of the presentation of the Queen's Colour.

On his farewell as the inspector in 1995, Barraclough flew a bombing sortie in a Tornado – the 57th anniversary of his first flight in the RAF.

For six years in the 1970s he was editorial director of the defence magazine *NATO's Nations*. He was also a co-author, with General Sir John Hackett, of the bestselling book *The Third World War*, to which he contributed the air aspects.

In 1980 he became president of the Air Power Association, and the next year sponsored the Barraclough Trophy, awarded annually to the unit or individual member of the RAF who has made an outstanding contribution to RAF public relations in the previous year.

Barraclough was chairman of the Royal United Services Institute for Defence Studies, and then vice chairman of the Air League, receiving its Gold Medal for distinguished services to British aviation. He was elected a Fellow of the Royal Aeronautical Society and was a Liveryman of the Guild of Air Pilots and Air Navigators.

In 2002 he was approached to support an initiative to commemorate all those who had lost their lives in Coastal Command. He was appointed chairman of the Maritime Air Trust, and under his guidance and management, the trust launched a formidable fundraising programme with the Duke of Edinburgh as its very supportive patron. On March 16, 2004, the Queen dedicated a sculptured tribute and roll of honour in the south cloister of Westminster Abbey. Barraclough – who, aged 86, handed over the reins of the trust to a former chief of the air staff, Sir Peter Squire – always considered it an honour to have been associated with the project.

Barraclough settled in Bath, where in later years he was invited to be chairman, and later president, of the city's Royal Crescent Society, an organisation he led with his usual vigour, and to acclaim, in countering the adverse effects of un-managed tourism.

He was a fine sailor and horseman. He navigated the Irish yacht *Clarion* to success in her division of the Fastnet Race in the Admiral's Cup in 1973. In the winter he rode regularly to hounds wherever he found himself, and he followed three-day eventing with keen interest. He was a past president of the RAF Modern Pentathlon Association and of the Combined Services Equitation Association. He listed amongst his hobbies, "stilt walking (retired)".

John Barraclough was a tall man with a commanding presence, but an unassuming manner. After being diagnosed with terminal cancer, he displayed stoical courage.

Shortly before his death, he paid tribute to his wife Maureen (née McCormack), whom he had married in 1946 (and had died in 2001), writing that "her devoted and unselfish support during a taxing career was quite simply immeasurable". They had a daughter.

CAPTAIN JIM FUTCHER

Captain Jim Futcher (who died on May 10, 2008 aged 86) was a senior captain with British Airways awarded the Queen's Gallantry Medal (QGM) in recognition of his calm and courageous conduct after Palestinian terrorists hijacked his VC-10 airliner in November 1974.

On the night of November 21, Futcher was at Dubai airport to meet the inbound Flight 870 from London. After the VC-10 had been refuelled, he and his crew were to take over for its

continuing flight to the Far East.

During the brief stop, four men disguised as airport workers left the passenger lounge and ran towards the airliner, firing guns as they approached. A stewardess standing by the aircraft's steps was shot in the back but survived. It was only once they were on board that the hijackers realised that there was no pilot and they threatened to shoot the passengers if one did not arrive immediately.

Futcher did not hesitate to go to the aircraft, and the VC-10 took off with 27 passengers, eight airport workers (who had been cleaning the aircraft) and a crew of 10. The hijackers ordered Futcher to fly to Beirut, but the authorities had closed the airport and ringed it with security forces.

The aircraft refuelled at Tripoli before putting down in Tunis, where it was immediately surrounded by troops. The hijackers decided to make a stand, and demanded the release of seven Palestinian terrorists, five held in Cairo and two in the Netherlands. They set a deadline of 24 hours, threatening that if it was not met, they would shoot one hostage every two hours. When the deadline duly passed, they executed a German banker and dumped his body on the tarmac.

As intense diplomatic discussions took place, Futcher attempted to establish some kind of relationship with the hijackers, who were by now extremely excitable, and to reassure his terrified passengers. The terrorists held in Cairo were brought to Tunis and taken to the aircraft, resulting in the release of seven hostages from the VC-10. But if Futcher hoped that this gesture would calm the hijackers, he was mistaken; the new arrivals indicated that they intended to die "for the cause". The following morning, the two terrorists from the Netherlands arrived, and the remaining hostages were released – leaving

Futcher, the co-pilot and the flight engineer on board.

The hijackers were informed over the radio that all Arab governments as well as the Palestinian Liberation Organisation (PLO) had condemned their actions. Increasingly desperate, they now sought political asylum in Tunisia; but this was refused, and they were ordered to surrender. In reply they set two deadlines for their demands to be met; otherwise they would blow up the aircraft and their hostages.

The deadlines passed and they stated that, at 7 a.m. the next morning, they would detonate the explosives they had placed in the cockpit. Futcher made one last effort to make the 11 terrorists see reason. He tried to persuade them that if they blew themselves up, together with the flight crew, the world would condemn them, but he went on: "If you release us and kill yourselves, you will be martyrs." They fell silent, and Futcher returned to the flight deck.

At 7 a.m. a gunman approached the cockpit. Convinced that he and his colleagues were about to be killed, Futcher was surprised when the terrorists' leader told him they had decided to surrender.

At a press conference hastily arranged after his release, Futcher's initial comment was: "I'm not a brave man. Anyone would have gone out." But his actions and conduct received international acclaim. He received a 'well done' message from Peter Shore, the Secretary of State for Trade and Industry and in due course he was given more generous recognition. In addition to being awarded the QGM, presented to him by the Queen in July 1975, he was awarded the Founder's Medal by the Guild of Air Pilots and Air Navigators, the British Airline Pilots Association Gold Medal and a Certificate of Commendation from British Airways.

The son of a Canadian Pacific Railway sign writer, James Edward Futcher was born on June 17, 1921 in the Thunder Bay district of Canada. His parents returned to England in 1926 and he was educated at Collingdale High School. His first job was with the Metal Box Company, but in February 1942 he joined the RAF and volunteered for aircrew. He was selected to be a navigator and trained in Canada.

After completing his training, he remained in Canada and joined No. 525 Squadron tasked with delivering bomber and transport aircraft to war theatres in Europe, the Middle East and the Far East. In March 1947 he joined BOAC as a navigator on flying boats before transferring to the Argonaut airliner. He was one of the few navigators to be selected for training as a pilot and he qualified in April 1953. He flew as a first officer on Argonauts before transferring to the Britannia. In 1964 he joined the VC-10 fleet as a first officer, was promoted to captain in January 1969 and a senior captain first class five years later.

In January 1974 Futcher commanded the VC-10 that took the Queen and the Duke of Edinburgh to the Commonwealth Games in New Zealand. This was the same aircraft that was involved in the hijack later that year.

In February 1979 Futcher was again in command of a Royal Flight when he took the Queen and the Duke to Saudi Arabia and the Gulf States. A month later he retired from British Airways having accumulated over 20,000 flying hours.

For all his heroism, Futcher was a modest man. Highly respected by his professional colleagues, his easy-going personality, generosity and charm also won him many friends.

He was an accomplished golfer who played on courses all over the world. As a member at Camberley Heath, Surrey, he won the club's match play and foursomes' championships. He was also a proficient tennis player and athlete.

Jim Futcher married Eileen Hughesman in March 1949 who died in November 2007. They had a son and a daughter.

THE VENERABLE HEWITT WILSON

The Venerable Hewitt Wilson (who died on June 29, 2008 aged 84) had the distinction of being the longest-serving RAF chaplain-in-chief in the service's 90-year history.

The post, which carries the honorary rank of air vice-marshal, is the senior chaplain's appointment in the RAF. Wilson was appointed in 1973 and served for seven years. This was a period that covered turbulent times in the service, including a morale-sapping manpower redundancy scheme, during which Wilson's strong leadership, compassion and understanding were much in evidence.

His post also carried with it the appointment of canon and prebendary of Lincoln Cathedral, an establishment with a unique relationship with the RAF, and in particular with Bomber Command.

John Hewitt Wilson was born on St Valentine's Day in 1924 at Worcester, Massachusetts, where his father was working. His family returned to farm near Cork, in Ireland, when Wilson was two. He was educated at Kilkenny College and Mountjoy School in Dublin before entering Trinity College, Dublin, to graduate with a First in Oriental languages and Theology in 1947.

Wilson was an outstanding sportsman and earned his university colours at rugby, athletics and tennis. He went on to play rugby threequarter for Leicester and also for the RAF when he was the only non-international to play for it regularly.

After graduation, Wilson served for three years as a curate at St George's Church, Dublin before taking a commission in the RAF Chaplain's Branch in 1950. For the first 10 years of his service, he served on flying stations, most notably in Aden and Germany.

Wilson's gentle, easy-going and caring manner allowed him to establish a unique relationship with the station officers, airmen and their families. He liked nothing better than the company of young fighter pilots and their ground crew – not a breed that always readily looks upon the padre as a chum – and enjoyed sitting in their crew rooms or in the bar at 'happy hour' listening to their tales and banter. He also developed a well-tuned ear for the state of morale in the unit, which was of great value to the station commander, to whom the chaplain always had direct access.

Wilson served as the staff chaplain to the RAF's chaplain-in-chief, the Venerable Frank Cocks, who later became the Bishop of Shrewsbury – a period that had a profound influence on his approach on his later career and ministries. In 1963 he was appointed the senior chaplain at the RAF College Cranwell, an appointment described by a colleague as "an inspired choice". He then served as the assistant chaplain-in-chief at the HQ Far East Air Force, and in 1969 he filled a similar appointment at the RAF's biggest headquarters, Strike Command at High Wycombe. Three years later he was appointed honorary chaplain to HM the Queen, and the next year he was made chaplain-in-chief.

Wilson set, expected and demanded high standards of his chaplains, seeking their views on key matters (asking them to give it to him straight), before deciding on which course of action to take or recommend. He could be hard but was always fair and consistent in his dealings with those who needed a sharp reminder of what was expected of them. There was never any malice, the 'rocket' was delivered in a quiet, gentle manner in his Irish lilt, and the matter was then never mentioned again. Together with his sincerity, integrity and sense of fun and humour, these qualities made Wilson a most effective, respected and well-liked chaplain-in-chief. In 1977 he was appointed CB.

On his retirement from the RAF in 1980, Wilson was appointed archdeacon emeritus and canon emeritus of Lincoln Cathedral, the latter a unique distinction shared with only one other RAF chaplain.

In 1991 he was appointed rector of Somerton, the Heyfords and Rousham where his uncomplicated faith and straightforward ministry soon revitalised the four parishes. He and his wife provided unstinting hospitality, and they immersed themselves in every activity in the region. Wilson formed close relationships with the USAF personnel at the nearby Upper Heyford airbase, who benefited from his service experience of relationships with local communities and how best to avoid conflict over any controversial issue.

So respected was he by the Americans that he was asked to marry the colonel's daughter in the ecumenical station chapel, which meant obtaining a special licence from the Archbishop of Canterbury. One parishioner described his 10-year ministry as "a golden age for the Cherwell valley".

Wilson became chaplain in 1995 to the Worshipful Company of Coachmakers and Coach Harness makers, a City livery company involved with the automotive and aerospace manufacturing industries. His wise counsel, commitment, warm personality and sense of humour were much in evidence and appreciated by members. He went on to become an honorary assistant to the court and then chaplain emeritus.

Wilson enjoyed the theatre and travelling and he maintained his great love for sport.

Hewitt Wilson married Joan Weir in 1951 with whom he had three sons and two daughters.

COLONEL DON BLAKESLEE

Colonel Don Blakeslee (who died on September 3, 2008 aged 90) served in the Royal Canadian Air Force and the RAF before transferring to the USAAF, where he was considered one of the finest combat fighter leaders of the Second World War.

On January 1, 1944 Blakeslee was appointed to command the 4th Fighter Group based at Debden in Essex. The role of the group was to escort the Eighth Air Force's long-range bomber force deep into enemy territory. A forceful, no-nonsense man, he left his pilots in no doubt what he expected of them when

he addressed them for the first time: "We are here to fight," he began. "To those who don't believe me, I would suggest transferring to another group. I'm going to fly the arse off each one of you. Those who keep up with me, good; those who don't, I don't want them."

His group was equipped with the P-47 Thunderbolt, a fighter he had little time for. He worked hard to be re-equipped with the P-51 Mustang, and when higher authority approved, he was told that his pilots had to be operational within 24 hours of receiving them. He agreed, instructing his pilots to "learn how to fly them on the way to the target".

In March 1944, Blakeslee led the first Mustangs over Berlin escorting a daylight-bombing raid. In just four months his aggressive leadership led to the group achieving its 500th 'kill'. On June 21, he led his fighters (known by the bomber crews they escorted as their 'little friends') on the first 'shuttle' bombing mission to Russia by Eighth Air Force Flying Fortresses, a flight of 1,470 miles. Blakeslee and his pilots landed in the Ukraine after being airborne for seven hours in their single-engine fighters.

By his own admission Blakeslee was not a very good shot

and he flew very close to his adversary before opening fire. He was credited with 15-and-a-half victories, but when there was a multiple claim he always allowed the junior pilot the credit. Many believe that he destroyed at least 30 enemy aircraft.

His greatest asset was his outstanding ability as a leader in the air. One eminent aviation historian wrote: "He was everywhere in the battle, twisting and climbing, bellowing and blaspheming, warning and exhorting. His ability to keep things taped in a fight with 50 planes flying at 400 mph was a source of wonder." One of his pilots described him as "George S. Patton Jr. in a P-51 Mustang".

Blakeslee forged the 4th Fighter Group into one of the most formidable and successful USAAF fighter combat units – many claim it was the best. By the end of the war it had become the top-scoring American fighter group. Having flown more than 400 operational sorties since transferring to the USAAF, he was finally grounded in September 1944.

Donald James Mathew Blakeslee was born on September 11, 1917 at Fairport Harbour, Ohio. As a boy he watched the Cleveland National Air Races and became fascinated with flying. In 1939 he and a friend bought a light aircraft and learnt to fly but when the friend crashed it, he left Ohio in October 1940, to cross the Canadian border and join the RCAF.

After completing his training, he arrived in England in May 1941 and joined No. 401 (RCAF) Squadron flying Spitfires from Biggin Hill. Engaged on sweeps over northern France throughout 1941, he was credited with destroying a Messerschmitt Bf 109 and damaging others. He also destroyed two aircraft on the ground during strafing attacks.

He later transferred to No. 133, one of the three US-manned 'Eagle' squadrons of the RAF, and during the Dieppe operation in August 1942 he shot down a Dornier bomber, probably destroyed a Focke-Wulf Fw 190 and damaged two others. He was awarded the DFC after completing 120 operations.

In September, the Eagle squadrons were transferred with their Spitfires to the USAAF's 4th Fighter Group, and Blakeslee

took command of the 335th Squadron. The unit was soon re-
equipped with the P-47 and in April 1943 he achieved his
first success when he shot down a Fw 190, followed shortly
afterwards by a second. In May he was promoted to lieutenant
colonel and became the group's executive officer, continuing
to fly in combat. As one of the most experienced American
fighter pilots in Europe, he was asked to lead the recently arrived 354th Fighter Group on its initial operations. This was
the first unit to be equipped with the P-51 Mustang, and he
was able to claim another victory on the type. His experience
with the 354th convinced him that the Mustang was superior
to his own unit's P-47s. A few weeks later he was promoted to
colonel to command the 4th Fighter Group.

After he was grounded, Blakeslee returned to the United
States to command an airfield in Florida. He remained in the
USAAF and commanded a fighter wing and his later assign-
ments included two tours in Germany and one in Korea.

He saw service in Vietnam and retired from the air force in
1972, when he went to live in Florida.

Blakeslee was one of America's most decorated pilots. He
was twice awarded America's Distinguished Service Cross as
well as a Silver Star and numerous DFCs and Air Medals.

Most fighter pilots enjoyed playing the role, sporting artwork on the noses of their aircraft as well as the tally of their
scores. But for all his aggression and flamboyance in the air,
this was not Blakeslee's style. His aircraft bore no artwork and
no 'victory' crosses beneath the cockpit.

In later years, many aviation artists chose to paint a particular ace's finest moment, usually an event relating to one of
their air combats. The only painting Blakeslee ever officially
approved was one that shows him standing in front of his Mustang pointing to his watch as he stands alongside a Russian officer. It depicts his arrival in Ukraine after his unique flight in
June 1944 when he led the 4th Fighter Group across Germany
and Eastern Europe using only a map on his knee and a watch.

He was greatly admired in the American fighter pilot community, which recognised him as one of the two most out-

standing pilots in the European theatre, the other being Colonel 'Hub' Zemke.

In retirement Blakeslee was a private man who shunned publicity: but in July 2001 he agreed to visit Duxford with three other American 'aces' for the Flying Legends Show.

Don Blakeslee married his wife Lee on his return to the USA in 1944 and they had a daughter. His wife predeceased him.

FLIGHT LIEUTENANT 'BLONDIE' WALKER

Flight Lieutenant 'Blondie' Walker, (who died on November 9, 2008 aged 91), was a dashing and courageous fighter pilot who excelled at very low-level flying to attack ships with rockets. Many of his attacks were carried out at night in his single-engine Hurricane and his exploits earned him two DFCs.

Walker was a flight commander on No. 6 Squadron, a unit with an outstanding reputation during the North African campaign. In recognition of its tank-busting exploits in the desert, each aircraft was adorned with a flying can-opener. When Walker joined in September 1943, the squadron had turned its attention to attacking shipping and was soon transferred to support operations in Italy.

Based initially in Corsica, Walker flew at 20 feet to attack

enemy shipping holding the fire of his four rockets until he
was 200 yards from the target. Losses were high on both sides
and, with coastal shipping avoiding daylight sailings, Walker
pioneered night attacks, at which he became an acknowledged
expert and leader.

In June 1944, off Elba, Walker attacked a destroyer in the
harbour and scored hits before pulling up steeply over cliffs.
When he landed his ground crew removed leaves and twigs
from his aircraft's radiator. In that month, he was credited with
destroying a number of patrol boats, schooners and barges. He
was awarded an immediate DFC for his "outstanding keenness
and devotion to duty".

The squadron then transferred to the Balkan Air Force for
operations in the Adriatic and on July 10, Walker destroyed a
ferry. A week later, as he attacked a small ship off the Yugoslav
coast, his aircraft was hit and he ditched a mile off the enemy
coast. He tried to paddle away from the coast as Spitfires circled overhead, and after two hours, a US flying boat landed
and picked him up under enemy fire.

Two weeks later he was attacking a ship that was sheltering
beneath a cliff when his Hurricane was badly damaged by flak,
and he was forced to bale out over an island. He landed in the
sea but was able to paddle ashore. For four days he lived off his
survival rations of barley sweets and Horlicks tablets and fresh
water he found at a deserted cottage. He marked out an SOS
on the beach using seaweed and on the fifth day, two Spitfires
flew close by. He fired his flares and they turned towards him.
A few hours later a US Catalina landed to pick him up and
he paddled out to the aircraft in his dinghy. The crewman ex-
claimed, as he pulled him aboard: "Not you again!" It was the
same crew that had come to his aid a fortnight earlier.

By this time Walker had flown 169 operational sorties, and
it was decided to rest him. Over the course of the next month
he 'borrowed' Hurricanes to visit his friends in Corsica, Yugoslavia and Italy, then returned to England when he was awarded a Bar to his DFC.

The son of a stonemason and builder, Arnold Edgar Walker, always known as 'Blondie', was born on April 4, 1917 in Halifax and educated at Heath Grammar School. He left school early to join the family's building firm and at the age of 18 found himself in charge following the death of his father. This meant that he was in a reserved occupation, but he was passionate about flying and on the outbreak of war he immediately volunteered for the RAF.

Having completed his pilot training in Canada under the British Commonwealth Air Training Plan, Walker was commissioned and converted to the Hurricane. He was sent to the Middle East, sailing to Freetown in Sierra Leone before flying across the desert to Khartoum and on to Port Said. The first part of the journey was in a lumbering German-built Junkers 52 transport of the South African Air Force. As it approached to land at Fort Lamy, the gunners defending the airfield, believing they were under attack, opened fire on it but missed.

In August 1942 Walker joined No. 94 Squadron, which soon afterwards received four Hurricanes donated by Lady MacRobert who had lost her three sons serving in the RAF, one of them with No. 94. Their names and coat of arms were painted on the nose of the aircraft and Walker was allocated 'Sir Roderic', which he flew during the North African campaign.

On September 2, he was patrolling over Suez when he was vectored on to a Junkers 88 bomber. He hit it with his first shots and pursued it to low level, where another burst set one of the engines on fire. The bomber crash-landed in the desert. By this time Walker had almost run out of fuel, only just managing to land at an RAF airfield; as he turned off the runway, the engine of his Hurricane died. Later in the day he took a light aircraft and landed alongside the German bomber to examine the effects of his shooting. He met the pilot who appeared to be pleased that his war was over.

Shortly afterwards, Walker had the stressful experience of shooting down an American aircraft. He had been ordered to intercept a low-flying aircraft that was approaching a convoy. With no Allied activity reported in the area, he was given clearance to attack, and he sent the 'enemy' spiralling into the sea. At the subsequent court martial, Walker was completely exonerated as the American aircraft was 150 miles off course and had failed to display the mandatory identification codes.

In April 1943, the engine of his Hurricane failed and he was forced to land in the desert where he spent the next two days before his mechanics arrived to carry out repairs. After scraping out a rough strip he was able to take off.

At the end of his time with No. 94, Walker did not want an instructor's job so he volunteered to transfer to No. 6 Squadron, which was training with new rockets prior to joining the war in Italy.

On his return to England in October 1944 he became an instructor at an armament practice camp in the New Forest flying Typhoons. He was released from the RAF in 1946 and returned to re-establish his building company in Halifax, which had been shut down during the war. He wrote a short memoir of his wartime experiences with the dedication: "To my two ground crew – without your fabulous service of my aircraft, I would not be alive today."

In the early post-war years Walker built over 2,000 council houses and 1,000 private houses and he continued to construct houses in West Yorkshire for the next half century. He also established building interests in Perth, Western Australia and for 40 years he shared his time between Halifax and Australia. He was a liberal councillor in Halifax during the early 1950s and was elected president of the Halifax Building Trades Council.

In whatever endeavour, Walker was a fierce competitor. His golf swing was not pretty but he played off a handicap of four. He first skied at Kitzbuhel in 1948 and returned virtually every year until he was 80. He loved fast cars, fast skiing and beautiful women. He was known in the town as 'Halifax', some locals even assuming that he was the Earl of Halifax.

'Blondie' Walker was married three times and had a daughter and three stepsons; a son predeceased him.

AIR COMMODORE PETE BROTHERS

Air Commodore Pete Brothers (who died on December 18, 2008 aged 91) flew throughout the Battle of Britain and was one of the RAF's most distinguished fighter pilots, credited with destroying at least 16 enemy aircraft.

Brothers was a flight commander on No. 32 Squadron and had been blooded in May 1940 during the hectic, and often chaotic, fighting during the Battle of France when he downed two enemy fighters.

As the Battle of Britain opened in July 1940, the squadron was operating Hurricanes from Biggin Hill and was soon involved in furious fighting. Flying three, and sometimes four, times a day, Brothers shot down seven fighters and a bomber over Kent before the end of August.

On one occasion he returned home after a particularly difficult day to learn from his wife that a bomb splinter had entered through an open window and shattered the mirror as she was applying her make-up. Years later he commented: "It was then that I decided the war had become personal."

Leading his flight of eight aircraft during one patrol, he encountered about 100 enemy bombers. He dived to attack them but before he could open fire he was engaged by a number of Messerschmitt fighters. Despite being heavily outnumbered he was able to break away and close on a bomber, which he shot down. Later in the day on a second sortie, he shot down a fighter.

In order to relax as he was returning from combat, Brothers would open the cockpit canopy and light up a cigarette. After a particularly exhausting day late in August, he woke the following morning to discover that a line of bomb craters crossed the officers' mess lawn a few yards from his bedroom and there were many spent anti-aircraft shells scattered around the base. He had heard nothing.

At the end of August, No. 32 was reduced to eight pilots and was rested. Brothers was sent as a flight commander to No. 257 Squadron, which had also suffered heavy losses and where morale was very low. Between them, Brothers and the new CO, Squadron Leader Bob Stanford-Tuck, helped to restore the confidence of the inexperienced pilots. When he and his wingman jointly destroyed a bomber he would not claim the victory for himself but insisted that it was all the work of his inexperienced colleague. On September 15, Brothers shot down two bombers over London. Two days earlier he had been awarded the DFC for his "courage and initiative".

Peter Malam Brothers was born at Prestwich on September 30, 1917 and educated at North Manchester School, a branch of Manchester Grammar School. When he was 16, and still at school, he learnt to fly at the Lancashire Aero Club and gained his civil pilot's 'A' licence. He joined the RAF in 1936, trained as a pilot, and joined No. 32 Squadron at the end of the year to fly Gauntlet bi-plane fighters. He remained with the squadron for four years.

After the Battle of Britain, Brothers trained as a flying instructor and on promotion to squadron leader he formed and commanded No. 457 (RAAF) Squadron flying Spitfires. On March 26, 1942 he shot down a Messerschmitt Bf 109 and a month later probably downed another enemy fighter. In June he was given command of No. 602 (City of Glasgow) Squadron leading it during the ill-fated Dieppe raid in August. His pilots destroyed five enemy aircraft and he himself claimed a fighter. One of his pilots was forced to bale out over the sea and Brothers orbited his dinghy until rescue arrived.

By now Brothers had been identified as one of the RAF's outstanding fighter pilots and he was promoted to wing commander to lead the Tangmere Wing of three Spitfire squadrons. He led them on sweeps deep into France as the RAF took the offensive to the Luftwaffe. During one of these operations on January 26, 1943 he shot down a Focke-Wulf Fw 190. In June he was awarded a Bar to his DFC and rested from operations.

In 1944 Brothers took command of the Exeter Wing, leading his six squadrons on attacks against transportation targets and enemy airfields on the Brest Peninsula and in Normandy. Heavily involved in the lead-up to the Allied invasion in June 1944, his squadrons operated in support of the beachhead.

On August 7 he achieved his 16th and final success when he shot down a Focke-Wulf Fw 190 over the River Loire. Later he wrote of this period: "With great excitement we participated in the invasion of Europe, sweeping over the beaches and deep into France, top dogs now, hammering the enemy in the air and on the ground." He was awarded the DSO for his "courage and brilliant leadership".

After attending a staff course in the USA, Brothers served at the Central Fighter Establishment. Despite his outstanding war record, he was not offered a permanent commission in the peacetime RAF and in 1947 he left to join the colonial service. Two years as a district officer in Kenya, however, convinced him that it was not the life he wanted, and in 1949 rejoined the RAF.

To his surprise, Brothers was posted to command a Lincoln bomber squadron, No. 57. He flew operations during the Malayan Emergency, his being the first bomber squadron to participate in the campaign.

After attending the Staff College and serving at the headquarters of Fighter Command, he was appointed the wing commander flying at Marham in Norfolk where he flew the Valiant V-bomber. As a group captain he served in the plans division at SHAPE Headquarters in Paris. On promotion to air commodore he commanded the Headquarters, Military Air Traffic Organisation.

In 1968, Brothers started a five-year appointment as the

RAF's director of public relations. This job was particularly demanding, and involved guiding and advising defence correspondents during the Cold War when national security was paramount. His success in winning the respect of the press and other media was due in part to his war record; but he was also an outstanding communicator, and his fine sense of humour, often directed at himself, helped him negotiate many difficult situations.

In 1964, he was appointed CBE. After leaving the RAF in 1973, he formed Peter Brothers Consultants Limited and finally retired in 1986.

Brothers was made a Freeman of the Guild of Air Pilots and Air Navigators in 1966 and was a member of the technical committee and of its court. He was elected Master of the Guild in 1973-74. He gave great support to the Battle of Britain Fighter Association being appointed its deputy chairman in 1993 taking over as chairman in 2003. He quickly brought his delightful sense of fun to the running of the association and led by example, attending a multitude of Battle of Britain commemorative events.

He was a great supporter of the Battle of Britain Memorial Trust and campaigned for the monument on the Thames Embankment. He was also patron of the Spitfire Association of Australia and president of his local branch of the Air Crew Association at Hungerford, Berkshire.

When it was announced that RAF Bentley Priory, Fighter Command's headquarters during the Battle of Britain, was to close in 2008, he strongly supported the campaign to save the historic building insisting: "This is our [RAF] home, as HMS *Victory* is for the navy."

An inveterate cigar smoker and a connoisseur of malt whisky, Brothers was a keen golfer, sailor and fisherman and a great raconteur.

Pete Brothers married in 1939 Annette Wilson who died in 2005. They had two daughters.

AIR CHIEF MARSHAL SIR NEIL WHEELER

Air Chief Marshal Sir Neil Wheeler (who died on January 9, 2009 aged 91) enjoyed an outstanding wartime career – at the time of his death he was the RAF's most highly decorated officer – and later made a notable contribution to the British aerospace industry.

Having been a regular peacetime officer, in the early months of the war Wheeler was instructing on out-dated bombers. But in the spring of 1940, he decided he should take a more active part; after a highly irregular visit to the Air Ministry, he managed to wangle a posting to the top-secret Photographic Development Unit at Heston, the brainchild of the brilliant and unorthodox Sidney Cotton.

Wheeler found himself flying unarmed Spitfires, modified to fly over long ranges to cover distant areas in search of targets, particularly naval ones. Flying at very high altitudes in an unheated aircraft for three or four hours, Wheeler found the cold his biggest enemy. On one occasion at 28,000 feet over Germany, the moisture collecting in his oxygen mask froze and he passed out; he regained consciousness at 1,500 feet over Kiel Harbour.

The small force of Spitfires modified for photographic reconnaissance was much in demand. Wheeler commanded a flight at Wick to photograph targets in Norway, and obtained excellent results, despite bad weather. Later he was one of the pioneers of low-level reconnaissance, specialising in taking photographs of radio and radar sites in France and the Netherlands. Flying from an airfield in Cornwall he photographed Brest Harbour from low level in the face of heavy anti-aircraft fire. He completed 56 operations and was awarded the DFC.

After recovering from serious injuries sustained in a car crash, Wheeler was promoted to wing commander, and in November 1942 took command of No. 236 Squadron equipped with the Beaufighter. One of three squadrons forming the North Coates Strike Wing, No. 236 had lost its CO and a flight commander and been badly mauled attacking a convoy off the Dutch coast. Wheeler recognised the low morale and immediately reviewed and revised the tactics.

He recommended that the three squadrons should attack together and he established a period of intense training when everyone was expected to match his own high standards. He was adamant that a fighter escort was essential and vowed that no matter how much pressure was put on him he would refuse to lead a wing strike without an escort.

Wheeler received an enthusiastic response from his crews, who saw him as strict but fair. And on April 18, 1943 his methods were put to the test; an important, heavily defended convoy had been sighted off the Dutch coast and Wheeler was ordered to attack. He led 21 Beaufighters, and their large escort of long-range fighters, across the North Sea at 50 feet. His timing and navigation were perfect, and despite the intense anti-aircraft fire from the escorting flak ships, hits were scored on the major merchant ships; the largest, and principal, target – the *Hoegh Carrier* – exploded and sank.

All the Beaufighters returned safely, and the attack represented the turning point in the fortunes of the Strike Wings, which went on to achieve great success along the Dutch and Norwegian coasts. Wheeler was awarded a Bar to his DFC.

Throughout the summer of 1943 he led numerous successful strikes off the Dutch Frisian Islands, sinking many merchant ships carrying raw materials from Scandinavia to Rotterdam. With the introduction of the rocket projectile, Wheeler's Strike Wing became an even more effective force.

His arduous and extremely successful tour came to an end in August 1943 when he was awarded the DSO. The citation described him as "an outstanding leader with cool courage and infectious confidence".

The son of a British-born director of music of the South African Police, Henry Neil George Wheeler was born in Pretoria on July 8, 1917. He was educated at Waterkloof House School, Pretoria and at St Helens College, Southsea in Hampshire before being awarded a Dominion Scholarship to the RAF College Cranwell, where he trained as a pilot. He gained his lifetime's nickname of 'Nebby' after an instructor described him as "nebulous" – his reports as a cadet were satisfactory but modest, giving little indication of his subsequent glittering career. On graduation he flew antiquated bombers with No. 207 Squadron before transferring to the photographic-reconnaissance role.

After attending a course in the USA in 1944, Wheeler served on the strategic planning staff in the Cabinet Office until June 1945. In May 1947 he became responsible for flying at RAF Changi, in Singapore and at the outbreak of the Malayan Emergency in June 1948 he went to command the RAF task force at Kuala Lumpur. He returned to England at the end of 1949 and two years later commanded the flying wing of three bomber squadrons at RAF Marham in Norfolk.

In March 1954, Wheeler moved to the Air Ministry to fill an appointment in the directorate of operational requirements. It was to prove an invaluable introduction into this important and specialist arena when he took up senior posts in the organisation in later years. He returned to Cranwell in 1956 as the assistant commandant, where his somewhat stern and tough demeanour hid a deep concern for cadet affairs. Once, whilst he was at a formal dinner, some cadets removed the wheels of his car. Wheeler was not amused, and the alleged ringleader received a severe admonition (30 years later, however, he would be appointed as the RAF's chief of the air staff).

Wheeler commanded the large RAF airbase at Laarbruch in Germany and after attending the Imperial Defence College, he served in the Defence and Policy Research Staff at the Air Ministry. When serving as the senior air staff officer at the Headquarters RAF Germany, his elder brother, Norman, was chief of staff at the Headquarters British Army of the Rhine.

At the end of their tours they attended an investiture together at Buckingham Palace when both were appointed CB.

In 1966, Wheeler returned to Whitehall where he was the assistant chief of defence staff, operational requirements and a year later, on promotion to air marshal, he became deputy chief with the added responsibility of tri-service requirements.

In February 1969 Wheeler returned to Singapore as the commander-in-chief of the Far East Air Force. This was a sensitive time for international relations in the area as the British government had already announced plans for the withdrawal of military forces from the region. He returned to Britain in 1969 to become a member of the Air Force Board as the Air Member for Supply and Organisation and at a time when the RAF was significantly increasing its combat air capability and the infrastructure required to support it.

His experience made Wheeler uniquely qualified for his appointment as Controller Aircraft in the Procurement Executive in June 1973. He had extensive knowledge of operational requirements, research and service engineering, and supply support, in addition to his senior command and operational flying appointments. His time in the role coincided with many discussions on European collaborative projects, including the Jaguar strike aircraft and a number of helicopter proposals. But the biggest and most important programme involved the multi-role combat aircraft, later the Tornado. All these had significant political and military dimensions, and Wheeler's knowledge and firm negotiating skills proved great assets.

On retirement from the RAF in January 1976, his services were much in demand. He was responsible for military affairs at Rolls-Royce, where his experience and international contacts were invaluable as he travelled widely to promote the company's products.

Wheeler could be a tough man to work for. He demanded the best from his people and would frequently quiz them to substantiate their views; but once he had established their worth, he trusted them, and was happy to delegate. He also looked after his staff and his personal pilot in the Far East found that he never interfered with the progress and execution of the flight. He and his wife were always very considerate and would never fail to find time to thank the air and ground crew after every flight.

In 1986 he was appointed the Master of the Guild of Air Pilots and Air Navigators. He was elected a Fellow of the Royal Aeronautical Society and was made a Companion of the Chartered Management Institute. He was a vice president of the Air League.

An avid fisherman Wheeler was president of the Flyfishers Club. He was a keen supporter of the South of England Agricultural Show and of aviation art – the eminent aviation artist Frank Wootton captured some of his wartime exploits on canvas.

In addition to his three gallantry awards, Wheeler was appointed OBE (1949), CBE (1957), CB (1967), KCB (1969) and GCB (1975), and awarded an AFC in 1954.

Sir Neil Wheeler married, in 1942, Elizabeth Weightman, then a WAAF officer serving as a photographic interpreter. They had two sons and a daughter. His nephew General Sir Roger Wheeler was chief of the general staff from 1997 to 2000.

SQUADRON LEADER TOM McPHEE

Squadron Leader Tom McPhee (who died on February 22, 2009 aged 91) piloted one of the Mosquitos that flew on Operation Jericho, a daring low-level attack to breach the walls of Amiens prison to liberate members of the French Resistance who were due to be shot the following day.

During early 1944, news reached London that up to 120 prisoners were to face execution, some on February 19 and the RAF was ordered to attack the prison in an attempt to free them. Two days before the executions 18 crews of No. 140 Wing, commanded by Group Captain 'Pick' Pickard (famous for his appearance in *Target for Tonight*), were briefed using a

replica model of the prison.

The aim was to fly as low as 25 feet and drop delay-fused bombs to blow two holes in the walls that surrounded the prison while a second group was to open up the ends of the cruciform-shaped prison and destroy the German quarters to aid the escape of the prisoners. McPhee and his navigator were assigned to this task.

The weather on the day was appalling, but it was decided that the attack must go ahead. The 18 Mosquito bombers took off in blizzard conditions at 11 a.m. to rendezvous with their fighter escort. Three bombers were forced to turn back but the leading section from No. 487 (RNZAF) Squadron attacked the north and east walls successfully, and a few minutes later McPhee and his fellow pilots of No. 464 (RAAF) Squadron attacked the prison and blew the ends off the main building.

The attacks were of pinpoint accuracy, and the third wave of aircraft was not required and ordered to return to base. Whilst circling to observe the results, Pickard was shot down by a German fighter – he and his long-serving navigator, Bill Broadley, were killed.

Casualties in the prison were high with 102 prisoners killed by the bombing or German machine-gun fire; 50 German staff were also killed. But 258 prisoners escaped including 12 who were due to be shot the following day.

Amongst those who remained at large was Raymond Vivant, a key leader of the Resistance who had been captured a few days earlier and was awaiting interrogation. Five days after the attack, a message was received in London from the French Resistance which read: "I thank you in the name of my comrades for bombardment of the prison." A post-war analysis of the operation concluded: "The attack on Amiens prison will remain one of the RAF's epics."

Thomas McPhee was born at Greenock on November 30, 1917 and educated at Preston Technical College. He began his working life as a draughtsman at Vauxhall Motors in Luton but joined the RAF to train as a pilot in September 1938. His younger brother James also joined the RAF and flew Hurricane fighters during the Battle of Britain.

McPhee joined No. 139 Squadron at the end of 1940 to fly Blenheims on daylight bombing attacks. They encountered fierce anti-aircraft fire and casualties on the Blenheim squadrons were high. He attacked the port facilities at Rotterdam, Boulogne and Calais and during a shipping sweep over the North Sea he sank two small ships.

In early 1941, formations of six Blenheims, with a strong fighter escort, were sent to bomb airfields in northern France with the aim of enticing German fighters to join combat with the RAF escorts. McPhee flew on a number of these operations and bombed German-occupied airfields at St Omer and Abbeville.

On April 7 he and his crew flew in tight formation with the squadron commander to attack the Ijmuiden steelworks in daylight. The two aircraft met intense enemy fire, but McPhee maintained his position and the target was bombed from 50 feet. On leaving the area his aircraft was attacked by an enemy fighter, which damaged one of the Blenheim's engines. The enemy pursued the aircraft halfway across the North Sea before McPhee was able to shake it off. He returned to base and made an emergency landing.

McPhee was awarded an immediate DFM. A comrade recalled: "We congratulated him but he was visibly annoyed that his crew – who had been on all his sorties – were neglected and not mentioned."

On May 27, McPhee flew his 40th and final sortie on No. 139 when, still a sergeant, he led eight aircraft to attack the airfield at Lannion near Brest. He delivered his attack from 50 feet, scoring a direct hit on a hangar.

He was then commissioned and, after a rest tour as an instructor, in December 1943, he and his close friend and permanent navigator, Geoff Atkins, joined No. 464 Squadron. They flew night-intruder attacks against German airfields, and in February 1944 started to bomb the V-1 launching sites and storage depots in the Pas de Calais. By April, No. 464 began attacking road and rail targets in preparation for the Normandy landings.

On the night of June 5 – as the Allied invasion force crossed the English Channel – McPhee took off to attack enemy road convoys and railway junctions near the beachhead, and the following night he flew two sorties to attack motor transports and railways. Throughout June he flew numerous night attacks to strafe and bomb trains and railway installations to prevent enemy reinforcements reaching Normandy. By the end of June, McPhee had completed 72 operations.

He was awarded an immediate DFC for his "high standard of leadership and outstanding devotion to duty". He continued to fly on non-operational duties for the rest of the war and was released from the RAF in December 1945 when he received the Air Efficiency Award.

After the war, McPhee returned to being a draughtsman and worked for de Havilland Aircraft Company before moving to Bristol to work for Rolls-Royce until he retired.

He maintained a close friendship with his navigator and his Blenheim air gunner and they both attended his golden wedding celebrations. He was an accomplished self-taught artist, and he had a wide knowledge and appreciation for fine wines.

Tom McPhee married Elvina Duncan in June 1941 who died in 2007. They had two daughters.

COLONEL 'ROSY' du TOIT

Colonel 'Rosy' du Toit (who died on February 13, 2009 aged 90) was one of South Africa's outstanding wartime fighter pilots and leaders who fought in Abyssinia, the North African desert and Italy, ending the war with his Spitfire Wing in Austria.

In October 1943, with the Allied armies becoming established in southern Italy, du Toit was appointed the deputy leader of No. 7 (SAAF) Wing. His three squadrons of RAF and SAAF Spitfires were engaged in ground-attack operations in support of General Montgomery's Eighth Army in Italy and the partisans in Yugoslavia.

During November, du Toit led his squadrons on an audacious attack against an enemy landing ground in Yugoslavia. Four enemy aircraft were destroyed, others were damaged and enemy gun positions were eliminated. He was awarded an immediate Bar to an earlier DFC with the citation commending him for his "gallant leadership, great skill and courage".

He continued to lead the wing throughout the harsh winter, strafing and bombing enemy gun emplacements and motor transports as Montgomery attacked the Gustav Line. In July 1944, at the age of 26, du Toit was promoted to colonel and took command of No. 8 (SAAF) Wing with four Spitfire squadrons.

The Germans had withdrawn north of Rome to the Gothic Line and the Allies launched a major operation to attack their lines of communication. Flying in support of the US Fifth Army, du Toit led his Spitfires strafing road and rail targets and dive-bombing bridges in an attempt to cut off the enemy's supplies.

On April 9, 1945 the Allies' final offensive commenced when No. 8 (SAAF) Wing were in the forefront of the attacks. By the time of the German capitulation on May 2, du Toit and his squadrons were close to the Austrian border and a few weeks later moved to Modernhof where they became the first South African unit to be stationed in pre-war German-occupied territory. Du Toit was awarded the American DFC and appointed CBE, the latter a unique distinction for such a young officer.

The son of a headmaster, Stephanus Francois du Toit was born on January 28, 1919 at Groot Marico, Western Transvaal and educated at Helpmekaar School, Johannesburg. Whilst studying engineering at Witwatersrand University in 1937 he enrolled as a pupil pilot with the Transvaal Air Training Scheme and transferred to the South African Military College at Roberts Heights where he trained as a pilot. It was at this time that he gained his nickname 'Rosy' – he always kept his uniform immaculate and carried with him at all times a yellow duster (a rosy), to give a final polish to his buttons and leather webbing.

Du Toit was commissioned into the South African Air Force on September 6, 1939, the day South Africa declared war on Germany. He joined No. 41 Squadron flying the Hartebeest bi-plane aircraft in direct support of South African ground forces throughout the little-known campaigns against the Italian East African Empire.

During an operational flight near the Kenyan border, the engine of du Toit's aircraft failed and he made a forced-landing in a remote area. He set fire to his aircraft and spent the next few days walking through the bush giving slip to the local tribesmen who were intent on relieving him of his rifle. As the ground forces advanced into Abyssinia and Eritrea, du Toit flew many sorties strafing and bombing enemy positions. In August 1941 he landed behind enemy lines to pick up a fellow pilot who had been shot down.

During the major offensive against Gondar, du Toit's aircraft was hit by ground fire and set alight. He managed to clear the area by making a crash-landing on a road before returning on foot with the assistance of Ethiopian patriots. During the intense fighting over the next two months, he had to make two more emergency landings after his aircraft had been set on fire. The Italian forces surrendered at the end of November and the East African campaign was over. For his services, du Toit was mentioned in despatches.

The squadron moved to North Africa to become part of the Desert Air Force in the campaigns against the Axis forces. In July 1942, du Toit joined No. 4 (SAAF) Squadron flying the Kittyhawk fighter bomber and in September was promoted to major to command the squadron. He led from the front and for the next 12 months he was in constant action.

During the fierce fighting around Alam el Halfa in September 1942 he shot down a Messerschmitt Bf 109. In October he led his squadron to a notable victory when they intercepted a large force of Stuka dive-bombers with a heavy fighter escort. Two-thirds of the Stukas were shot down, one by du Toit. In a later attack against an enemy landing ground, his squadron destroyed enemy transports and du Toit silenced two anti-tank posts.

During an assault on the enemy airfield at Gambut on November 11, du Toit shot down a Bf 109 before being engaged in a 30-minute running fight with five enemy fighters. When they ran out of ammunition, he escaped and landed with his aircraft out of fuel and sporting several bullet holes.

As the Eighth Army advanced, he and his squadron moved forward in the desert providing support. On one occasion he attacked a tank and saw it topple off a cliff. On April 22, 1943 he provided top cover for other squadrons from his wing as they shot down 24 giant Messerschmitt Me 323s into the sea as they made a last desperate effort to re-supply Rommel's army with fuel. He described it as "terrific carnage, as the aircraft crashed and burst into flames. It was as if the sea was on fire."

In June 1943, du Toit was awarded the DFC and rested.

Du Toit resigned from the SAAF in 1950, having become disillusioned with the new national government's re-structuring of the armed forces, which he felt disadvantaged the country's minorities. He worked in the sugar industry until 1962, when he established a farm near Salisbury in Southern Rhodesia. Over the next 16 years he developed a first-class cattle farm but, following the political deterioration in 1973, he decided to leave and emigrate to the United States. Initially he worked as a ranch hand in New Mexico but soon rose to become general manager of a 60-hectare ranch. In 1983 he returned to South Africa, where he pursued his love of climbing and walking in the Western Cape.

Rosy du Toit married his first wife Jean, an American army nurse in 1946 and she died in 1964. His second marriage ended in divorce. He married his third wife Doreen in 1984.

FLIGHT LIEUTENANT WALTER MORISON

Flight Lieutenant Walter Morison (who died on March 26, 2009 aged 89) escaped from Stalag Luft III in June 1943 when he and a colleague attempted to steal a German aircraft to fly to Sweden: their audacious effort was thwarted at the last moment and he soon found himself imprisoned in Colditz Castle, where he remained for the rest of the war.

Morison's path to captivity had begun on the night of June 5/6, 1942, when he took off in his Wellington to bomb Essen. As he crossed the Dutch/German border his aircraft collided with another bomber. He was the only member of his crew able to parachute to safety, but on landing badly damaged his shoulder.

After a few weeks in hospital he arrived on July 28 at Göring's 'show camp' on the outskirts of Sagan, 100 miles south-east of Berlin. He soon discovered that the principal pastime was attempting to escape, and he described it as a game

Welch and Morison (right).

that was "like an English field sport played by the rules, which both sides understood". These rules were to endure until March 1944, when, after the Great Escape, the Germans shot 50 prisoners.

By the spring of 1943, the escape organisation at Sagan had been placed on a formal footing under the control of Squadron Leader Roger Bushell ('Big X'), one of those shot a year later. Morison became a member of the 'Gadget Factory' making tools, ventilation systems and pumps to be used in the tunnels for the Great Escape a year later. He and his team considered themselves as 'sub-contractors'.

He also hit on the idea of building a glider, and convinced Lorne Welch, a colleague who shared the same hut and had an excellent and imaginative engineering brain, that it was a feasible idea. They approached 'Big X', but before they could put the plan into action, they were given the opportunity to escape.

Welch and Morison were chosen to escape by 'borrowing' a German aircraft, and homespun Luftwaffe uniforms were run up for the purpose. On June 10 they were among 22 prisoners who shambled out of the compound 'guarded' by two of their number, both of whom spoke German and were dressed in the bogus uniforms. Once out of the camp, the party dived into surrounding woods, where Morison and Welch exchanged their clothes for the Luftwaffe uniforms before heading for a nearby airfield.

While all the other POWs were soon recaptured, Morison

and Welch made it to an airfield near Küpper after living rough for a week. Overnight they had a rough shave and tried to make their uniforms presentable. The following morning they picked the lock of a security gate and strolled on to the airfield.

They found a small training aircraft, a Junkers W34, parked by the control tower and boarded it only to discover that it had to be started by an external handle. While Morison remained in the cockpit, Welch was about to start the aircraft when the rightful crew appeared.

The two RAF flight lieutenants saluted the German crew, who assumed they were ground crew and ordered them to start the aircraft. As soon as it taxied away, Morison and Welch made themselves scarce. The following day they wandered around the airfield looking for another suitable aircraft before finding a small bi-plane. But as they tried to start it, the pair were apprehended; the game was up. A few hours later they were welcomed back to Sagan by the commandant, who rewarded them with six weeks in the 'cooler'.

They were threatened with a court martial and execution for wearing German uniforms and for espionage. Instead, they were transferred to Colditz.

Walter McDonald Morison was born on November 26, 1919 at Beckenham, Kent and was educated at Stowe. After a year at Trinity College, Cambridge, he volunteered for the RAF on the day war broke out. He was already a glider pilot and was soon accepted for pilot training. After being commissioned, he joined No. 241 (Army Co-operation) Squadron in February 1941, flying the Lysander.

Morison's time with No. 241 was short and he was transferred to a bomber training unit as an instructor on Wellingtons before joining No. 103 Squadron in May 1942. His second operation was on Bomber Command's first 1,000-Bomber Raid when 1,046 bombers attacked Cologne on the night of May 30/31. Six nights later he took off for Essen on his third and final operation.

The basic qualification to be in Colditz was to be a member

of the 'Prominenten', or an inveterate escaper. Morison's escaping activities, however, were over and he took on the job of running the canteen, participated in theatre productions and studied for accountancy exams. Compared to Sagan, he found Colditz a relatively comfortable place with friendly guards; he did, though, express irritation at the incessant patter of the bridge players.

Finally, in April 1945, the American army arrived and Morison and his fellow prisoners were freed. A few days later he was flown back to England and in July was released from the RAF.

Morison qualified as a chartered accountant, and in 1960 became the senior partner in Morison and Stoneham, where he remained until his retirement 21 years later.

He was a founder and long-time trustee of the Colt Foundation, a charity that promotes research into medical and environmental health problems arising from conditions at the workplace. He became the trust's chairman, finally retiring at the age of 88. He continued his gliding activities after the war, but then transferred his interests to sailing off the south coast and across the Channel to Brittany.

Like many of his breed, Morison was quintessentially unassuming and modest. When asked what he had done in the war he replied: "Not a lot. Taught some people to fly. Dropped some bombs. Taken prisoner. Escaped. Tried to borrow an aircraft from the Luftwaffe. Caught. Sent to Colditz. That was all there was really. A very ordinary war." He wrote about his wartime experiences in *Flak and Ferrets – One Way to Colditz*.

Walter Morison met his physiotherapist wife, Joan Devas, shortly after returning from Colditz. She died in 2005. They had two sons and two daughters.

AIR MARSHAL SIR MICHAEL GIDDINGS

Air Marshal Sir Michael Giddings (who died on April 5, 2009 aged 88) saw considerable action as a fighter pilot during the siege of Malta in 1942. He went on to fill senior appointments as a test pilot and later had responsibility for future projects and operational requirements. After his service he was a highly respected inspector for the Department of Environment.

On July 21, 1942, Giddings took off in a Spitfire from the aircraft carrier *Eagle* as one of a group of 31 sent to reinforce Malta. As the formation approached the island, a cultured voice gave instructions to turn on to a northerly heading. This perplexed the leader who queried the order when the gruff voice of an RAF controller immediately told him to continue on an easterly heading – thus foiling a German attempt to lure the Spitfires to Sicily.

Over the next three months, Giddings flew with No. 249 Squadron. Early in August, a crucial convoy departed from Gibraltar with supplies and fuel for the island. Giddings and his fellow pilots provided cover as the convoy came under intense attack as it approached Malta. Only four merchantmen and the tanker *Ohio* reached the safety of Valetta harbour.

During August and September, intelligence indicated that the Germans were building up their air forces for a new offensive against the island. Giddings flew on sweeps to strafe enemy aircraft on Sicilian airfields but, on the morning of October 11, the Axis air forces mounted their final blitz against Malta in an effort to subdue the island's tenacious resistance.

Over the next 14 days, Giddings was scrambled three or four times each day to intercept German bomber formations and their fighter escorts. He had already damaged two Messerschmitt Bf 109 fighters when he was scrambled on the 17th. He damaged a Junkers 88 bomber before a fierce dogfight developed with the escorts when he shot down a Bf 109 over St Paul's Bay.

On the 24th, over 40 German and Italian fighter-bombers were detected approaching Malta, and seven Spitfires of No. 249 were scrambled. Giddings attacked a gaggle of Italian Macchi 202s and hit one, which exploded in front of him. He fired at another, which streamed smoke from its engine, but before he could see the final results, he was forced to break away. Five days later, as he was taking off, a constructor's truck appeared on the runway and he crashed into it at high speed sustaining a broken wrist and arm. He returned home in November.

Kenneth Charles Michael Giddings was born on August 27, 1920 in Walthamstow and educated at Ealing Grammar School. He was conscripted into the RAFVR in 1940 and was trained as a pilot in the USA. On his return to the United Kingdom he was commissioned and joined No. 122 Squadron flying Spitfires on sweeps over France.

After recovering from his injuries, Giddings returned to flying as an instructor on fighters and in the summer of 1944 he was appointed a flight commander with No. 118 Squadron flying the Spitfire IX. During the airborne operations at Arnhem, he shared in the destruction of a Messerschmitt Bf 109. The squadron was re-equipped with the Mustang and provided a long-range fighter escort for the bomber force. In March 1945 over Bremen, he engaged a Messerschmitt Me 262 jet fighter and damaged it. He went on to command No. 129 Squadron in April and after VE Day he took the squadron to Norway. He was awarded a DFC for his "great skill and determination".

Giddings attended the Empire Test Pilot's School in 1946, before spending the next three years at the Royal Aircraft Establishment, Farnborough testing the new jet fighters. He was awarded the AFC for his work. After a period at the

headquarters of Fighter Command, he took command of the
flying wing at RAF Waterbeach where he flew Meteors and
was the first station officer to fly the new Supermarine Swift.
The Swift proved troublesome as a fighter and Giddings was
involved in the efforts to improve its capabilities and the development of tactics. At the end of his tour of duty, he was
awarded a Bar to the AFC and moved to the Central Fighter
Establishment to command the tactics wing.

In 1958 Giddings was one of a number of fighter pilots
transferred to Bomber Command to command one of the
new V-bomber squadrons. The commander-in-chief, Air Marshal Sir Kenneth Cross, himself a former fighter pilot, wanted
to inject some new blood and thinking into the force and
Giddings took command of No. 57 Squadron operating the
Victor. In 1960 he was promoted to group captain to serve on
the operational staff at Bomber Command.

In 1962 he returned to the test-flying arena when he was
appointed the Supcrintendent of Flying at the Aeroplane and
Armament Experimental Establishment (A&AEE) at Boscombe Down. He was an ideal choice for this appointment.
With his wide experience of test flying, fighter operations
and his recent flying on the Victor, he was well placed to
supervise the development of the later marks of the RAF's
fighter and bomber aircraft and their associated guided and
unguided weapons. He also took every opportunity to fly
other trials aircraft. On one occasion he flew a Beverley transport for a NATO officer's field day when an earth excavator
– the heaviest load to be dropped by parachute at the time
– fell from its pallet after leaving the aircraft and excavated a
very large hole in Salisbury Plain. The episode signalled the
end of the demonstration.

After two years as the director of Aircraft Projects in the MoD
and a period as the air officer commanding the Central Reconnaissance Establishment, much of Giddings' later service was
spent in the area of operational requirements. In 1969 he was
appointed the assistant chief of the air staff (operational requirements). He was heavily involved in international discussions for

the multi-role combat aircraft (MRCA). Following two years as the chief of staff at No. 18 (Maritime) Group, Giddings' final appointment was as deputy chief of defence staff (operational requirements) and he retired from the RAF in June 1976.

From 1979 to 1991 he was an independent panel inspector with the Department of Environment and was appointed to a number of high-profile public inquiries. He presided over those for four sections of the M25 and for some of the motorway plans in the Manchester region. In May 1982 he was the inspector for the year-long inquiry – the longest ever held at the time – for the Kirkhamgate-Dishforth Scheme, which resulted in the extension of the M1 motorway to link with the A1(M).

Giddings resigned from the acrimonious 'Archway Inquiry', into a proposed motorway extension in north London, which would have entailed the destruction of almost 200 homes, after he and his family received numerous threats and considerable harassment, which became the subject of a police inquiry. His intellect, integrity and dignified conduct attracted considerable praise and sympathy.

A keen golfer and gardener, he also listed music as one of his interests. This bland statement hid a significant talent. He was a very accomplished pianist and wrote many pieces including numerous scores for television programmes, amongst them the theme tune for the powerful drama *Cathy Come Home*, which was first broadcast in November 1966.

Michael Giddings, who was appointed KCB (1975) and OBE (1953), married Elizabeth McConnell in 1946 with whom he had two sons and two daughters.

WING COMMANDER DOUGGIE OXBY

Wing Commander Douggie Oxby, (who died in Toronto on April 10, 2009 aged 88), was involved in the destruction of 22 enemy air-craft, making him the highest-scoring Allied night-fighter navigator of the Sec-ond World War, an achievement that earned him four gallantry awards.

Oxby had already gained major successes over Malta and North Africa when, in the spring of 1944, he joined No. 219 Squadron, which was equipped with the night-fighter version of the Mosquito. In September he teamed up with the CO, Wing Commander Paddy Green, and over the next few months they were to become the RAF's most successful night-fighter crew operating over north-west Europe.

Flying from an airfield near London, they opened their ac-count on the night of September 23, when they were on an intruder sortie near Cologne and shot down a Messerschmitt Bf 110 night-fighter. Ten days later they had the unusual dis-tinction of shooting down three enemy bombers in the space of a few minutes. Using his airborne intercept radar, Oxby picked up a small force of aircraft and 'homed' Green on to the target. Three Junkers 87 dive-bombers were preparing to attack the bridge at Nijmegan. Guided by Oxby, Green closed in and shot one down. Debris from the enemy aircraft hit the Mosquito but the crew moved in and shot down the other two aircraft before heading for an airfield near Brussels where they landed on one engine.

After moving to the former Luftwaffe airfield at Amiens, Green and Oxby soon had another success when they shot down a Junkers 88 bomber.

Two months later, they brought down a second – this attack was so precise that they fired only 71 rounds from their cannons before the enemy bomber caught fire and the crew were seen to bale out. On the night of February 24, they achieved their ninth and final success when Oxby brought the Mosquito behind an enemy contact and Green visually identified a Junkers 87, which he shot down. For their achievements, Green was awarded a DSO and Oxby received the DFC.

The squadron had a 'rogue' Mosquito, which all the pilots found very difficult to fly. On March 1, Green decided to air test this aircraft in an effort to identify the problem, electing to leave Oxby on the ground. Shortly after take-off, the aircraft crashed and Green was killed.

Oxby was taken off operations and sent to be an instructor at a fighter training unit. Two weeks later it was announced that he had been awarded the DSO.

Douglas Alfred Oxby was born on June 10, 1920 in Cardiff and attended the city's Canton High School before going to the technical college. He worked as a barrister's clerk before joining the RAF in June 1940 as a ground-radar operator.

Bored with watching for enemy bombers off the coast of Wales, he volunteered for the new aircrew duty of radio operator (air) in June 1941. He trained on Blenheim night-fighters at Prestwick where he joined up with an Australian pilot, Mervyn Shipard. They were to fly together for the next two years and become one of the RAF's outstanding night-fighter crews.

After joining No. 68 Squadron equipped with the Beaufighter, they shot down a Heinkel bomber raiding Liverpool on November 1, 1941 but the next six months was very quiet. Threatened with an instructional tour, they volunteered to go to the Middle East to see some action. They took a Beaufighter to Egypt via Gibraltar and Malta arriving in a sandstorm. Assigned to No. 89 Squadron near the Suez Canal, they found little enemy activity and in June 1942 they transferred to a night-fighter detachment in Malta where they remained for four months. In

July they scored three quick victories against German bombers.

During the Axis air force's final blitz against the island, Shipard and Oxby destroyed three Heinkel bombers (and probably a fourth) in rapid succession. On the night of October 14/15, Oxby carried out a successful interception at 22,000 feet – he declined the use of oxygen in order that his pilot could obtain the benefit of the little that was left. They also flew five intruder sorties against enemy airfields in Sicily as well as attacks on E-boats and convoys. Oxby was awarded a DFM for his "exceptional ability and determination".

Returning to Egypt, they joined a detachment in the desert to provide support for the Tobruk offensive. On the night of December 12, they patrolled north of Tobruk shooting down two Junkers 88 bombers in the space of only a few minutes. On January 8, they accounted for two more bombers and then another two a week later in the Gambut area. During his time in the Middle East, Oxby used his radar to intercept 21 enemy contacts and this had resulted in the shooting down of 13 aircraft and probably two others. He received a Bar to his DFM and a field commission.

In June 1943, Oxby and his pilot Shipard, who had become the RAAF's highest-scoring night-fighter pilot of the war, returned to Britain where Oxby became an instructor at a training unit for radar operators. He remained in the RAF after the war serving as an instructor at an air navigation school but most of his time was spent in fighter-related appointments including periods at the Central Fighter Establishment and at Headquarters Fighter Command. In June 1962 he was appointed the assistant air adviser to the British High Commissioner in Ottawa. When he retired from the RAF in March 1969 in the rank of wing commander, he emigrated to Canada where he served as a civil servant until 1984.

Oxby was a quiet, private man who enjoyed reading and classical music. He was always conscious of the human losses for which he was responsible. With the help of his son, he was finalising his wartime memoirs, which he was dedicating to the memory of the aircrew of the RAF and the Luftwaffe who failed to return. He made little fuss of his unique awards and modestly claimed that he was no hero.

Douggie Oxby was married twice. He had a son from his first marriage.

SQUADRON LEADER JOHN PATTISON

Squadron Leader John Pattison (who died at Hawkes Bay, New Zealand on September 11, 2009 aged 92) was one of the few remaining New Zealanders who fought in the Battle of Britain during which he was shot down and severely wounded; he recovered to have a distinguished war and was awarded the DSO and DFC for gallantry.

Pattison arrived in Britain at the end of July 1940, and with the RAF short of fighter pilots he was rushed through battle training in a few days. With just a handful of sorties flying Spitfires, he joined No. 266 Squadron at Debden in Essex during an intense phase of the battle on August 26.

On his first operation the squadron intercepted a force of 40 enemy bombers and their fighter escort. Pattison became separated from the rest of his squadron, ran out of fuel and made a wheels-up landing in a field bristling with anti-aircraft obstacles. He was greeted by pitchfork-wielding farmers who took him for a German. Two weeks later he was posted to No.

92 Squadron based at Biggin Hill.

After the major engagements of September 15, the Luftwaffe switched its attacks to London. On September 23, a Messerschmitt Bf 109 attacked Pattison over Gravesend. He received serious wounds to his right thigh from a cannon shell and he crash-landed as he attempted to land at West Malling airfield. He spent the next eight months in hospital, but recovered to rejoin the squadron in June 1941.

John Gordon Pattison was born on January 27, 1917 at Waipawa and educated at Wanganui Collegiate School before going to work on his father's farm. In January 1939 he joined the Civil Reserve of Pilots and learned to fly on Tiger Moths at the Hawkes Bay and East Coast Aero Club. With many others of his countrymen he volunteered for service with the RAF the day after war was declared. He completed his training and sailed for England.

A month after returning to operational flying following his serious injury, Pattison was made an instructor. A dashing pilot, he did not always set a good example to his students. He was not averse to some daring escapades and once 'borrowed' another pilot's Hurricane (without his knowledge) to get himself to a party. Later, he was reprimanded and lost three months' seniority for flying his Spitfire under the Severn railway bridge. In April 1942 he returned to operations and joined No. 485 (NZ) Squadron, one of three that made up the Kenley Wing.

On April 26, 1942 he was taking part in a sweep over northern France when his formation was 'bounced' by a force of Focke-Wulf Fw 190s. Four of the New Zealanders were hit and two were lost. The engine of Pattison's Spitfire was damaged but he managed to glide across the Channel before baling out near the Sussex coast. After 90 minutes in his dinghy, he was rescued by an air-sea rescue launch.

Over the next 12 months he flew on many sweeps and low-level strafing attacks against transport targets over France. In July 1943 he was awarded the DFC for "his determination, zeal and courage".

After a spell as the chief flying instructor of a fighter training unit, Pattison returned to operations in March 1944 with No. 66 Squadron. Armed with bombs, he attacked targets in his Spitfire IX during the pre-invasion offensive, including the new V-1 sites in the Pas de Calais region. On July 6 he was flying an offensive support mission when he intercepted a Messerschmitt Bf 109 near Chartres. He attacked the enemy fighter and registered hits before the German pilot baled out. A month later he was flying a similar operation when he engaged and shot down a Focke-Wulf Fw 190 near Montrichard. The squadron had just moved to a makeshift airstrip in Normandy, where Pattsion flew many armed-reconnaissance sorties armed with bombs and cannons.

Pattison was appointed to command his old squadron, No. 485 (NZ), in September and he led it with great verve and tenacity as it supported the advancing armies through France and Belgium into the Netherlands. He destroyed many enemy vehicles. When No. 485 was withdrawn from the front line to convert to the Tempest, Pattison was rested and given a staff job with HQ 84 Group.

On March 20 he was awarded the DSO and the citation concluded that "he has set the highest standard of skill and courage and shown the finest qualities of leadership both in the air and on the ground".

After being discharged from the RAF in January 1946 Pattison returned to New Zealand. For the rest of his life he farmed in Waipawa before retiring to Havelock North.

Fearless in combat, Pattison was the epitome of the colourful fighter pilot. He was never afraid to enjoy himself or take on authority and his sense of humour remained sharp and direct throughout his life. When asked about his wartime flying he commented: "Wonderful times to have lived through and with fantastic mates."

He remained a champion of the 485 (NZ) Squadron Association, rarely missing their annual dinners. At the 2005 reunion he was presented with a working scale model of the Spitfire he was forced to abandon in April 1942. He noted that the engine did not give off the sound of "the Rolls-Royce Merlin twelve-cylinder symphony" but he agreed it was like meeting up with a faithful friend again.

To commemorate the 50th anniversary of D-Day in June 1994, President Chirac appointed him to the Légion d'Honneur.

John Pattison and his wife had four sons.

FLIGHT LIEUTENANT 'LEW' CODY

Flight Lieutenant 'Lew' Cody (who died on October 31, 2009 aged 91) was engaged in flying operations from the first day of the Second World War to the last, including bombing missions during the Battle of France and the Battle of Britain. After the Battle of El Alamein he dropped paratroopers on the island of Kos and then flew on the three major airborne assaults in Europe.

Cody left for the Middle East in July 1942 to join No. 216 Squadron flying unarmed Hudsons in the transport role. He flew countless re-supply and casualty evacuation flights in support of the Eighth Army operating into rudimentary desert landing grounds, sometimes just hours after the withdrawal of German troops. On other occasions, as the army retreated, he took off as the airstrips came under enemy shellfire.

In September 1942, Cody flew men of the Long-Range Desert Group into Kufra Oases, the first of a number of such operations. On the night of October 23/24, 1942 as the Battle

of El Alamein began, he flew one of four Hudsons behind
enemy lines. Each aircraft carried eight dummy parachute
troops, which were dropped to divert the enemy's attention;
the dummies were equipped with time-delay fuses, and were
set to explode after landing on the ground. Over a period of
30 minutes, each aircraft released flares and dropped their 'par-
achutists'. The close attention of light flak confirmed that the
enemy was well aware of the 'airborne landing'.

In mid-November the RAF established in great secrecy a
landing ground deep inside enemy territory where two Hurricane squadrons were deployed to carry out attacks in the enemy's rear area. Cody flew in the initial supplies and supported
the outpost until it was withdrawn a few days later.

After flying 700 hours in a year, Cody left to instruct at the
Dakota training unit in Palestine, but his rest was short-lived.
On the night of September 14, 1943, he flew one of six Dako-
tas that made a night, low-level approach to the island of Kos
in the Aegean, where he dropped men of the 11th Battalion
Parachute Regiment.

The Germans soon gained air superiority, and the presence
on Kos became untenable. During this ill-fated operation he
made numerous landings on the basic airstrip delivering more
troops and supplies for a fighter squadron and evacuating casualties before the island fell. Cody then dropped supplies to the
garrison on Leros before it also fell. Finally, on two consecutive
nights at the end of October, he flew a nine-hour sortie from
Cairo to drop men of the Greek Sacred Squadron on Samos,
the last Aegean island in Allied hands. He was awarded a DFC.

The eldest of seven children, Alfred 'Lew' Cody was born on
May 15, 1918 within the sound of Bow bells. He was brought
up in Clerkenwell and educated at the local school. An outstanding boxer, he was London Boy's Club flyweight champion; it was a skill he put to frequent use during his off-duty
time in the RAF.

After two years' service as an ordinary seaman in the RNVR,
in November 1938 he enlisted in the RAF and trained as an

observer before joining No. 40 Squadron equipped with the obsolescent Fairy Battle.

His squadron was sent to France on September 2, 1939. Halfway across the Channel, the aircraft's engine failed and the pilot was forced to ditch. Cody was picked up by a rescue launch but was unable to speak – he had a month's pay in his mouth.

He flew reconnaissance sorties during the 'Phoney War' before the squadron re-equipped with the Blenheim. After the German blitzkrieg on May 10, 1940, they were immediately in action. The losses in the Blenheim force were amongst the highest and his was the only aircraft of four to return from the squadron's first operation. By early June, most of the original crews had been lost and on two more occasions his was the only aircraft to return.

During the height of the Battle of Britain, he attacked the German invasion barges gathering at the Channel ports. After 35 operations he was one of a handful of survivors and rested. He was awarded the DFM for his great courage and determination.

Cody was trained as a pilot and commissioned. His flying career continued to be full of incidents. On his first operation as a pilot, his Blenheim was badly damaged by flak over the Netherlands and – with most of his controls shot away and no hydraulics – he made a belly landing back at his base. Soon after, he left for the Middle East.

Early in 1944 he returned to Britain to join one of the new squadrons preparing for the airborne invasion of Europe. Cody went to No. 233 at Blakehill Farm near Swindon and on the night of June 5/6, he joined a stream of 362 transport aircraft dropping men of the 3rd Parachute Brigade at Toufreville. The following night he dropped supplies to the paratroopers at Ranville.

Ten days after the invasion Cody took supplies to one of the hastily prepared landing strips (B2) in Normandy and on his return flight brought back 22 wounded, the first of many such 'casevac' flights.

On September 18 he took off for Arnhem, but the glider he was towing broke loose over Suffolk. A second attempt the following day was successful. As the situation on the ground became desperate, he flew resupply sorties over the next two days when his aircraft was badly damaged by flak on each occasion.

On January 9, 1945 Cody took off from Eindhoven in poor weather. Another aircraft struck his Dakota and six feet of the aircraft's wing disappeared. With his slight build, he could control the aircraft only by standing, while his co-pilot placed both feet on the starboard rudder pedal. Yet he managed to land the heavily laden transport and was awarded the AFC.

Cody's final airborne operation was to tow a Horsa glider on Operation Varsity, the crossing of the Rhine. On the last day of the war he was ordered to fly to Copenhagen, which had just been liberated. His was the first Allied aircraft to land and he was amazed to find a posse of German officers paraded to surrender to him before the Danish Resistance arrived. On his return via Lübeck he brought 30 POWs back to Britain, his final wartime sortie.

In June, Cody and his crew were selected to be Field Marshal Montgomery's personal crew. Cody celebrated the news in fine style and had to be woken the next morning for a VIP flight. His navigator taxied the aircraft from dispersal whilst the rest of the crew made a vain attempt to sober up their pilot – they failed. Cody missed his appointment with Monty and within days found himself posted elsewhere as a flying instructor.

A pugnacious and irreverent character, Cody's favourite phrase late at night was, "I can punch my weight". Fortunately, his wireless operator, who accompanied him everywhere, was well over six feet tall and a former commando. His navigator commented: "For all his high spirits on the ground, he was marvellous in the air and immensely brave. It was men like 'Lew' who won the war."

Cody remained in the RAF as a flying instructor and served in Rhodesia and with the Germany Training Mission before becoming a photographic interpreter. He left the RAF in 1964 and for five years, he and his wife ran a country pub at Thorpe Waterville in Northamptonshire.

He returned to flying, and from 1970 to 1976 was a flying instructor at King Faisal's Air Academy in Saudi Arabia. He then worked in the travel industry until he retired in 1987.

In addition to his three gallantry awards, Cody was also mentioned in despatches. A lifelong cricket fan and keen on boxing and motor racing, laughter and humour were an ever-present feature of Cody's life.

'Lew' Cody married, in March 1941, Marie Bulbrook who cared for him selflessly in his final years. They had a son and two daughters.

AIR CHIEF MARSHAL SIR THOMAS PRICKETT

Air Chief Marshal Sir Thomas Prickett (who died on January 23, 2010 aged 96) distinguished himself as a bomber pilot during the Second World War and later played a prominent role in the air planning for Operation Musketeer, the ill-fated Suez operation of 1956.

In July that year Prickett was attending the Imperial Defence College in 1956 when he and two colleagues were suddenly sent to the Air Ministry to form the planning staff for the Allied Air Task Force for Operation Musketeer.

In great secrecy they took over a basement office in the

ministry, earning the nickname 'the troglodytes'. Prickett was appointed the chief of staff to the air commander Air Marshal Denis Barnett. From the outset, Prickett and his colleagues found themselves working in a vacuum, with no clear idea of the political aim. At the insistence of the prime minister, Anthony Eden and the Foreign Office, many senior officers were kept in the dark, severely hampering military planning.

Prickett and his colleagues spent three months devising air plans and aiming to simplify the unnecessarily complex command structure – which Prickett described as being like something out of *Alice in Wonderland*.

In September he moved to Episkopi in Cyprus to prepare the air planning cell. He had much sympathy for the resident headquarters staff and their commander-in-chief, who had been sidelined throughout the planning phase. As for the Suez operation itself, he was adamant that politics continually interfered with the detailed conduct of the military action. While he praised the British military effort and the excellent co-operation of the French air staff, he summarised the conflict as a "monumental political cock-up".

In a letter to the *Daily Telegraph* in September 2002, Prickett detected similarities between Suez and the situation in Iraq. He concluded the letter with the words: "The present crisis has all the ingredients of confused and conflicting political and military aims. Is history about to repeat itself?"

Thomas Öther Prickett was born at Lindfield, Sussex on July 31, 1913 and educated at Haileybury College. From 1932 he spent five years in India working on sugar estates with Begg Sutherland, first as an assistant and later as manager. During this period he served as a trooper with the Bihar Light Horse, of the Indian Army (Auxiliary).

In October 1937 Prickett joined the RAF and trained as a pilot. He was assessed as above average and was immediately selected to be a flying instructor, a role he fulfilled for the next three years, first in England and then in Southern Rhodesia. Anxious to fly operations, he got himself sent to Egypt where in October 1941 he joined No. 148 Squadron flying Wellington bombers.

Prickett flew on his first bombing operation a few days after joining the squadron when he attacked Benghazi, a target that would become very familiar to him. Over the next few months, the fortunes of the hard-pressed British and Allied forces fluctuated greatly as they strove to meet the many demands placed on them. The ill-equipped bomber squadrons of the Desert Air Force strived to provide support.

Flying from forward landing grounds, Prickett and his crews attacked enemy ports, supply depots and airfields in North Africa. In November and December 1941, No. 148 was tasked to support British forces in Greece and Prickett dropped supplies on Crete and twice bombed Piraeus. In March 1942, the squadron was diverted to support the British evacuation from the Aegean area, and he bombed the airfields on Crete recently occupied by the Germans.

The following month, Prickett led a small detachment to Malta, from where they attacked the airfields on Sicily. After returning to the desert, he flew more operations until his 32nd and final one on July 13. He was awarded the DFC.

Prickett then spent six months in the USA as a senior flying instructor at No. 5 British Flying Training School based at Clewiston in Florida. Then in April 1943 he returned to operational flying, joining No. 103 Squadron as a flight commander. After just one flight in a Lancaster to familiarise himself with the aircraft, he flew his first operation, a 10-hour sortie to bomb the docks at La Spezia in Italy.

In the spring of 1943, Bomber Command's main offensive had begun and Prickett had joined No. 103 as the Battle of the Ruhr opened. He bombed the heavily defended major cities of the Ruhr with occasional sorties to Turin.

On the night of July 24, he took off for the first of four devastating raids against Hamburg. Accompanying him for experience was a major of the Royal Artillery serving at HQ No. 1 Bomber Group. On their return the major wrote a detailed report highlighting the effectiveness of the 'window' radar countermeasures, which had been employed for the first time. For the rest of his life, Prickett was deeply affected by the devastation and suffering caused by the Hamburg raids.

By now Prickett was beginning to suffer from spinal arthritis, a serious handicap on long sorties, but he never once turned back, continuing to fly on all the major operations. On August 17, he joined 595 other aircraft on the successful attack against the German research establishment at Peenemünde, where the V-1 and V-2 rockets were being developed and tested. After 30 operations he was rested and awarded an immediate DSO, the citation recording his "unflinching determination and magnificent courage and an outstanding example to the squadron".

In October 1943, Prickett returned to the USA for staff duties with the RAF Delegation in Washington, where he had particular responsibility for the very large bi-lateral aircrew flying training programme.

During the immediate post-war years Prickett was an instructor. He then converted to jet fighters, commanding the fighter bases at Tangmere and at Jever in northern Germany. He also served on the staff of the Middle East Air Force and in 1956 was selected to attend the Imperial Defence College.

After Suez he served in the Air Ministry's policy branch before becoming the senior air staff officer at No. 1 (Bomber) Group. This was at a time of the introduction of the Vulcan strategic bomber; he flew the aircraft himself in May 1960 leading a formation of the aircraft on a tour of South American capitals.

There followed two important appointments in the air ministry – in the operations and plans divisions. There was considerable restructuring of the RAF in the aftermath of the Duncan Sandys Defence White Paper of 1957, and Prickett's experience and calm approach proved highly welcome.

In September 1964 Prickett was appointed commander-in-chief Near East Air Force, commander British Forces Near East, and administrator, British Sovereign Bases.

In Cyprus, his outgoing personality and charisma won him

the trust of President Archbishop Makarios; aside from more weighty matters, Prickett persuaded Makarios to accept the setting-up of a wildlife reserve throughout the Sovereign Bases, in order to protect the huge numbers of migrant birds. Prickett also became a personal friend of King Hussein of Jordan, who admired not only his military record, but also his excellent horsemanship and enthusiasm for polo. The British Army in the Mediterranean also took warmly to their RAF C-in-C.

On his return to Britain in January 1967 he was appointed C-in-C Transport Command. A year later he was instrumental in expanding and transforming it into Air Support Command, when he was given increased responsibility for fulfilling the long-range strategic and tactical air support and assault roles.

Prickett's appointment in July 1968 as air member for supply and organisation gave him a seat on the Air Force Board as the RAF was introducing a new generation of 'fast jet' aircraft after the successive cancellations of the TSR-2 and its replacement, the American-built F-111.

He fought his corner astutely (and at times outspokenly) when dealing with both his peers and with politicians. On the cancellation of the F-111, he wrote directly to the responsible minister, reminding him of his privately given undertaking a year or so earlier, that he (the minister) would resign should anything happen to derail that aircraft. The letter was never answered.

In October 1970 Prickett took voluntary retirement from the RAF following an invitation by the Duke of Richmond to assist in the redevelopment of the Goodwood estate. He was tasked to regenerate the airfield and the motor racing circuit, both of which he accomplished with style, and he gave valuable assistance in the development of the estate's international equestrian events.

A large and powerful figure, Prickett was a strong personality with considerable presence. Held in the greatest esteem by his staff, he was known for his warm and generous nature.

He was appointed CB (1957) and KCB (1965).

Prickett's fine horsemanship derived from his days playing

polo in his pre-RAF days, when he served with the Indian cavalry. In later life he was an active president of the RAF Equitation Association, taking a particularly keen interest in its annual championships. He was also a passionate sailor and had part ownership of a racing yacht of the X-1 design.

Tom Prickett married his American wife Betty in 1942 and they had a son and daughter. Betty died in 1984. He married Shirley Westerman in 1985.

LIEUTENANT COLONEL LEE ARCHER

Lieutenant Colonel Lee Archer (who died on January 27, 2010 aged 90) was a member of America's segregated 'Tuskegee' air corps and recognised as the only black fighter 'ace' during the Second World War; subjected to racial discrimination and prejudice, both within and outside the army, he and his comrades none the less served their country with great distinction.

Strict racial segregation existed in the US Army when Archer volunteered to be a pilot. He and like-minded African-Americans were at first rejected because many people thought that black men lacked intelligence, skill, courage and patriotism. Eventually, in June 1941, a series of legislative moves by the US Congress forced the Army Air Corps to form an all-black combat unit, despite the War Department's reluctance. The pilots trained at a segregated Army Air Corps unit at Tuskegee Army Airfield, Alabama and for ever more became known as the 'Tuskegee Airmen'.

Lee A. Archer was born on September 6, 1919 in Yonkers and raised in New York's Harlem neighbourhood. He left New York University to enlist in the Air Corps in 1941 but, after rejection, trained in the infantry and then as a signaller. In December 1942 he was accepted for pilot training and left for Tuskegee. He graduated in July 1943, first in the order of merit, and was commissioned as a second lieutenant.

Archer was assigned to the 302nd Fighter Squadron of the 332nd Fighter Group, which had been formed amid great controversy in October 1942 as the first all-black USAAF fighter group. The group moved to Italy early in February 1944 and soon began operations flying the Bell P-39 Airacobra on ground-attack missions before converting to the P-51 Mustang, when their main role was to provide close escort to the USAAF's heavy bomber forces. In their red-tailed Mustangs they developed a reputation as one of the most effective fighter escort groups. It was claimed that they never lost a bomber, but post-war research suggests this might be a slight exaggeration. Nevertheless, the 'Red Tails' earned near-mythic status.

On July 18, 1944 they flew their first escort for a large formation of B-24 bombers. When a fierce air battle ensued over southern Germany, 11 Messerschmitt Bf 109s were shot down, one by Archer. The long-range Mustangs were able to accompany the bombers all the way to the target and back, and the bomber pilots always felt safe once their 'little friends' had joined the formation. Many were unaware that all their 'friends' were black airmen.

On October 22, 1944, Archer took part in a sweep along the Danube. With his leader, he attacked a Heinkel bomber when seven Messerschmitts appeared on the scene. In the ensuing battle, Archer shot three of them down, the last as it attempted to land at an airfield.

The 'Red Tails' escorted bomber formations to attack the

oilfields of Romania, rail yards in Austria and long-range bombing operations to Regensburg and Munich. Archer shared in the destruction of another Messerschmitt and he was also credited with destroying six enemy aircraft on the ground, in addition to several locomotives, motor transports and barges. By the end of the war he had flown 169 missions.

The Tuskegee airmen proved their racist detractors wrong. They were credited with shooting down 109 enemy aircraft and they proved some of the USAAF's best pilots, many going on to forge distinguished careers once segregation in the military was ended in 1948.

Despite their prowess, few gallantry medals were received though Archer was awarded the DFC, the Air Medal with 18 clusters and a Distinguished Unit Commendation.

 Archer retired from the USAAF in 1970. He joined General Foods Corporation becoming one of the era's few black vice presidents of a major American company. He was an adviser on the deal that created the conglomerate TLC Beatrice in 1987, then the largest black-owned and managed business in the US. After retiring from General Foods in 1987, Archer founded the venture capital firm Archer Asset Management.

In 2005 Archer and three of his Tuskegee colleagues flew to Iraq to address active duty airmen serving in the current 332nd Group.

Archer lived long enough to see the service of the Tuskegee airmen fully, if belatedly acknowledged. In March 2007, about 350 airmen and their widows received the Congressional Gold Medal of Honor from President George W. Bush at a ceremony in the US Capitol. The present-day 99th Flying Training Squadron's aircraft are adorned with red tails in honour of the black airmen. Many streets and parklands bear their name and in August 2008, the City of Atlanta officially renamed a portion of State Route 6 in their honour.

On December 9, 2008 Archer and the remaining Tuskegee airmen were invited to attend the inauguration of Barack Obama. Honoured by the American Fighter Pilot's Association, Archer was described by a colleague as "extremely competent, sometimes stubborn but he had a heart of gold and treated people with respect. He demanded respect by the way he carried himself."

Lee Archer's wife Ina, whose name adorned the nose of his Mustang, died in 1996. They had three sons and a daughter.

AIR CHIEF MARSHAL SIR DEREK HODGKINSON

Air Chief Marshal Sir Derek Hodgkinson (who died on January 29, 2010 aged 92) specialised in maritime air warfare and will long be remembered for his 'Hodgkinson Report' – the most detailed post-war review into the career structure for the RAF's officers.

After entering the RAF on a short-service commission in 1936, Hodgkinson joined No. 220 Squadron, where he was one of the first pilots to fly the American-built Lockheed Hudson. On November 25, 1939 he was tasked to find the British submarine *Triad*, which the Admiralty believed was in trouble off the Norwegian coast. He located the submarine and over the next few days monitored its laboured progress until a destroyer could arrive and take it in tow.

For the next few months, and after the German invasion of Norway, he patrolled an area stretching from Heligoland Bight in the south to Stavanger in the north. At the end of May 1940, he and his squadron maintained constant patrols over the English Channel throughout the evacuation from the beaches of Dunkirk.

Whilst on a rest tour as a squadron leader, Hodgkinson and some of his fellow instructors were ordered to form scratch crews to take part in the third of 'Bomber' Harris' 1,000-Bomber Raids, the attack on Bremen on the night of June 25/26, 1942. The Hudsons were completely unsuitable for medium-level bombing over heavily defended German targets, and five were lost.

An enemy night-fighter set Hodgkinson's aircraft on fire. Despite being wounded, he managed to ditch his blazing aircraft in the sea, where it immediately sank; but he was able to join his badly injured navigator in clinging to the only piece of wreckage afloat, one of the main wheels. The rest of his crew perished.

Just as their strength was beginning to fail in the rough seas, the aircraft's dinghy suddenly appeared and they clambered aboard. Next morning they were washed ashore on a Dutch island and taken prisoner.

After recovering in hospital, Hodgkinson was sent to Stalag Luft III. He immediately contacted the escape committee and, as one of the senior officers, (though aged just 25), he joined the team under 'Big X', Squadron Leader Roger Bushell. Hodgkinson was responsible for some of the security measures and co-ordinated a complex network of lookouts during the excavation of escape tunnels with the additional responsibility for the security of the countless items of escape material from money to maps, and tools to escape clothes. After 18 months he was appointed as adjutant of the camp, placing him at the centre of important matters such as negotiations with the German authorities, Swiss inspectors and the Red Cross.

On the night of January 28, 1945, the camp was evacuated and the prisoners forced to march westwards during a cruel winter. As adjutant on the 'Long March', Hodgkinson was kept busy negotiating with his captors for food and shelter. He was liberated at the end of April, and for his services as a POW was mentioned in despatches.

William Derek Hodgkinson was born near Prestbury, Cheshire on December 27, 1917 and educated at Repton before joining the RAF.

On his return home at the end of the war, he served for 15 years in Coastal Command, commanding two squadrons (Nos. 210 and 240), the large airfield at St Mawgan in Cornwall and helping to set up the Australian Joint Anti-Submarine School at Nowra, New South Wales.

In 1961 he joined Lord Mountbatten, then chief of defence staff, as a personal staff officer with responsibilities for RAF issues and the Near and Middle East. The job had its hazards, principally the conflict of loyalties involved. But Hodgkinson quickly mastered the art of walking the tightrope between the air staff, who tended to think he had sold his soul to the devil, and Mountbatten, who was particularly severe on any member of his staff who he suspected might not be telling him the whole truth.

Perhaps Hodgkinson's finest moment came when Mountbatten was invited back to India for the first time since he had been viceroy. Asked to advise the government there (in the aftermath of the severe mauling their forces had received at the hands of the Chinese operating from Tibet), Mountbatten called on Hodgkinson to address Nehru on the use of the Indian Air Force.

Shortly after returning home, Hodgkinson was promoted to air commodore. Mountbatten wrote a farewell note to him saying: "Congratulations Derek, you have now got your foot on the bottom rung of the ladder."

After spending a year at the Imperial Defence College and another as commandant of the RAF Staff College, Andover, Hodgkinson assumed the post of ACAS (Operational Requirements).

It was in this post a year later, while he was deeply involved in the international negotiations for a future multi-role combat aircraft, that Hodgkinson was suddenly ordered to conduct an exhaustive study of the officer career structure, being told to "drag the current system out of the past and fit it for the next decade".

Despite his protestations, and those of his military and civilian superiors engaged in the vital negotiations regarding the future aircraft for the RAF, he was made to undertake both jobs; and by the end of the year he had produced a report which was largely accepted by the Air Force Board.

At the time, the RAF had a two-tier officer entrance scheme, with the majority commissioned on the supplementary list. This produced a breed of officers who, with much justification, felt they were treated as second-class citizens.

Hodgkinson's recommendation to abolish this list was accepted, and from then on it was established that promotion would go to those who proved their ability and potential in post rather than on how they had entered into the service. The implementation of the 'Hodgkinson Report' had a profound effect on the management and organisation of the officer corps for more than two decades, and some measures still exist in today's RAF.

Hodgkinson then returned full-time to his role in the development of the RAF's present front-line aircraft and equipment. The Anglo-French Variable Geometry Aircraft and American F-111 had been cancelled by the then Labour government, and in 1967 Hodgkinson successfully negotiated the British entry into the European Multi-Role Combat Aircraft Consortium.

The remainder of his time as ACAS (OR) was spent commuting between London, Rome, Bonn and Munich in a successful attempt to get the other members of the consortium to accept the RAF's air staff requirement for a deep-strike aircraft rather than the short-range battlefield aircraft they then favoured. The outcome was the Tornado.

After his demanding two years in the Air Ministry, Hodgkinson spent a year as senior air staff officer at Training Command, before going to Cyprus as C-in-C Near East Air Force, commander British Forces Near East and administrator of the Sovereign Base Areas. His arrival in Cyprus in 1970 coincided with the election of Ted Heath's Conservative government, and Hodgkinson was soon sent on diplomatic missions to Greece, Egypt, Israel and Jordan. As C-in-C NEAF he had to visit Malta, Gibraltar and Gan, where elements of his forces were stationed, as well as Oman, where a war against invading Yemeni forces was being fought. He also had to pay regular visits to the Shah of Iran, where his V-bombers had their forward bases.

Back in Cyprus, the split between Greek and Turkish Cypriots was becoming more pronounced. But Hodgkinson struck up a good relationship with Archbishop Makarios, and the Sovereign Base Areas remained largely unaffected by the ensuing trouble – until 1974, after Hodgkinson had left.

On his return home, Hodgkinson became air secretary responsible for managing the careers, including postings and promotions, of the RAF's 20,000 officers and NCO aircrew. Although immensely rewarding in most respects, this was not a particularly happy time for him as he had to deal with the major redundancies caused by the withdrawal from the Far East and the Gulf.

The RAF's transport force was cut in half, making some 400 aircrew officers redundant at a stroke, and many senior officers with excellent records also had to leave. Hodgkinson and his staff did all they could to mitigate this damaging blow, but the result adversely affected morale in the RAF for some years to come.

Hodgkinson retired in 1976. He was awarded a DFC in 1940 and an AFC in 1942, and appointed CBE (1960) and KCB (1971).

After leaving the RAF, he took on a number of voluntary posts serving both his local community and national organisations. The most rewarding was that of helping to run the Regular Forces Employment Association, which helps find jobs for soldiers, sailors and airmen when they retire. As vice chairman, chairman and eventually president he served the association for more than 12 years.

Hodgkinson was an excellent cricketer, representing the RAF both before and after the war. He served as president of the RAF Cricketing Association for a number of years and was a member of MCC. His other main interest was trout fishing. He tied all his own flies and used to fish in Hampshire at least once a week during the season, sending many of his best fish to a smokery at Stockbridge.

Derek Hodgkinson married Heather Goodwin in 1939 and they had a son and a daughter.

WING COMMANDER LUCIAN ERCOLANI

Wing Commander Lucian Ercolani (who died on February 13, 2010 aged 92) was a wartime bomber pilot decorated three times for gallantry in operations over Europe and in the Far East; he was later chairman of the family furniture company Ercol.

On the night of November 7/8, 1941, Ercolani took off in his Wellington of No. 214 Squadron to attack Berlin. The target was obscured by cloud, and Ercolani dropped his high-explosive bombs but decided not to release the incendiaries as, if dropped in the wrong place, they might cause confusion for the following aircraft.

Over Münster on the return journey, his aircraft was hit by anti-aircraft fire, and the incendiary containers caught fire. The crew's attempt to jettison them failed and the fire spread over the whole of the bomber's floor, filling the aircraft with smoke.

The flames eventually subsided, but were never completely extinguished, leaving the mid-section of the aircraft almost burned away with most of the fuselage fabric destroyed. The aircraft's wings and engines had also been damaged and the bomber steadily lost height and speed.

Despite the appalling state of his aircraft and his limited ability to control it, Ercolani decided to attempt to fly it to England. The journey took three hours; he crossed the enemy coast at 1,000 feet eventually having to ditch in the Thames Estuary.

When the aircraft hit the water, Ercolani was injured, and he went down with the sinking bomber – but the cockpit section floated to the surface, allowing him to join his crew in the dinghy. Despite his injuries, he took charge of the situation. Unfortunately, the dinghy floated into the North Sea and eventually along the English Channel. The searching aircraft and ships failed to find it, and the crew's efforts to paddle ashore were ineffective. Finally, after three days drifting in an open dinghy during bad November weather, Ercolani and his men were washed up on the southernmost point of the Isle of Wight.

Flying Officer Ercolani was awarded an immediate DSO – a very rare award for so junior an officer – for his "outstanding courage, initiative and devotion to duty".

The son of an Italian furniture designer and manufacturer brought to England in 1910, Lucian Brett Ercolani was born at High Wycombe on August 9, 1917 and educated at Oundle School where he excelled at sport. He left school in 1934 to work at his father's company, Ercol.

When war broke out he joined the RAF and trained as a pilot in Canada, returning in May 1941 to join No. 214 Squadron. In October the next year Ercolani left for India joining No. 99 Squadron near Calcutta.

The squadron was one of two Wellington long-range bomber units used to attack enemy airfields and river, road and rail supply routes. Ercolani led many of these missions over the ensuing months before the squadron switched to night bombing. Inadequate maps, appalling weather and poor aircraft serviceability due to lack of spares added to the hazards of flying during the 'Forgotten War'.

With the expansion of the strategic bomber force, and the introduction of the long-range Liberator in September 1943, Ercolani went to the newly formed No. 355 Squadron. He flew many sorties deep into enemy territory, some involving a round trip of 2,000 miles, to destroy the supply networks used to reinforce and support the Burma battlefield. An important and frequent target was the Siam-Burma railway built by Allied POWs.

In September 1944 Ercolani returned to No. 99 as the CO where he won the respect and affection of his airmen ('erks' in RAF slang) who affectionately dubbed him '*The* Erk'. He led many of the most difficult raids himself, often taking his heavy four-engine bomber as low as 100 feet to drop his delay-fused bombs as his gunners strafed any buildings or rolling stock.

He attacked supply dumps and Japanese headquarters and throughout the early months of 1945 regularly led forces of up to 24 Liberators against targets in Siam, southern Burma and on the Kra Isthmus, often in the face of heavy anti-aircraft fire. He was the master bomber for an attack against the railway system at Bangkok and was mentioned in despatches.

By the end of March 1945 the decisive battle for Central Burma was won and a few weeks later, the 'erks' of No. 99 bade a sad farewell to their popular CO. For his outstanding leadership and courage, he was awarded a Bar to his DSO.

Ercolani was appointed to command No. 159 Squadron, part of the Pathfinder Force, attacking targets in Malaya and flying a number of mining operations to distant ports, including Singapore – sorties of more than 20 hours duration.

On June 15, he led a force of Liberators to attack a 10,000-ton tanker, the *Tohu Maru*, which had been located in the South China Sea. The mission involved a round trip of 2,500 miles. Flying in appalling weather, some of the Liberators were unable to find the target, while some were damaged by enemy fire. Ercolani attacked at low level and made three separate bombing runs, registering successful hits on the tanker, which caught fire. Subsequent reconnaissance reports confirmed that it had sunk, a devastating blow to the Japanese troops depending on its vital cargo of fuel. Ercolani was awarded an immediate DFC.

He flew his last operation on August 5 when he attacked a target in Siam. Almost immediately, his squadron turned its attention to dropping food and medical supplies to the many POW camps spread across Siam and the East Indies.

Ercolani left the RAF in March 1946 and rejoined his father at Ercol. Owing to the scarcity of raw materials, new furniture had been rationed since 1942, and the particular achievement of the Ercolanis was to mass-produce the Windsor chair while conforming to the stringent requirements of cost and material laid down by the Board of Trade. At its peak of production, Ercol made around 3,000 Windsor chairs a week.

After many years as chairman and joint managing director with his brother, Ercolani formally retired in the mid-1990s but remained closely involved within the company until his death.

In 1980 he became Master of the Furniture Makers' Guild – his father had been a founder member. He was a great supporter of the Livery with a particular interest in the Company's Guild Mark scheme that gives awards for excellence in design and manufacture.

He took a great interest in young people and their education, whether it was Ercol's apprentices or those training in design. For some years he served as a governor at High Wycombe College. In 1992 the Council of National Academic Awards gave him an honorary doctorate in design. A year later he was made an honorary burgess of the town of High Wycombe in recognition of his lifelong contribution to the town's community.

He was a devoted supporter of the British Legion and had a great passion for classic cars and for sailing – his many forays to sea took him from Hamble to France, and to the Azores.

Lucian Ercolani married Cynthia Douglas in June 1941 and she died in 2004. They had a son and a daughter.

WING COMMANDER ALAN 'RED' OWEN

Wing Commander Alan 'Red' Owen (who died on February 13, 2010 aged 87) was one of the RAF's top night-fighter pilots of World War Two. He was credited with destroying at least 15 enemy aircraft.

Owen and his radar operator, Vic McAllister, joined No. 85 Squadron, equipped with Mosquitos, in August 1944. By that time they had already established a reputation as an outstanding team during operations in North Africa and Italy.

In the months after the D-Day landings and the Allied advance into France, No. 85's role was to undertake bomber support operations over Germany. The Mosquito night-fighter crews mingled with the RAF bomber streams seeking out enemy night-fighters attempting to attack the bombers. They also flew 'intruder missions' to attack enemy aircraft as they took off and landed at their airfields.

During a brief period in the summer of 1944, the squadron was also employed on patrols over Kent intercepting the V-1 flying bombs. On August 5, Owen destroyed one before resuming night operations. On the night of September 17/18, he destroyed two Messerschmitt Bf 110 night-fighters and by the end of the year he had destroyed seven more aircraft, including a Focke-Wulf Fw 190 over Hamburg, in addition to destroying aircraft on the ground.

When patrolling south of Frankfurt on December 22, Owen engaged a Junkers Ju 88 and shot it down. Seven minutes later his operator made contact with another night-fighter; Owen closed in and destroyed it. Before the patrol was over, a third contact was obtained and, after a 15-minute chase,

139

during which his target took violent evasive measures, Owen finally managed to get in a cannon burst and the Bf 110 went into a vertical dive and crashed.

For their work on No. 85, both Owen and McAllister were awarded DFCs and within two months they each received a Bar. The citation commented on their "exceptional skill" and described them as "fearless and devoted members of aircraft crew".

One of eight children, Alan Joseph Owen was born in Chelsea on July 8, 1922 and educated at St Mary's C of E School, Merton Park and at Wimbledon Technical College where he trained as a technical draughtsman before joining a local engineering firm at Cheam in Surrey. In January 1941 he followed two of his brothers into the RAF and trained as a pilot, his shock of red hair attracting the nickname 'Ginger' – later he was known as 'Red'.

Owen was selected to fly Beaufighters and he teamed up with Vic McAllister. They were to remain together throughout their operational flying appointments to become one of the RAF's most successful night-fighter crews.

The two sergeants joined No. 600 Squadron and in November 1942 moved with the squadron to North Africa. On the night of December 21/22 they gained the squadron's first success in that theatre when they shot down a Heinkel III bomber near Algiers. Return fire from the enemy bomber damaged the Beaufighter's undercarriage and Owen crash-landed at his base. As it slid across the airfield, the Beaufighter collided with a Spitfire, a concrete mixer and a fuel tanker – all of which some wag added to their tally on the squadron scoreboard – before finally smashing into a wall. The aircraft was completely wrecked.

A few weeks later Owen accounted for another Heinkel as well as an Italian four-engine bomber, which he intercepted at 20,000 ft north of Bône in Algeria. Both he and McAllister were awarded DFMs. Subsequently, operating over Sicily, the crew shot down three more aircraft and damaged two others before returning to England in November 1943 to be instructors.

Following his successes over Germany, Owen remained with No. 85 until June 1946, initially as a flight commander and later – at the age of 23 – as the CO. He left the RAF for civilian life but could not settle and in July 1947 rejoined as a flight lieutenant. He joined No. 13 Squadron in Egypt flying Mosquitos on aerial mapping photographic work. In July 1950 he returned to England and developed radar interception tactics at the Central Fighter Establishment.

After flying night-fighters in Germany, he converted to the Meteor jet fighter and assumed command of No. 39 Squadron in Malta, which later moved to Cyprus in case it was required for operations during the Suez crisis; in the event it did not see action.

After a period at the School of Land/Air Warfare at Old Sarum working as air liaison officer with the Army's Southern Command, Owen returned to the night-fighter role in April 1962 taking command of No. 23 Squadron.

This was in the early days of in-flight refuelling, and in October he led three of the squadron's Javelins on a non-stop flight from Britain to Aden setting up a Fighter Command record of eight hours 50 minutes. Two months later the squadron extended its range when Owen led 12 Javelins from RAF Coltishall in Norfolk to Singapore and back using in-flight refuelling and staging through the RAF's bases in Cyprus, the Persian Gulf and the Indian Ocean. In January 1964 he was awarded the AFC.

From October 1964 until his retirement from the service in July 1969, he served in the fighter operations division at the Ministry of Defence before being posted to a sector operations appointment near Jever in Germany. This was during the Cold War, when a primary function of the RAF was to monitor the incursions and activities of Warsaw Pact aircraft and to maintain the integrity of NATO airspace.

Following his retirement from the RAF, Owen worked for the British Aircraft Co-operation Commission in Saudi

Arabia for two years.

In 1974, he was appointed road safety officer at East Sussex County Council. After promotion to the position of county road safety officer, he transferred to a similar position with Kent county council before retiring in 1984.

For much of his life Owen enjoyed a vigorous game of squash, later choosing golf as his major sporting pastime.

'Red' Owen married Rita Drew in October 1945 and they had two sons and four daughters.

WING COMMANDER BOB DOE

Wing Commander Bob Doe (who died on February 21, 2010 aged 89) was the joint-third most successful fighter pilot during the Battle of Britain credited with 14 victories and two shared.

Yet Doe had struggled to become a pilot, barely passing the necessary exams to gain his wings. He lacked confidence, was poor at aerobatics and did not like flying upside down – not an auspicious beginning for a fighter pilot. On August 15, 1940 – dubbed *Adler Tag* (Eagle Day) by Hermann Göring and the day he claimed he would destroy Fighter Command – the twenty-year-old Doe was on standby with his Spitfire of No. 234 Squadron at Middle Wallop in Hampshire waiting for his first scramble. Years later he confessed: "I knew I was going to be killed. I was the worst pilot on the squadron." When the scramble bell rang, Doe was filled with dread but he took off; the fear of being thought a coward was more powerful than the fear of death.

One hour later Doe landed to find that four of his colleagues had failed to return; but he had shot down two Messerschmitt Bf 110 fighters south of Swanage. The next day, he destroyed a Bf 109 fighter and damaged a bomber; and two days later he accounted for another Bf 109.

The battle intensified, and Doe's outstanding memory was to be of continued tiredness, which produced the ability to sleep anytime and anywhere. By the end of August, he had destroyed five aircraft. On September 4, his squadron intercepted a large force of Bf 110s over the south coast near Chichester. Doe shot down three and the following day accounted for a Bf 109 over Kent. More successes followed, including shooting down a Heinkel bomber but by September 7, just three weeks after arriving at Middle Wallop, the squadron's 15 pilots had been reduced to three.

Doe was rested for a short period before joining No. 238 Squadron as a flight commander, this time flying the Hurricane. On September 30 he claimed another Heinkel bomber after a head-on attack but by this time the Luftwaffe was sending most bombers over at night and the intensity of the day fighting reduced. He shot down a Bf 110 on October 1 and seven later days claimed his final victory on what turned out to be the last major daylight bombing raid of the battle, when he shot down a Junkers 88 bomber near Portland.

At the beginning of October Doe learnt that he had been awarded the DFC "for his outstanding dash and an eagerness to engage the enemy at close quarters". This "dash" almost proved his undoing a few days later. As he cleared some cloud his aircraft was hit repeatedly and he was badly wounded in the leg, lower back and arm. He baled out and landed in a sewage drainage pit on Brownsea Island. It was his last action during the battle. In just eight weeks he had risen from being his squadron's junior pilot to be a flight commander with at least 14 victories. A few weeks later he was awarded a Bar to his DFC.

The son of a head gardener, Robert Francis Thomas Doe was born at Reigate on March 10, 1920. A shy, sickly boy he left school at 14 to work as an office boy at the *News of the World*. He was one of the first young men to apply to the RAF Volunteer Reserve and started to train as a pilot at a civilian flying school. He gained a short-service commission in the RAF in March 1939.

After recovering from his wounds, Doe rejoined No. 238 in December. On January 3, 1941 his aircraft suffered an engine failure on a night sortie and he made a force-landing. His restraining harness broke and he smashed his face into the gunsight. One eye had fallen out, his jaw was broken and his nose was almost severed; he also broke his arm.

After undergoing 22 operations at East Grinstead Hospital he earned his place as a member of the Guinea Pig Club (an exclusive organisation for those who had undergone plastic surgery). He was flying again within four months of his crash. A series of training posts followed at a fighter school and in October 1943 he volunteered for service in India.

Two months later he formed No. 10 Squadron, Indian Air Force, at Risalpur in the North-West Frontier Province, the last Indian Air Force squadron to be formed during the war. He arrived to find 27 pilots, most of them Indian, about 1,400 men and 16 Hurricanes. The rest was up to him.

Flying Hurricanes IICs, known as 'Hurri-bombers', armed with four 20-mm cannons and two 500-lb bombs. Doe worked his squadron hard, and once it was declared operational it moved to Burma to fly ground-support missions in support of the Fourteenth Army's operations in the Arakan and the Kaladan Valley. After a particularly successful raid led by Doe in support of an amphibious landing, No. 10 received a commendation from the commander of the Arakan Group.

Doe's Indian squadron flew intensively, attacking ground targets that were sometimes just a few hundred yards ahead of friendly troops, as General Slim began his southern advance into Burma and towards Rangoon. In April 1945 Doe left the squadron to attend the staff college at Quetta. For his services with the Indian Air Force he was awarded a DSO for his "inspiring leadership and unconquerable spirit and great devotion to duty". At the end of the war he was tasked to run the air display for Indian Victory Week.

Doe remained in the RAF and after appointments with the Royal Auxiliary Air Force he was sent to Egypt in May 1950 to command No. 32 Squadron equipped with Vampire jet fighters. He had never flown a jet before, so on his way to the squadron he managed to stop off at a maintenance unit and borrow a Vampire for a few hours to familiarise himself. By the time he left in May 1953, No. 32 had built up a reputation for *esprit de corps* envied by all the other RAF and army units on the base.

He returned to Britain to join the Fighter Gunnery Wing as a senior instructor. A series of staff appointments followed including two years with the chiefs of staff secretariat. This placed him in the corridors of power, and the boy who had left school at 14 had to learn how to write minutes, which would be scrutinised and re-worded by secretaries and read by the chiefs. Doe found this job to be the most difficult and challenging appointment of his career. In April 1966 he opted for premature retirement.

Doe settled in Tunbridge Wells, where he joined a family-owned garage business before moving on to Rusthall, Kent to establish his own very successful garage and contract hire and self-drive car company. He took a passionate interest in his garden and three greenhouses and in his large family.

Much admired but always modest, Doe never considered himself a hero saying that he had been "just doing my duty". But he did write about his wartime experiences in *Bob Doe, Fighter Pilot* (1989).

Bob Doe was married three times and had five children and three stepchildren.

FLIGHT LIEUTENANT TOM FLETCHER

Flight Lieutenant Tom Fletcher (who died on March 10, 2010 aged 95) was the RAF's most decorated air-sea rescue pilot and was once recommended for the Victoria Cross.

On October 2, 1942, a Spitfire pilot was forced to bale out over the English Channel landing in the sea four miles off the French coast on the edge of a minefield. When his leader transmitted an emergency call, the naval authorities at Dover decided it was impossible to get a launch through the minefield and too dangerous for rescue by a Walrus amphibian aircraft. Despite this, Fletcher immediately volunteered to go, taking off in his Walrus with a Spitfire squadron providing an escort.

He arrived on the scene just as another Spitfire squadron was engaging enemy fighters trying to interfere with the rescue. He located the dinghy, landed 150 yards away and taxied towards the survivor who failed to grasp the boathook on the first pass as he fell out of his dinghy.

In the strong wind and choppy sea, Fletcher tried again, and the pilot was hauled on board. He then taxied clear of the minefield and took off, just clearing a floating mine. Throughout the rescue, the Walrus had come under heavy fire from shore batteries.

The air officer commanding of No. 11 (Fighter) Group strongly recommended Fletcher for the award of the Victoria Cross, writing: "Sergeant Fletcher was fully aware of the risks involved when he volunteered for the task. He carried out the rescue with conspicuous gallantry...he ignored all dangers and through coolness, considered judgement and skill, succeeded in picking up the fighter pilot."

In the event, Fletcher was awarded an immediate DFM, the next highest gallantry award available for a SNCO at that time.

Tom Fletcher was born on September 7, 1914 at Leigh in Lancashire and educated at Leigh Grammar School. Although his job as a commercial traveller for a medical equipment business was, at the beginning of the war, classified as a reserved occupation, he volunteered to be a pilot in the RAF, joining up in June 1940.

On completing his flying training, he joined No. 43 Squadron to fly Spitfires as a sergeant pilot. An effervescent, outspoken and sometimes rebellious character, Fletcher did not see eye-to-eye with his CO, who had him transferred to another Spitfire squadron flying coastal patrols. This role fitted him well for air-sea rescue duties and he joined a flight at Hawkinge, which soon became No. 277 Squadron.

Flying a Lysander spotting aircraft during the summer of 1942, Fletcher found a number of aircrew in the sea and directed RAF high-speed launches to rescue them. By the time of his exploit in the minefield in October he had already helped to save nine airmen.

On December 14, 1942, six men were found adrift on a raft 10 miles east of Dover. Fletcher touched down in the rough seas even though he knew it would be impossible to take off again.

In failing light he made three passes picking up the men one by one – although several of them were swept from the raft. Even as his Walrus started to take in water, he succeeded in recovering one of the survivors. By now it was completely dark, and Fletcher reluctantly abandoned the search and started to taxi towards Dover. The aircraft continued to ship water, and it took him almost two hours to make the harbour – where the harbour master reprimanded him for not getting permission to bring the sinking aircraft into port. The survivors for whom Fletcher had gone to such lengths were German sailors.

Fletcher was awarded an immediate bar to his DFM, one of only 60 awarded in the Second World War.

In the summer of 1943 Fletcher picked up seven more ditched aircrew, including a USAAF fighter pilot and a Belgian Spitfire pilot. Then, on October 3, he went in search of a Typhoon pilot reported in the sea too near the French coast for a launch to attempt a rescue. Fletcher found three dinghies, landed and picked up the occupants – survivors from an RAF bomber. Having taken them back to base, he immediately took off again, finally locating and rescuing the Typhoon pilot.

The sea was too rough for a take-off, and he began the long taxi back to England. A Royal Navy launch was sent to assist, but then the Walrus lost a float. The attempt to tow the aircraft failed, and it started to sink. Fletcher, his crew and the survivor had to abandon the aircraft and transfer to the launch. He was awarded an immediate DFC.

In the spring of 1944, Fletcher took off to rescue a Canadian fighter pilot. The dinghy was so close to the French coast that he had to fly over enemy-held territory to approach it, so that he would be in a position for an immediate take-off. Throughout the rescue he was under heavy anti-aircraft fire and his crewman was wounded. The pilot was snatched from the sea as Fletcher taxied past and brought back to England.

Fletcher later rescued an American bomber crew from the Somme Estuary and on April 30, he picked up a Spitfire pilot – his final rescue. He had by now saved more people than any other rescue pilot.

Remaining in the RAF after the war, in July 1945 Fletcher was attached to the High-Speed Flight as the search and rescue pilot when Group Captain E.M. Donaldson broke the world speed record off the Sussex coast in a Meteor jet. He later served as an instructor at the search and rescue training unit. In 1948 he was badly burned when his Mosquito crashed during a training sortie at the Central Flying School.

Fletcher trained as a fighter controller, but returned to flying in 1956 before continuing his career at ground control centres in Fighter Command. He retired from the RAF in 1964.

He spent three years with the company RFD, redesigning life-saving equipment and working on the design of rafts carried in larger aircraft, including Concorde. In 1968 he joined the Ministry of Agriculture, Fisheries and Food, where for 10 years he was a higher executive officer responsible for EEC subsidy payments to farmers.

Fletcher helped to establish the Shoreham Air-Sea Rescue Museum and assisted for many years at the annual air shows at Shoreham and Farnborough. He had a keen interest in motor racing, travelling around the country in a caravan to attend meetings.

Tom Fletcher married Mabel Berry in March 1941 and she died in 2003. They had a son.

COLONEL 'BUD' MAHURIN

Colonel 'Bud' Mahurin (who died on May 11, 2010 aged 91) was one of the US Army Air Forces' outstanding fighter aces in Europe during World War Two; he went on to serve in the Pacific and later became a POW after being shot down during the Korean War.

Mahurin arrived in Suffolk in January 1943 and joined the Eighth Air Force's 63rd Fighter

Squadron, which was part of 56th Fighter Group, to fly the
P-47 Thunderbolt, a robust long-range fighter escort. Before
experiencing combat he nearly killed himself when he carried out aerobatics around a Liberator bomber. Caught in
the aircraft's slipstream, he collided with the bomber and was
forced to bale out. He expected to be court martialled, but his
commander fined him $100 and "chewed him out". Five days
later, on August 17, Mahurin atoned by shooting down two
Focke-Wulf Fw 190s as he escorted bombers on the Schwein-
furt-Regensburg raid.

Whilst escorting bombers to Bremen on October 4, he shot
down three Messerschmitt Bf 110s. After further successes on
long-range escort missions, he became the Eighth Air Force's
first 'double ace' (10 victories) on November 26, in a raid over
Bremen. As the Messerschmitt Bf 110s came after the bombers
he was escorting, Mahurin and the rest of the 56th Fighter
Group waded in. He shot the wing off his first victim and
as the gunners in the bombers blasted away at anything that
came too close, including USAAF P-47s, Mahurin avoided
their 'friendly fire' and found a second Bf 110, which he sent
down in flames. His third target tried the Germans' favourite
– but least effective – evasive tactic; diving away. Virtually no
other aircraft could out-dive the 'Seven-Ton Milk Jug', and
Mahurin caught and destroyed his quarry.

During that winter, Mahurin's outstanding marksman-
ship accounted for another five enemy aircraft. Then, in
March 1944, as he escorted bombers to Berlin, the Luftwaffe
launched more than 400 fighters. The USAAF escort of 800
fighters accounted for 87 of the enemy, Mahurin destroying a
Focke-Wulf Fw 190. Shortly after he achieved his third triple
victory in a single day when he shot down two Fw 190s and a
Junkers bomber. These successes made him the highest-scoring USAAF pilot at the time with 19 aircraft destroyed and
two shared.

On March 27, he attacked a Dornier bomber over northern
France and he shared in its destruction, but his P-47 was hit
by return fire and he was forced to bale out. He landed in a

haystack and was hidden by the Resistance; they arranged his escape and he arrived back in England six weeks later. It was American policy not to allow evaders to return to operations, so Mahurin headed back to the USA.

Walker Melville Mahurin was born on December 5, 1918 in Benton Harbour, Michigan. He studied engineering at Purdue University before joining the US Army Air Forces in September 1941. Having graduated as a pilot in April 1942, he was assigned to the 63rd Fighter Squadron.

On his return to America in the summer of 1944 Mahurin was put in command of the 3rd Fighter Squadron at Luzon in the Philippines. Flying a P-51 Mustang, he scored his only aerial victory in the Pacific in January 1945 when he shot down a Japanese bomber. Promoted to lieutenant colonel he became the commander of the 3rd Air Command Group.

He stayed in the military after the Second World War and was working in the Pentagon for the secretary of the air force when the Korean War broke out. He quickly "got up to speed on jets", and in December 1951 left for Korea on a 90-day tour of temporary duty with the 51st Fighter Interceptor Wing, serving as a special assistant to the wing commander.

Determined to see action, he soon arranged a transfer to command the 4th Fighter Interceptor Wing, flying the F-86 Sabre jet from Kimpo in South Korea. On January 6, 1952 he shot down a MiG-15 and six weeks later accounted for a second. On March 5 he shot down a third and shared in the destruction of another.

On May 13, while strafing ground targets, Mahurin's Sabre was shot down by North Korean ground fire. After crash-landing, and breaking his arm in the process, he was captured.

Mahurin spent 16 months in a North Korean POW camp. He was confined to a small cell and fed only enough water and food to keep him alive. He was subjected to 'brainwashing' and forced to endure sub-freezing conditions with minimal clothing. Interrogations sometimes lasted all night while standing at attention, deprived of sleep and threatened with execution if he did not answer questions. The North Koreans insisted that he sign a confession that he and the US had waged 'germ warfare'.

He finally agreed to write a 'confession', but one so full of inaccuracies and implausibilities that any Western reader would know it was fiction. Unknown to him, the war had already ended. He was released in September 1953, well after the war's end, and was promoted to full colonel.

On his return to the United States, Mahurin and other former POWs were shocked to learn that some Americans, including the Democrat Senator Richard B. Russell, thought that those who signed confessions should be dishonourably discharged. The Defense Department thought otherwise.

After his release from Korea in 1953, his experience in brainwashing provided America with invaluable material to develop courses in survival techniques.

Mahurin was appointed vice-commander of the 27th Air Division, but his prospects of further promotion had been reduced. He resigned his commission in 1956 to accept a senior position in the aircraft industry. He later used his wartime call sign 'Honest John' as the title of his autobiography published in 1962.

Mahurin was the only US Air Force pilot to shoot down enemy aircraft in the European theatre of operations and the Pacific and in Korea.

He was awarded the Distinguished Service Cross, the Silver Star and the Distinguished Flying Cross. The British government awarded him the DFC for his "exemplary aggressiveness and outstanding leadership in action".

Walker 'Bud' Mahurin had two sons and a daughter during his first marriage, which ended in divorce. For 40 years he was married to his second wife.

AIR COMMODORE PAT KENNEDY

Air Commodore Pat Kennedy (who died on May 2, 2010 aged 92) fought with distinction in the Burma campaign and in the immediate aftermath, when his squadron was one of the first to fly to the Dutch East Indies following a serious outbreak of fighting against Indonesian nationalists.

Within days of the Japanese surrender in August 1945, Doctor Soekarno proclaimed the Republic of Indonesia, which created a dangerous situation, in particular on Java, where Allied forces struggled to reassert control. With Indonesian revolutionaries determined to fight for independence, both the RAF – which had been deployed largely to discover the location of the many thousands of POWs and internees in unknown jungle camps – and returning Dutch forces were targeted.

The RAF quickly deployed two Thunderbolt fighter-bomber squadrons including Kennedy's No. 81 Squadron. For the next few months No. 81 shouldered the responsibility for all offensive operations notably providing close support to ground units searching for POWs in Western Java.

The flying conditions were arduous and often dangerous, as Kennedy and his pilots provided this support and escorted RAF Dakotas dropping supplies to the many isolated POW camps. The Thunderbolts were also called on to mount strafing sorties against rebel strongholds and to bomb airfields and ammunition dumps. As some RAF squadrons were withdrawn, No. 81 Squadron remained, and Kennedy attracted widespread praise for his efforts in the air and on the ground. The citation for the DSO he was awarded concluded: "He had a prolonged and excellent record of gallantry and devotion to duty."

Patrick Ascension Kennedy was born on May 5, 1917 (Ascension Day) in County Tipperary and educated at Newbridge College near Dublin. In February 1938 he joined the Royal Ulster Rifles as a rifleman and sailed with the 2nd Battalion for France in early October 1939 as part of the British Expeditionary Force. With the German invasion of the Low Countries, the regiment moved into Belgium and was heavily engaged. A series of fighting retreats culminated in a withdrawal to Dunkirk and on June 9, the resourceful Kennedy and a few of his colleagues discovered a rowing boat and headed for a destroyer sailing for Folkestone.

After returning from France, the duties of guarding the Sussex coast did not satisfy Kennedy's restless nature so, in January 1941, he took advantage of a scheme allowing army personnel to transfer to the RAF to train as pilots. He completed his training in Canada before joining No. 123 Squadron based in Iraq flying Hurricanes. The squadron then moved to Persia to protect the oilfields from the threats in the north before transferring to Egypt from where it operated over Crete.

In October 1943 Kennedy left for India and six months later joined No. 4 Squadron, Royal Indian Air Force, as a flight commander, flying Hurricanes in the tactical reconnaissance and ground-attack roles in support of the Fourteenth Army. Kennedy flew many reconnaissance sorties over the mountainous Arakan, often in adverse weather, to gain valuable information on Japanese troop concentrations and movements before leading formations of aircraft in attacks against them.

When supporting the 81st West African Division, cut off in the Kaladan Valley, Kennedy and his pilots attacked enemy positions within 300 yards of friendly troops. During two of these sorties, Kennedy's Hurricane was badly damaged by ground fire but he succeeded in returning to an airfield.

As the Fourteenth Army advanced towards Rangoon, No. 4 Squadron bombed Japanese strongpoints and supported Indian troops landing at Kangow, when it laid a dense smoke screen to enable the troops to land safely. After moving further south, Kennedy led more 'smoke screen' sorties described by one pilot as "hair-raising and involving flying very low, having to distinguish the bomb line on the ground and then drop the containers". In March 1945 the squadron was rested and Kennedy received the DFC. Shortly afterwards he took command of No. 81 Squadron.

Kennedy returned to England in 1947 and spent two years at the Central Fighter Establishment. In January 1950 he was appointed to command No. 6 Squadron flying Vampire jet fighters. Over the next two years, the squadron was based in Jordan, Iraq and Egypt and was viewed as the best squadron in the Middle East Air Force.

No. 6 exercised regularly with the Arab Legion under the command of Glubb Pasha and established a very close relationship with King Abdullah and the Jordanian people. Shortly after receiving its RAF squadron standard, the King presented the squadron with his personal standard, making it the only RAF squadron to be granted two royal standards. For his outstanding leadership of No. 6 Squadron, Kennedy was awarded the AFC.

After three years at the Air Ministry, Kennedy took command in July 1958 of No. 31 Squadron flying Canberra aircraft in the tactical reconnaissance role from its base at Laarbruch on the Dutch-German border. A very popular CO, he guided the squadron to a number of successes in the annual NATO competitions and evaluations.

In May 1964, Kennedy commanded the V-bomber base at Marham but within three months he was faced with major difficulties. A Valiant bomber was found to have fatigue cracks in the wing and, after exhaustive tests, it was decided to scrap the whole Valiant force. The shock of the loss of the Valiants, and the period of uncertainty that followed, gave Kennedy a testing time. At the end of his tour he was promoted to air commodore, but shortly after taking up his post at HQ 1 (Bomber) Group he took voluntary retirement.

Kennedy joined the British Aircraft Corporation and moved

to the Middle East to work on the development of a national air defence scheme for King Idris of Libya. On September 1, 1969 a group of army officers, including 27-year-old Colonel Muammar Gaddafi, launched a coup, and Kennedy was confined to his hotel room. Not liking this, he immediately commandeered a taxi and told the driver to head for Tunis. On arrival, he handed over his watch as payment and boarded an aircraft for England.

After a brief spell in BAC's guided weapons division at Stevenage, Kennedy moved to Warton in Lancashire, dealing with international business particularly with Oman.

In 1984 he and his wife bought Lindeth Fell on the shores of Lake Windermere, which they established as a country house hotel. Kennedy developed the extensive gardens, designed by Thomas Mawson in the early 20th century, and remained actively involved in their care and maintenance until late in his life. Lindeth Fell won the *Good Hotel Guide's* 'Country Hotel of the Year Award' for 2009.

Pat Kennedy married Diana Clark in September 1958 and they had four daughters.

GROUP CAPTAIN MIKE JUDD

Group Captain Mike Judd (who died on August 22, 2010 aged 92) was a veteran of the fighting in the North African desert campaign and was recognised as one of the RAF's outstanding fighter-bomber pilots.

In early 1944 Judd was given command

of a wing of three Typhoon squadrons and, in the build-up to
D-Day, attacked the V-1 launching sites and the coastal radar
units in the Pas de Calais. On June 1, he attended a meeting
at 21st Army Group and was briefed on the operational plan
for the Normandy invasion and the role his wing would play.
With knowledge of this top-secret information, he was not allowed to fly for the next few days for fear of being shot down
and captured. He found it particularly frustrating to stand by idly
as his pilots took off to attack enemy gun positions.

But just after dawn on June 6, Judd took off from an airfield in Hampshire leading two of his squadrons. He had been
ordered to destroy two German 88-mm gun batteries that
overlooked the Normandy beaches and which posed a serious
threat to the Allied forces as they went ashore. Each aircraft
carried two armour-piercing 1,000-lb bombs.

The low cloud base hindered the attack but the Typhoons
dived onto their targets. As he pulled away he saw the scale of
the invasion fleet and he later observed: "I knew this was an
historic moment I would never forget."

On the following day, Judd's Typhoon was badly damaged
by anti-aircraft fire as he attacked enemy positions. The aircraft's hood simply disappeared and a large hole was blown in
one of the wings. It was only with difficulty that Judd managed to keep control of the aircraft as he was escorted back
across the Channel to make an emergency landing. For the
next three weeks, he continued to lead his wing against rail
and road targets and, on June 27, he and his comrades started
operating from temporary airstrips in Normandy.

Flying daily in support of Montgomery's army, the Typhoon wings attacked any transports they could find. Judd
and his pilots also bombed the bridges over the rivers Orne
and Odon as the Germans started their retreat eastwards. After
being moved to airfields in the Netherlands, the Typhoons attacked trains and the railway system in an attempt to interrupt
the movement of the V-2 rockets to their dispersed sites.

At the end of January 1945, Judd was finally rested and two
weeks later it was announced that he had been awarded the

DSO for his "brilliant work as an outstanding pilot with a fine fighting spirit".

Michael Thomas Judd was born on September 19, 1917 at Scotney, Hampshire and educated at Gresham's School, Holt before going to Wadham College, Oxford where he read Greats. He gained a good degree, which led to the award of a Laming Travelling Fellowship at Queen's College. In August he left for France but within a month, war was declared and he returned to England and was called up.

During his time at Oxford, Judd had been commissioned into the RAF Volunteer Reserve and trained as a pilot with the university air squadron, in which two of his close friends were Leonard Cheshire and Richard Hillary, later the fighter pilot who wrote *The Last Enemy*.

Judd completed his pilot training in December 1939 and was assessed as above average, which, to his great disappointment, led to his selection to be a flying instructor rather than his heading to Fighter Command. He left for Montrose to instruct at an advanced flying training school, where his skill was soon apparent. He rose to become a flight commander and after almost 18 months as an instructor, he was awarded the AFC.

In September 1941 he sailed for the Middle East, where he joined No. 238 Squadron to fly Hurricane fighters providing support for the Eighth Army. Returning from one sortie he flew into a sandstorm and was forced to land in the desert, recovering his aircraft the following day. On another occasion, his aircraft was hit by anti-aircraft fire and he had to make a wheels-up landing on the beach but he soon registered his first success. Whilst supporting an Allied convoy, he attacked a Junkers 88 bomber and damaged it. The Admiralty later confirmed that it had crashed into the sea.

In April 1942 Judd was promoted to squadron leader and appointed to command No. 250 Squadron equipped with the American-built P-40 Kittyhawk fighter fitted with long-range fuel tanks. He led his squadron against enemy supply dumps and airfields strafing aircraft on the ground. He destroyed a Ju 87 Stuka bomber and damaged another.

The German Panzer armies relied entirely on re-supply from mainland Europe. On May 12, intercepted enemy radio transmissions indicated that a large formation of Luftwaffe transport aircraft was heading for Libya from Crete. Judd took off at the head of his squadron to escort a Beaufighter squadron and intercepted 12 lumbering troop-carrying Junkers off the coast. Judd shot down two of the aircraft as his pilots attacked the others – only two of the Junkers escaped.

As the Eighth Army prepared to counter-attack Rommel's Army, Judd attacked supply dumps and motor transports. During these sorties he damaged two enemy fighters and on October 22 he destroyed a Messerschmitt Bf 109. He continued to lead the squadron until November when he was rested and awarded the DFC.

After a brief spell in East Africa, he was sent to the USA to discuss air tactics in support of ground forces and to fly and assess the latest American ground-attack fighters. A year later, in January 1944, he returned to the UK to join No. 83 Group and was soon placed in command of No. 143 Wing equipped with three RCAF Typhoon squadrons.

In addition to his gallantry awards, he was also mentioned in despatches and received the Air Efficiency Award. In November 1945 he left the RAF.

After the war, Judd left Britain to set up home in Houston, Texas where he established a partnership in oil exploration. When small production oil drilling became unprofitable, he worked for a firm of stockbrokers eventually joining the board of directors. He finally retired at the age of 82.

A charming man with a keen wit, his primary hobby was golf and he was particularly proud of his hole in one at the Houston Country Club's ninth hole.

Mike Judd married in 1943 and had two daughters. In 1952 he married his second wife Ann with whom he had two sons and two daughters.

WING COMMANDER 'BUTCH' BARTON

Wing Commander 'Butch' Barton (who died on September 2, 2010 aged 94) became a fighter ace during the Battle of Britain and went on to lead his squadron with distinction during the fierce air battles over Malta.

Barton was flight commander of the Hurricane-equipped No. 249 Squadron based in Yorkshire when it was transferred to Boscombe Down on August 14, 1940; the aim was to reinforce the hard-pressed fighter squadrons in the south. He was immediately in action and the following day he shot down a Messerschmitt Bf 110 fighter and damaged a second.

On August 16, Barton's deputy, Flight Lieutenant J.B. Nicolson, was attacked and his Hurricane caught fire. Despite suffering burns, Nicolson immediately attacked another German fighter before being forced to bale out. He was later awarded a Victoria Cross, the only pilot in Fighter Command to receive the supreme award for valour.

Over the next three weeks, Barton's successes mounted. On September 3, now flying from North Weald in Essex, his Hurricane was hit by the return fire from a Dornier bomber and he was forced to bale out. On his return to the squadron later in the day he was ribbed by his colleagues for allowing himself to be shot down by a bomber.

When his CO was wounded, Barton led the squadron into battle during the most hectic phase of the Luftwaffe's onslaught, sometimes flying four times in a single day. On September 15, the day of the greatest air battle, Barton shot down a Dornier bomber over the Thames Estuary and damaged a second.

By the end of the Battle of Britain on October 31, Barton had accounted for two more enemy fighters and damaged two others. He was awarded the DFC for his "outstanding leadership".

The son of a Canadian civil engineer and a Scottish mother, Robert Alexander Barton was born on June 7, 1916 in Kamloops, British Columbia. He was educated in Vernon, a weekly steamship journey from his home in Penticton. When he was 19, he went to a recruiting office in Vancouver and was accepted into the RAF. He travelled to England to take up a short-service commission in January 1936.

After training as a pilot he joined No. 41 Squadron flying bi-plane fighters. Following the outbreak of war, he joined the newly formed No. 249 Squadron whose CO was Squadron Leader John Grandy later chief of the air staff and a marshal of the Royal Air Force.

In December 1940, Barton was promoted to take command of No. 249 Squadron and he destroyed two more enemy fighters. In May 1941 his squadron was ordered to prepare for service in Malta and on May 19 its Hurricanes were transferred to *Ark Royal* in Gibraltar. Two days later, Barton took off from the aircraft carrier at the head of the squadron and set course on the long flight to Malta.

Barton opened his account in Malta on June 3 when he shot down an Italian bomber, the squadron's first victory over the island. Five days later he destroyed another bomber over the sea, this time at night. At first light, he returned to the scene to search for the Italian crew. Two were found and rescued to become POWs.

Under Barton's leadership, No. 249 Squadron was one of the most successful fighter squadrons on the island. His own successes mounted but he strongly disapproved when one of his pilots was ordered by higher authority to shoot down an air-sea rescue aircraft, which had red crosses on its wings.

On July 31, Barton was lucky to survive when the engine

of his Hurricane failed as he took off and he crashed through some sturdy Maltese walls. He was injured and suffered second-degree burns, which kept him in hospital for several weeks. Yet by September he was back leading the squadron and was soon involved in a fierce combat with Italian fighters, during which he was credited with shooting down one and damaging another. On November 22 he achieved his final victory when he shot down a Macchi C.202 fighter near Gozo.

After two years' continuous and intense fighting, he was rested and returned to Britain in December. His deputy, Tom Neil (himself a Battle of Britain ace), wrote:

> "I was very conscious of the squadron's debt to him. Small and slight in stature, in no way a heroic figure and unassuming almost to a fault, he was a wonderful leader and one of the best fighter pilots it would be my good fortune to meet."

The citation for a Bar to his DFC concluded "his excellent leadership inspires the pilots under his command".

Following a spell as chief instructor at a fighter-training unit, Barton took command of the fighter airfield at Skaebrae in the Orkneys. He later commanded North Weald and served at HQ Fighter Command responsible for tactics. He was mentioned in despatches and in June 1945 was appointed OBE.

In August 1945 he was posted to India where he spent two years closely involved in the arrangements for the creation of the Pakistan Air Force following partition in India.

Barton served on a number of fighter stations and commanded RAF Acklington in Northumberland. His final appointment was on the operations staff in the Air Ministry and he retired in February 1959. During his career he had always tried to maintain the highest standards of chivalry, once severely reprimanding an inexperienced colleague who had finished off a damaged German aircraft, killing the pilot as he was attempting to crash-land over England.

On his return to Canada he lived a quiet life. Much of his

time was devoted to caring for his wife, who for a long time was in poor health, and every year they wintered in Arizona. His great passion was fishing in the rivers and lakes of British Columbia where he was regarded as one of the region's finest fly fishermen.

'Butch' Barton's ashes were sprinkled on his favourite lake in British Columbia on the morning of September 15, Battle of Britain Day. He married Gwen Cranswick in September 1939 and they had a son.

GROUP CAPTAIN GEOFF WOMERSLEY

Group Captain Geoff Womersley (who died on October 28, 2010 aged 95) was one of the RAF's outstanding pilots of Bomber Command's Pathfinder Force and was awarded two DSOs and a DFC.

Womersley had already completed more than 50 bombing operations over Europe when he was appointed to command No. 139 Squadron, a specially equipped Mosquito squadron of the Pathfinder Force's Light Night Strike Force. In addition to marking targets with flares and target indicators, this force of fast mobile bombers flew 'spoof' raids to confuse the German air defence forces as well as 'nuisance' raids designed to deprive the industrial work force of a good night's sleep.

After taking over the squadron in February 1944, Womersley soon completed 26 operations against Germany's most heavily defended cities, including Berlin, Munich and Frankfurt. On numerous occasions he acted as 'master bomber' with the role of directing other bombers on to the various coloured markers that indicated the aiming point for the target. This frequently involved Womersley remaining over the target, under fire, for long periods until the attack was complete.

On the night of May 12, he led nine of his Mosquitos in support of another squadron tasked to drop mines in the Kiel Canal. It was No. 139 Squadron's task to drop flares to mark the route and to illuminate the target for the low-flying bombers. The raid was a great success and the canal was closed for many days. On another occasion, Womersley descended to low level over Mannheim, in the face of intense anti-aircraft fire, in order to give accurate instructions to the main force of bombers above. For this he was awarded a Bar to an earlier DSO.

The son of a mill owner, Geoffrey Harland Womersley was born at Bingley, Yorkshire on November 19, 1914 and educated at Bradford Grammar School. He joined the RAF in January 1936 and trained as a pilot at the RAF's flying school in Egypt.

His flying career started on the bi-plane bombers of No. 102 Squadron before it re-equipped with the Whitley. Immediately after the outbreak of war he dropped propaganda leaflets over German cities and bombed the German seaplane bases on Heligoland and Sylt. On the night of May 11, 1940, however, Womersley flew on the RAF's first raid on a German town when 37 aircraft bombed the road and rail communication links at Mönchengladbach.

His squadron was called on to support the British Expeditionary Force and on May 22, his aircraft was hit by flak on the German-French border and he and his crew were forced to bale out. On the ground he inadvertently stumbled into a group of German soldiers. He immediately started walking in the opposite direction and a few hours later he came across

British soldiers. From there he managed to get to Paris and on to the last flight to England from Le Bourget airport. Throughout his life he would refer to the "luck of the Womersleys".

He went on to complete 30 operations, most against road and rail targets in Germany, before he was rested to become a bombing instructor – a task he considered more dangerous than operations.

His return to operations in August 1942 coincided with the formation of the Pathfinder Force and he immediately volunteered, joining No. 156, one of the force's original four squadrons. In his Wellington he attacked targets in Germany and in Italy (the latter often involving missions of nine hours duration), dropping flares to illuminate the targets.

Womersley was recognised as one of the most fearless pilots, and in January 1943, while still a junior flight lieutenant, he was awarded the DSO. The citation concluded: "He has displayed outstanding ability and pressed home his attacks with unusual courage in the face of enemy fighter and anti-aircraft opposition."

After the squadron had re-equipped with the Lancaster, Womersley went on to complete 25 operations during the Battle of the Ruhr. A few months after receiving his DSO he was awarded the DFC for "pressing home his attacks with grim determination".

In April 1943, he joined the air staff at the headquarters of the Pathfinder Force where he worked directly for its commander, Air Vice-Marshal Donald Bennett. Ten months later he took command of No. 139 Squadron.

After attending the USAAF Staff College, Womersley was promoted to group captain to command the Pathfinder airfield at Gransden Lodge near Cambridge, where he flew a number of operations with the resident RCAF Lancaster squadron. He left the RAF in November 1945.

Early in 1946, Donald Bennett established British South American Airways, whose civilianised RAF bombers flew routes to the Caribbean and South America. Many of his ex-Pathfinder crews joined him including Womersley. The airline later used the ill-fated and unpopular Avro Tudor, one of which was lost without trace in the Bermuda Triangle. Womersley was one of the aircraft's few fans, describing it as "the best civil airliner flying".

On May 10, 1954, following the airline's merger with BAOC, Womersley flew a Comet into Rome airport where another crew took over for the flight to London. Shortly after take-off, the aircraft suffered an explosive decompression and crashed into the sea off Elba: there were no survivors. He remained with the airline until 1968, retiring as one of its senior Boeing 707 captains.

Womersley was a well-built, impressive-looking man with a natural presence, admired for his unflappability and modesty. One wartime colleague described him as "the epitome of the bomber leader – he inspired confidence in all his men".

A scratch golfer in his youth, he played to single figures until he was in his late 80s. His golf clubs accompanied him everywhere, sometimes stowed in the cockpit of his aircraft.

Geoff Womersley married his childhood sweetheart, Dorothy Allsop, five days after the war broke out in September 1939. She died in 2002 and they had a daughter.

BILL FOXLEY

Bill Foxley (who died on December 5, 2010 aged 87) was considered the most badly burned airman to survive the Second World War; his example and support became an inspiration to later generations who suffered similar severe disabilities.

Foxley was the navigator of a Wellington bomber that crashed immediately after taking off from Castle Donington airfield on March 16, 1944. He escaped unscathed but, hearing the shouts of a trapped comrade, he went back into the aircraft despite an intense fire.

He managed to drag his wireless operator free, suffering severe burns in the process. "The plane was like an inferno,"

he said later. "I had to climb out of the astrodome at the top and that is when I got burned." His sacrifice was not rewarded, however, as his comrade died shortly afterwards, as did two other crewmen.

Foxley was admitted to Queen Victoria Hospital, East Grinstead with horrific burns to his hands and face. The fire had destroyed all the skin, muscle and cartilage up to his eyebrows. He had lost his right eye and the cornea of the remaining eye was scarred, leaving him with seriously impaired vision.

He came under the care of Sir Archibald McIndoe, the pioneering plastic surgeon, and over the next three-and-a-half years he underwent almost 30 operations to rebuild his face, including procedures to give him a new nose, and build up what was left of his hands.

He finally left hospital in December 1947, when he was discharged from the RAF as a warrant officer. Though he did his best never to let on, he was rarely free from pain for the rest of his life.

A notable witness to his courage was Winston Churchill. During a brief convalescence in 1946 in Montreux, Foxley and a fellow burns victim, Jack Allaway, found themselves in the gardens of the house where Churchill was painting. After watching how the two men manipulated cups of tea with their disfigured hands, Churchill walked over and offered each a cigar.

William Foxley was born in Liverpool on August 17, 1923. He was 18 when, in 1942, he joined the RAF to train as a navigator. Posted to Bomber Command, he was nearing the end of his training course when his Wellington crashed.

After being discharged from the RAF he worked in the retail trade in Devon but he wanted to return to Sussex and be near to East Grinstead. For many years he had a distinguished career in facilities' management at the London headquarters of the Central Electricity Generating Board where he was the terror of the contractors. Many of the workmen were unaware that he was nearly blind, and when a re-decoration job had been completed Foxley would press his face to within a few inches of the wall and glare at it for seconds, not letting on that it was the only way he could inspect the paintwork.

Foxley had to overcome very public horror of his scarred features. Commuting daily by train from Crawley to London, the seat next to him often remained empty. Passengers who moved to take up the seat would change their minds at the last moment, prompting Foxley to tell them: "It's all right. I'm not going to bite you."

In 1969, he appeared (with officer rank for effect) in the film *Battle of Britain* as the badly burned pilot who is introduced to a WAAF officer, played by Suzannah York, in a celebrated scene set in an RAF operations room.

The hospital ward at East Grinstead had been full of men who had suffered severe burns. Such was their indomitable spirit that they formed the association known as the Guinea Pig Club, in honour of McIndoe's pioneering and unproven surgery. Considered by its members to be more exclusive than any smart London club, the Guinea Pig Club provided a support network for burns victims throughout their lives. Foxley once commented that being a 'pig' meant "everything" to him.

Nor did he restrict his support to veterans of the Second World War. Foxley was an inspiration to others and gave immense encouragement to those badly burned during the Falkland's conflict as well as in Iraq and Afghanistan.

With two fellow 'pigs', he set up the charity Disablement in the City, which grew into Employment Opportunities, of which the Duke of Edinburgh was president. After developing into a nationwide organisation, Employment Opportunities merged in 2008 with the Shaw Trust.

Foxley also devoted a great deal of his time to raising funds for the Blond McIndoe Research Foundation even getting sponsored, aged 80, to abseil down a fireman's tower. "There's nothing to it," he said afterwards.

Unable to play sport, Foxley took to long-distance running and would often run 12-18 miles a day, an activity he kept up until he was in his 70s. Twice he trained for the London Marathon, but minor injuries thwarted his participation on both occasions. He rode a bicycle to the supermarket until a few months before his death, and regularly paraded at the annual Service of Remembrance at the Cenotaph.

The nature of Foxley's injuries left him unable to smile or communicate his emotions. The most animated feature of his reconstructed face was its glass eye, which glinted when it caught the light. None the less, he never lost his positive approach to life. When asked how his experiences had affected him, he would reply: "It's your personality that will come through, whatever. I've never let it worry me too much; I've just got on with it."

Bill Foxley, a remarkable and courageous man, married his wife Catherine, who worked at East Grinstead Hospital, in 1947 and she died in 1971. He had two sons and a daughter from a brief second marriage.

BARBARA HARMER

Barbara Harmer (who died from cancer on February 20, 2011 aged 57) earned her place in the record books on March 25, 1993, when she flew as first officer on a British Airways' Concorde from London Heathrow to JFK Airport in New York.

For 10 years she remained Concorde's only woman pilot to fly regular commercial services, until October 2003 when the world's only Mach 2 civil jet was withdrawn from service

by its two operators, British Airways and Air France, in the wake of the catastrophic accident to an Air France Concorde in July 2000.

Barbara Harmer had been flying the long-haul DC-10 with British Caledonian when the airline merged with British Airways in 1987. One of only 60 women pilots flying with the national airline at that time, she was chosen in 1992 for the intensive six-month conversion course for Concorde.

In May 1999 she took the Manchester United football

team to play Bayern Munich in the Champion's League final in Barcelona, a flight which she described as one of the most exciting of her career. "I felt quite emotional as I taxied the Concorde out on to the runway," she remembered later, "with British flags flying and thousands of people wishing the team luck on the way."

Most of her flying was on the North Atlantic routes, but she never lost her sense of wonder at seeing the world from 60,000 feet as she travelled at 1,350mph.

The youngest of four daughters, Barbara Harmer was born in Loughton, Essex on September 14, 1953. Educated at a convent school after the family moved to Bognor Regis, she left at 15 to become an apprentice hairdresser.

But after five years she decided that she wanted more excitement in her life.

She applied for a job as a trainee air traffic controller at Gatwick Airport, at the same time paying for flying lessons. For the five years she worked at Gatwick she scraped together the money for enough flying lessons to gain her private pilot's licence.

She obtained a bank loan of £10,000 to build up her flying hours and flew as an instructor at Goodwood Flying School. For two years she studied by correspondence course for her commercial pilot's licence, which she finally obtained in May 1982.

Her tenacity to succeed was put to a stern test after she had qualified. It took 100 applications before she found a job with Genair, a small commuter airline operating from Humberside Airport, before she joined British Caledonian in March 1984 to fly the BAC-111, later converting to the DC-10.

After Concorde was withdrawn from service Barbara Harmer retrained and became a British Airways captain on long-haul routes flying the Boeing 777 until she took voluntary redundancy from the airline in 2009.

Her affection for Concorde never wavered. "Concorde is so smooth it doesn't really get the adrenaline going – but there's nothing else like it in the world," she said. "Even pilots stop and stare. It has an aura about it."

Barbara Harmer always led an adventurous life. She was a fully qualified commercial offshore yacht master and often commanded the crew of *Concorde* in international yachting events. She had won several races, and, despite knowing she was seriously ill, had intended to take part in a transatlantic event in her French-built 10-and-a-half-metre *Archambault 35* in 2013.

A keen gardener, she had created a Mediterranean-style garden at her home overlooking the sea at Felpham, West Sussex. She became an inspiration to very many women and was much in demand for speaking engagements.

For 25 years she lived with her partner Andrew Hewett.

AIR MARSHAL SIR GEOFFREY DHENIN

Air Marshal Sir Geoffrey Dhenin (who died on May 6, 2011 aged 93) rose to the top medical appointment in the RAF; earlier in his career, in the 1950s, he distinguished himself during two British nuclear tests, flying a Canberra jet aircraft through the mushroom clouds to gather radiation samples.

In 1953 Britain undertook two atomic test firings in the Australian desert, 300 miles north of Woomera. At the time, Dhenin was serving at HQ Bomber Command as the principal medical officer responsible for aviation medicine. He was also a pilot, and his appointment required him to fly the latest RAF bombers. In September that year he flew a modified Canberra to Australia in preparation for the tests, Operation Hurricane.

When the first weapon was detonated on October 13, Dhenin was already airborne at 30,000 ft. As soon as the mushroom cloud developed, he turned towards it and placed a wing tip, with a sensor attached, into the cloud to obtain radiation readings. Using special instruments, his observer calculated the probable dose rate. Once assured that the rate "would not be suicidal", Dhenin turned for the centre of the cloud.

It was very dark inside the cloud, and the aircraft was buffeted dramatically, but Dhenin was just able to maintain control. The transit was successfully completed and he made two further passes through the cloud, one through the top and one through the base, before returning to Woomera. It was the first time that an aircraft had flown through a mushroom cloud.

After landing he released the pod with the sensors in a secure area and taxied to the decontamination centre. The sortie ended for him and his crew with an ice-cold shower and a change of clothing. He later commented: "We have seen Dante's Inferno."

The aircraft was found to be highly radioactive, and tests showed that the crew had exceeded the permitted radiation dose. Dhenin was summoned to the chief scientist (Dr William Penney), who congratulated him and then said: "Go home boy; you have done enough. I cannot authorise such a thing a second time."

Although Dhenin and his crew had been scheduled to carry out the sampling of the second nuclear test, they were withdrawn from the operation. Dhenin was awarded an immediate AFC.

In 1957 he was again called on to obtain samples from a nuclear explosion. He flew a Canberra to Christmas Island, where he was 'master sampler' for Operation Grapple, Britain's H-bomb test. Valiant aircraft dropped three bombs and Dhenin took off after the second detonation on May 31, to fly through the cloud above 50,000 feet to obtain radiation samples. For his work at Bomber Command and during Operation Grapple he was awarded a Bar to his AFC.

Geoffrey Howard Dhenin was born on April 2, 1918, the day after the formation of the RAF, and educated at Hereford Cathedral School and St John's College, Cambridge. He completed his medical studies at Guy's Hospital in London.

He joined the RAF in February 1943 as a junior medical officer and served on bomber stations in Lincolnshire. One night in October 1943, a Lancaster bomber had to return from a raid with an engine failure. The aircraft crashed near the airfield, disintegrated and caught fire.

Dhenin was immediately on the scene with a RAF Regiment gunner to find the injured rear gunner trapped in his crushed turret. Although there was a high-explosive bomb in the blazing wreckage, Dhenin administered medical aid as he and the airmen tried to release the man. For 30 minutes they worked in the intense heat before a crane arrived to lift the wreckage. Displaying a total disregard for the acute danger and his own safety, Dhenin then crawled under the raised wreckage and released the gunner, one of only two survivors of the seven-man crew.

Dhenin was later awarded the George Medal for his outstanding courage; his colleague received the BEM for gallantry.

Two days after D-Day, Dhenin joined a mobile field hospital, and throughout the campaign in north-west Europe was involved in evacuating casualties by air. He was mentioned in despatches.

In 1945 Dhenin trained as a pilot, and was one of a few doctors to be employed as a flying medical officer. After serving on bomber stations and at the Institute of Aviation Medicine at Farnborough, in 1950 he joined, No. 1 Flying College Course, a post-graduate course for experienced senior aircrew. His ability was recognised when, on graduation, he was appointed to the staff. He then qualified as a senior specialist in radiology and in 1953 went to HQ Bomber Command, where he was the deputy principal medical officer (flying).

After attending Staff College, he spent a year on external study and received the London Diploma of Public Health and the Chadwick Gold Medal and Prize. He commanded the RAF Hospital in Cyprus from 1960 to 1963 before returning to Britain to command the hospital at Ely. In 1968 he served as director of Health Research at the MoD and in 1970 was appointed honorary physician to the Queen.

For three years from 1971 he was the principal medical officer at RAF Strike Command, and during this period he was elected a Fellow of the International Academy of Aerospace Medicine. In 1974 he was promoted to air marshal; for four years he served as director-general of Medical Services (RAF), the first active pilot appointed to the post.

During the Queen's Silver Jubilee Review of the RAF, all branches of the RAF created a ground display to illustrate their roles. Dhenin, a man who cared deeply for the RAF family, chose the theme 'Total Medical Care', which one senior officer said typified his attitude and his personality. He was appointed KBE (1975) and elected as a Fellow of the Royal Aeronautical Society.

Dhenin retired from the RAF in March 1978 and for two years was advisor, National Guard, Royal Saudi Air Force.

A keen sportsman, he was president of the RAF's Sub-Aqua Association and of its Judo Association. He was a very keen golfer and was captain of Wentworth GC in 1981; he continued to ski until his late 80s.

Geoffrey Dhenin was greatly admired by both the medical and flying fraternities in the RAF. His courage and flying skills had been amply demonstrated during the nuclear tests, and he continued to fly bombers for many years. An RAF medical colleague remarked: "He was greatly revered as a doctor by all of us."

He married Evelyn Rabut in 1946 who died in 1996, and in 2002 he married, secondly, Syvia Howard. He had a son and two daughters from his first marriage. A second son pre-deceased him.

AIR COMMODORE PETER CRIBB

Air Commodore Peter Cribb (who died on June 20, 2011 aged 92) was one of the most successful and gallant master bombers of the Pathfinder Force; he flew more than 100 wartime operations, including one when he made an unauthorised raid on Hitler's retreat at Berchtesgaden.

Cribb was already a veteran of more than 70 missions when he returned to operations in May 1944 to fly the Lancaster. He attacked targets in the lead up to D-Day, often acting as the master bomber directing the main force against rail yards and gun emplacements.

In July he was appointed to command the newly formed No. 582 Squadron and flew 16 daylight sorties in support of the Normandy landings. On July 18 he was the deputy master bomber when more than 1,000 bombers pulverised the

German Panzer divisions in front of Montgomery's stalled army in Caen.

Cribb also controlled more than 700 bombers which attacked the V-1 sites before the bombing campaign resumed its efforts against major oil targets in Germany.

On October 3, he was master bomber for the attack on the sea walls of Walcheren Island. Coastal gun batteries dominated the approaches to the important port of Antwerp; the aim was to breach the walls and flood the island, most of which was reclaimed polder below sea level.

As the first to arrive at the head of 252 Lancasters, he orbited the target and directed eight separate waves of bombers, correcting the aiming point with flares and markers, to widen the initial breach. The sea poured in forcing the German defenders to abandon their carefully prepared positions. Cribb was the last to leave the target after a brilliantly controlled attack, which allowed the Canadian ground forces to capture the island and open the port of Antwerp. Newspapers hailed the achievement with the headline "RAF sinks an island".

On promotion to group captain at the age of 25, Cribb was appointed to command the Pathfinder airfield at Little Staughton in Bedfordshire and shortly afterwards he was awarded a Bar to an earlier DSO. Frustrated at being desk bound, he flew unofficially on a number of operations. On April 24, 1945 he learned that a force of Lancasters was to bomb Hitler's Bavarian retreat at Berchtesgaden but the Lancaster squadron on his airfield was stood down.

Determined not to miss this final attempt to eliminate Hitler, Cribb commandeered a Lancaster and some bombs and made up a crew from the senior executives on his station. He took off at dawn, catching up the main force as it was approaching the target. He dropped his bombs and obtained an excellent aiming point photograph.

Anxious to get back to Britain before anyone realised what he had been up to, Cribb returned on a direct route at top speed – but to no avail. Air Vice-Marshal Donald Bennett, head of the Pathfinder Force, had tried to contact him and his deputy, only to be told that they were airborne "on a 10-hour navigation exercise". It was reported that when he learned the truth Bennett "hit the roof".

The son of a wool merchant, Peter Henry Cribb was born on September 28, 1918 in the Yorkshire Dales and educated at Prince Henry Grammar School, Otley before gaining a cadet-ship in September 1936 to the RAF College, Cranwell where he trained as a pilot.

Cribb joined No. 58 Squadron to fly the Whitley bomber and on the outbreak of war flew convoy patrols before the squadron reverted to the bombing role. He attacked German-occupied airfields in Norway and Denmark. Following the German blitz into the Low Countries, he bombed road and rail systems used by the Germans to transport reinforcements, and during a hectic period in June he flew numerous sorties in support of the British Expeditionary Force. After completing 25 operations he was rested.

In December 1941 Cribb was promoted to squadron leader and joined the RAF's first Halifax squadron, No. 35, as a flight commander. He attacked major industrial targets in Germany, before turning his attention to the German battleship *Tirpitz*, which was at anchor in a fjord near Trondheim.

Bad weather and a smoke screen severely hampered the low-level attack and the force returned the following day. As he approached in poor visibility, Cribb's Halifax hit the sea and the tail wheel was ripped off. After he had landed the intelligence officer asked him at what height he had delivered his attack. Cribb replied: "I don't know. The altimeter reads in feet, not fathoms." Cribb flew on the first 1,000-Bomber Raid on the night of May 30, 1942. Shortly afterwards, he was awarded the DFC.

No. 35 became one of the founder squadrons of the new Pathfinder Force and Cribb – who was rated an "exceptional pilot" – flew on the first raid mounted by the new force when he attacked Flensburg on the night of August 18/19. He went on to attack the heavily defended targets in the Ruhr, often returning with his Halifax damaged by enemy gunfire. By January 1943 he had completed 60 operations and was awarded his first DSO.

During this period, he shared a bleak Nissen hut with his Canadian colleague, 'Shady' Lane. The winter of 1942-43 was especially cold, and both men were anxious to avoid being the last into bed, and thus responsible for switching out the lights. Eventually Cribb solved this problem by using his .38 revolver to shoot them out. Due to the cold and an alcoholic haze, he frequently missed. In the morning his batmen would wake him with a cup of tea and inquire; "Shall I reload sir?"

Cribb was given command of the Bomber Development Unit working closely with the eminent scientist R.V. Jones to develop new bombing, navigation and electronic countermeasure aids. He frequently flew on operations unofficially to test new equipment and tactics. In May 1944 he returned to the Pathfinder Force to start a third tour of operations.

In May 1945, Cribb left for Ceylon where he flew Liberators on mercy missions to drop food and medical supplies to the POW camps spread across the Far East. He served in India and commanded the airbase at Peshawar during the difficult period of Indian Partition.

After a period with Coastal Command and at the Air Ministry on technical intelligence duties, he served at HQ Bomber Command responsible for operational plans and policy at a time when the V-bombers were entering service. He was appointed CBE.

In 1957 Cribb was sent to Germany, where he commanded three fighter squadrons and took every opportunity to fly the Meteor and Hunter fighters. In 1961, on promotion to air commodore, he served in Aden as the senior air staff officer, having responsibility for operations in the Radfan and along the Yemen border.

Two years at the MoD left him disillusioned with the Wilson government's defence cuts, and disdainful of "the ponderous bureaucratic existence in Whitehall". Accordingly, he resigned in 1967.

Cribb moved with his family to Western Australia, where he was manager of one of the state's first giant iron ore mines before starting his own business in Perth. He was active as a Rotarian, magistrate, and charity worker.

A keen sportsman in his youth, he played rugby for the Yorkshire Wanderers once breaking his nose during a warm-up match against the All Blacks. In later life he was a blue-water yachtsman and game fisherman. A modest man, he never spoke of his wartime experiences unless pressed to do so and then only to relate the episodes he found amusing.

Peter Cribb married Vivienne Perry in December 1949. They had three sons.

SIDNEY GOLDBERG

Sidney Goldberg (who died on July 27, 2011 aged 88) fled Nazi Germany for England, where he intercepted Luftwaffe wireless traffic to provide crucial intelligence to the RAF.

A German Jew born in Leipzig on March 20, 1923, Sidney Goldberg was only 10 when his uncle, who had trade contacts in England, helped him escape to London. He was educated at the Jewish Free School, and though his parents managed to join him shortly before the outbreak of war, many of his family perished in Auschwitz.

As soon as he was 18, Goldberg volunteered for service with the RAF Volunteer Reserve. Rejected for aircrew training after failing an eyesight test, he served on a number of airfields before, in August 1942, answering an official request for German speakers. He was one of 15 German linguists, most with backgrounds similar to his, when he joined No. 381 Wireless Unit.

It was the task of this 50-strong unit (of whom only three or four were linguists) to intercept Luftwaffe aircraft radio transmissions and gather intelligence. Arriving at Bône, in Algeria, shortly after the Operation Torch landings, and using a captured German Type FuGe 16 VHF receiver, Goldberg monitored the heavy Luftwaffe fighter activity; his reports were passed to air headquarters, contributing to many successful interceptions by Allied fighters.

Goldberg's unit followed the Allied advance into Tunisia, and was based high in the Medjerda Mountains near the airfield complex at Souk-el-Arba. Though the risk of capture was lower for ground troops behind the front line than it was for German-Jewish aircrew volunteers, all faced the same fate if taken prisoner; they were treated as subhuman traitors by the Nazis.

In March and April 1943, the Germans tried desperate measures to reinforce their positions in Tunisia using giant six-engine Messerschmitt Me 323 transport aircraft. Signals intercepted by Goldberg and his small unit were credited with helping Allied fighters to destroy most of this air fleet.

After the fall of Tunis, Goldberg's unit moved to Cap Bon to cover the invasion of Sicily, and in August they landed at Catania. With the steep decline of the Luftwaffe fighter force, radio traffic had lessened considerably and, after a few months, Goldberg and his unit returned to England to prepare for D-Day.

On June 5, Goldberg embarked in *Hilary*, the HQ ship for Force J, to cover the landings of the 3rd Canadian Infantry Division on Juno beach. He landed at Arromanches and his unit moved steadily eastwards with the front-line ground forces as they advanced into the Netherlands.

Support was given for the airborne landings at Arnhem and on October 4, Goldberg and his unit made a critical breakthrough when they realised from their intercepts that the Messerschmitt Me 262 jet fighter, which posed a serious threat to Allied bombers, had been switched from its deadly fighter role to bomber duties – which would have far less impact on the overall Allied campaign.

The unit also intercepted wireless traffic of the Luftwaffe flak batteries and were able to warn Allied flying units of their presence and activity.

At the conclusion of hostilities, Goldberg was sent to Lingen in Germany when he and his German-speaking colleagues became interpreters with the Air Disarmament Wings. They interviewed German scientists and gathered a wide array of technical information. In late 1945 Goldberg was released from the RAF in the rank of sergeant.

Goldberg worked for a number of textile firms and became well known in the industry both in the UK, in Europe and in Israel. He also became a mentor to young textile designers through the Prince's Trust.

From 1992 he served as the honorary national public relations officer of the Normandy Veterans Association and in 1994 organised many commemorative events for the 50th anniversary of the D-Day landings.

In 2004, the 60th anniversary, he was appointed a Chevalier de la Légion d'Honneur. In 2009, at Bletchley Park, he was one of 35 veterans presented with an award in honour of his wartime service by the Foreign Secretary.

Goldberg worked for numerous service associations and charities and served as a member of the National Executive Council of AJEX (Jewish ex-Servicemen). An avid reader of the *Daily Telegraph*, he enjoyed classical music and attending concerts.

Sidney Goldberg married his wife Sylvia shortly before he left for D-Day. She died in 2009. Their daughter, Rachelle, a concert violinist survived them.

Group Captain Billy Drake (who died on August 28, 2011 aged 93) was one of the leading Allied 'aces' of the Second World War.

Five days after the outbreak of the war, Drake and his colleagues of No. 1 Squadron flew their Hurricanes to a French airfield to provide support for the British Expeditionary Force. Throughout the bitter winter of the 'Phoney War' there was little action, but on April 19, 1940 Drake met the enemy for the first time. His formation attacked a flight of Messerschmitt Bf 109 fighters and, in the ensuing melee, Drake claimed one, the first of many successes.

When the blitzkrieg was launched on May 10, No. 1 Squadron was thrown straight into battle, its Hurricanes trying to provide support for RAF bombers which were suffering terrible losses, by engaging enemy fighters. In three days, Drake, always a highly aggressive pilot, shot down three Dornier 17s and shared in the destruction of another.

Three days later he had just succeeded in setting a Dornier on fire when he was attacked from the rear; despite being wounded in the back, he managed to bale out of his blazing Hurricane. After a spell in a French hospital he returned to England to be reunited with the survivors of his squadron. He admitted that the situation in France was "total chaos".

Drake spent much of the Battle of Britain training fighter

pilots but, after badgering old friends, he joined No. 213 Squadron flying out of Tangmere. On October 10 he probably shot down a Bf 109 before heading to Gravesend to join a reconnaissance flight whose job was to fly over the English Channel looking for incoming German raids. Flying a Spitfire he shared in the destruction of a bomber and damaged a number of others. In December he was awarded the DFC.

The son of an English doctor who married an Australian, Billy Drake (a descendant of Sir Francis Drake) was born on December 20, 1917. After attending a number of schools that did not suit his lively temperament, he was sent to be educated in Switzerland – a country he came to love greatly, not least for the opportunities it gave him for skiing. On seeing an advert in *Aeroplane* magazine, he joined the RAF just before his 18th birthday and was commissioned a few months later having qualified as a pilot.

Drake joined No. 1 Squadron and flew the elegant Fury biplane fighter. In late 1938 the squadron received Hurricanes and nine months later they arrived in France.

In October 1941, he left for Freetown in Sierra Leone as a squadron leader to command No. 128 Squadron and to provide defence for the nearby naval facilities. Vichy French bombers occasionally strayed into the airspace and on December 13, he intercepted one which refused his orders to land; with some regret, he shot it down.

Life in Sierra Leone was too quiet for the restless Drake and his efforts to see more action paid off at the end of March 1942 when he left to join a Kittyhawk fighter-bomber squadron in the Western Desert. Two months later he was given command of No. 112 (Shark) Squadron and so began a period of intense action during which Drake accounted for over 30 enemy aircraft, 15 of them during strafing attacks against enemy landing grounds.

On June 6 he was leading his squadron on a bombing attack over Bir Hacheim in support of the Free French. Spotting four Bf 109s, he dived on them; all four were shot down, one by

Drake. The French commander signalled, "Bravo! Merci pour le RAF!" to which the RAF commander responded, "Merci pour le sport!"

Over the next few weeks Drake destroyed at least five aircraft on the ground and in mid-July he was awarded an immediate Bar to his DFC for a raid on Gazala which "grounded the German fighter force for three days".

During the retreat to El Alamein, Drake was in constant action destroying at least three more aircraft in the air and two on the ground. After a brief respite, operations gathered momentum again and in September and early October, he added to his score as he attacked enemy airfields; amongst his victims in the air, were two Italian Macchi fighters.

In the latter part of October, Drake claimed a German bomber and a fighter. Over the next few days he destroyed more fighters, two Stuka dive-bombers and two transport aircraft on the ground. At the end of October, two months before he was rested. he was awarded the DSO. During his time in command of No. 112 he had destroyed 17 aircraft in the air with two others shared, a total exceeded in North Africa only by one other pilot, the Australian-born Group Captain Clive 'Killer' Caldwell.

After six months in a staff post Drake was back on operations commanding a Spitfire Wing in Malta. Providing escort to USAAF bombers attacking Sicily he claimed two enemy aircraft destroyed on the ground and he shot down an Italian fighter on July 7, his 25th and final victim in air combat (having shared in the destruction of three others). He added an American DFC to his decorations.

After returning to England in December 1943, Drake commanded a Typhoon Wing and attacked the German V-1 sites in the Pas de Calais. With his great experience of fighter and ground-attack tactics he was sent to instruct at the RAF's Fighter Leaders' School. Despite being in a training appointment, he frequently absconded for a day to take part in attacks against targets in France. Finally his operational career came to an end in August 1944 when he was sent to the US Command

School in Kansas before returning to join the staff of the Supreme Headquarters Allied Expeditionary Force.

Drake spent the first few years after the war in operational headquarters, first in Japan and then in Singapore but his great love was the fighter environment. In 1949 he was posted to the Day Fighter Leader's School as a senior instructor, an appointment much to his liking and where he converted to jets. This was followed by his appointment as wing commander at Linton-on-Ouse near York where he commanded three Meteor fighter squadrons.

In 1956 Drake became the controller of Fighter Command's Eastern Sector but he still found time to persuade colleagues to allow him to fly their fighters two or three times a month. Two years later he left to be the air attaché in Berne, Switzerland spending the next three years in the country, a period he enjoyed greatly.

Returning to England in 1962, he took command of the RAF's fighter training base at Chivenor in Devon where he flew the Hunter. A dedicated fighter pilot who had little interest in administration and staff work, he recognised that his flying days would soon be over so decided to retire, leaving the RAF in July 1963.

Drake went to live in Portugal at the time that the Algarve was becoming popular as a holiday destination and he acquired several properties. He contracted cerebral meningitis, which forced him to give up drinking (something he did not regret), but none the less he established 'Billy's Bar'. Initially this was successful but by 1993 he decided to return to England.

Billy Drake was held in high estimation in the RAF as one of its most colourful and successful fighter pilots, and as a man who led from the front and inspired all those that flew with him. His great professionalism was accompanied by an infectious enthusiasm for life and for his mischievous sense of humour and bonhomie. He lived life in the fast lane, spoke his mind and could be irreverent but he was great company and times were never dull when with him.

His great passion was skiing. He captained the RAF ski

team and made annual trips to the home of one of his sons in Switzerland taking to the slopes until his early nineties.

Billy Drake's two marriages were dissolved. He had his two sons with his first wife.

AIR CHIEF MARSHAL SIR BRIAN BURNETT

Air Chief Marshal Sir Brian Burnett (who died on September 16, 2011 aged 98) enjoyed a life of constant achievement in two widely differing spheres. After filling very senior appointments in the RAF, he embarked on a second career as chairman of the All England Lawn Tennis Club presiding over the Wimbledon Championships for 10 years.

Burnett's name came to world prominence in 1938, when he was the navigator and second pilot of a Wellesley bomber that completed a record-breaking non-stop flight from Ismailia in Egypt to Darwin in Australia.

On October 24 four single-engine Wellesley aircraft of the RAF's Long-Range Development Unit (LRDU) arrived in Ismailia to prepare for the flight. Three were selected for the record attempt, and these included Burnett's aircraft, whose pilot was Flight Lieutenant Andrew Combe, with Sergeant Gray as the third pilot and wireless operator. Each took it in turns to fly the aircraft during their epic flight.

The three aircraft took off at dawn on November 5. There were immediate problems, as the undercarriage of Burnett's Wellesley would not retract. For an hour the crew cut a hole in the side of the aircraft through which they thrust the long arm of a fishing net (carried to pass messages between the crew in the narrow fuselage). After some wiggling, the undercarriage retracted. The route took the aircraft over the Persian Gulf, India and Singapore. Over Timor, one aircraft was forced to land with a shortage of fuel.

The two remaining aircraft arrived at Darwin with 20 gallons of fuel having completed the non-stop flight of 7,158 miles in just over 48 hours to establish a new world record. The crews were decorated with Burnett being awarded the AFC.

Brian Kenyon Burnett was born on March 10, 1913 in Hyderabad, India where his father was principal of Nizam College. He was educated at Charterhouse School, Heidelberg University and Wadham College, Oxford gaining a degree in Modern Languages. An outstanding sportsman, he gained a double blue at squash and tennis and represented the university at hockey. In the 1933 tennis match against Cambridge University, he beat his elder brother Douglas.

After learning to fly with the Oxford University Air Squadron, Burnett joined the RAF in September 1934. On gaining his wings he was posted to No. 18 Squadron to fly the bi-plane Hart bomber – the beginning of a long association with RAF bombers. Following completion of a specialist navigation course, Burnett was selected to join the LRDU in December 1937. Earlier in the year he had played squash for England against Scotland and achieved the unique double of being the RAF squash and tennis champion. He won the RAF tennis singles championship again in 1939.

At the outbreak of war, Burnett left for France with the Advanced Air Striking Force based at Rheims returning to HQ 4 (Bomber) Group in 1940. Anxious to gain operational experience, he was posted as the flight commander of a Whitley bomber squadron and attacked the docks at Kiel and

Hamburg before bombing the German battleships *Scharnhorst* and *Gneisenau* at Brest. Promoted to wing commander in May 1941, he took command of No. 51 Squadron.

According to one of his crew Burnett soon established a reputation as a "press on type". On the final bombing run over Hamburg, for example, his Whitley was caught in searchlights and he had to take violent evasive action to escape. Forced to abandon the run, he told his startled crew he was making another attempt. The majority of aircraft had left, so his aircraft attracted the attention of all the searchlights and anti-aircraft fire. He completed the attack and flew his damaged bomber back to base.

After seven months in command, Burnett was awarded the DFC and left for Canada to command an air navigation school.

In the early post-war years, tennis continued to feature large in his life. He was captain of the RAF team that beat the army, played in the Wimbledon Championships and was selected for an England team that toured Germany.

After three years in New York on the staff of the United Nations Military Staff Committee, Burnett returned to the Ministry of Defence on the Joint Planning Staff, helping with the implementation of the Marshall Plan and the establishment of NATO. He found time to win the RAF squash championship for the fifth time and beat his brother in the inter-service championships. In 1950 he and his brother had the rare distinction of being army and RAF champions in the same season.

In 1951 Burnett returned to the bomber role as the senior air staff officer at No. 3 Group at a time when the RAF's first jet bomber, the Canberra, was entering service and preparations were being made for the introduction of the V-bombers. In June 1954 he took command of RAF Gaydon as it opened as the RAF's first V-bomber base.

With his promotion to air commodore and appointment as director of Bomber Operations at the Air Ministry in June 1956, Burnett's steady rise to the top continued. He observed the dropping of Britain's first thermo-nuclear bomb at Christmas Island and was heavily engaged in the policy aspects of bomber operations during the Suez Crisis.

Senior appointments at HQ Bomber Command and as air officer commanding No. 3 Group followed when Burnett had the opportunity to fly the Victor bomber. In 1964 he was appointed vice-chief of the air staff (VCAS).

During Burnett's time as VCAS, there were many significant new developments in the RAF's capabilities and tasks, including the planning for the introduction of a new generation of combat aircraft. In addition, following Denis Healey's decision not to replace the Royal Navy's aircraft carriers, Burnett was charged with developing policy to provide land-based air support for the Fleet. Three years as the air secretary responsible for the career planning, promotion and appointments of RAF officers was followed by promotion to air chief marshal and an appointment as commander-in-chief Far East in May 1970. Based in Singapore for this tri-service appointment, Burnett had a huge parish extending from the Beira Patrol off East Africa to Australia and New Zealand.

He arrived just after it was announced that the Wilson government planned to withdraw British Forces from the Far East. While his main task was to implement this, he was tasked to organise a small UK, Australian, and New Zealand (ANZUK) force in conjunction with the Malaysian and Singapore armed forces. He was also the British representative at the South East Asia Treaty Organisation (SEATO) conferences.

As the time for withdrawal approached, the company of Burnett and his wife was in great demand by political and military leaders in the region. Finally, on October 29, 1971 he took the salute at the final closure of the command at a multi-national parade and flypast. Two days later, 16 ships of the Far East Fleet steamed past while Fleet Air Arm aircraft flew overhead. In March 1972 Burnett retired from the RAF.

His services were much sought after and, in April 1974, he was appointed chairman of the All England Lawn Tennis Club. A year earlier, 81 players of the Association of Tennis Professionals had boycotted the Wimbledon Championships and relations between the players and the club were still strained. Burnett's calm manner and his patient and tactful approach smoothed the way for reconciliation.

He made it clear more than once that he questioned the wisdom of escalating prize money but he, like Wimbledon, was reluctantly forced to go along with the American-led trend. There were times when, with his military background, he found it difficult to accept indiscipline as players increasingly flaunted their new found independence. However, what many players and their representatives regarded as coolness towards them on his part stemmed from a basic shyness, which masked a generosity of spirit and many acts of kindness.

In 1977, when the 17 year-old John McEnroe arrived at Wimbledon for the first time, it was Burnett who tried to steer him in the right direction as umpires repeatedly reported him to the referee's office for his extravagant outbursts. Burnett was also keen that the Royal Box should be utilised when members of Royalty were not in attendance. On one occasion there was an IRA scare at the box, with a bomb apparently timed to detonate at 3 p.m. After a search found nothing, Burnett remained with some of his guests and, with one minute to go, calmly suggested that they should take off their spectacles to avoid flying glass.

Much was achieved to develop Wimbledon before Burnett finally retired in March 1984 after 10 years' service as chairman of the Championships Committee.

He finally gave up skiing at 80, golf at 88 and tennis at 94. In 2009 he published his memoirs *A Pilot at Wimbledon*. An avid bridge player, he played twice a week until his death, having just returned from a holiday in the south of France.

Burnett was appointed CB (1961) KCB (1965), and GCB (1970). In 1969 he was appointed Grand Officer of the Order of the White Rose of Finland.

Brian Burnett married Valerie St Ludger in November 1944 with whom he had two sons. She died in 2003.

Colonel Henry Lafont (who died on December 2, 2011 aged 91) made a dramatic escape from Vichy-held Algeria and reached England to fly Hurricanes in the Battle of Britain; he was the last of the 13 French fighter pilots to fly in the battle.

When France capitulated in June 1940, Lafont was at the fighter school in Oran, Algeria and was said to be "mad with rage" to see France occupied. Although he and his fellow pilots were ordered not to attempt to escape six of them – including Lafont – decided to steal an aircraft and fly to Gibraltar.

Their leader was Réne Mouchotte who would later command a Spitfire squadron and be awarded a DFC before failing to return from a sweep over northern France in August 1943.

Mouchotte identified a twin-engine six-seat Caudron Goéland aircraft, which had sufficient fuel. What he and his comrades were unaware of, however, was that the propellers had been sabotaged in an attempt to prevent the aircraft taking off.

They stole aboard during the night and, at first light, started the aircraft. In the event, Mouchotte managed to drag the aircraft into the air at minimum speed and make a laborious climb. Using a map torn from a geography book, the crew

reached Gibraltar where they received a warm welcome.
A few days later they sailed for England to complete their
fighter-pilot training.

Henry Gaston Lafont was born in Cahors in the Lot region
on August 10, 1920. On leaving school he gained his pilot's
licence and joined the French Air Force in November 1938.

On arrival in England, Lafont and his colleagues converted
to the Hurricane and were sent to a squadron in Northern
Ireland before joining No. 615 Squadron at Northolt where
he flew patrols during the Battle of Britain.

Over the next few months he flew over 100 patrols and was
credited with shooting down two enemy aircraft. On February 26, 1941 he was the first of the pilots who had escaped to
England to achieve success, although he was the only one of
his formation of six aircraft to return safely to base.

In July 1941 Lafont became an instructor and trained more
than 60 French Air Force fighter pilots. Six months later he
left for the Middle East and joined the Groupe Alsace flying
Hurricanes on convoy patrols and fighter cover over Tobruk
when he probably shot down an enemy bomber. In May 1942
he volunteered for service in Russia with the Normandie
Squadron, but before joining was shot down and wounded.
He returned to England.

Throughout 1943 he flew with No. 341 Squadron on operations over France and the Low Countries. By the end of
the war he had completed 230 operational missions and he
was one of the few to be awarded the Ordre de la Libération,
instituted by General de Gaulle. He also won the Croix de
Guerre with three palms and the Croix de la Valeur Militaire.

Lafont remained in the French Air Force, serving at the 5th
Air Region Headquarters in Algeria during the conflict there
and spent six years serving in London. After losing his fighter
pilot medical category, he turned to helicopters. He retired
from the French Air Force in 1966.

In 1967 Lafont was appointed director general of the Paris
Air Show, the world's oldest and largest air show and held

at Le Bourget since 1909. During the late 1960s and early 1970s, the show emerged as a powerful international rival to the Farnborough Air Show, attracting all major international manufacturers, as well as representatives of the military forces of several countries. Lafont held the post until 1984.

In addition to his wartime awards, Lafont was appointed Commandeur de la Légion d'Honneur. In 2002 he published *Aviators of the Liberty, Memorial for the French Air Forces*.

At his funeral service at Les Invalides in Paris, the Colours of the French Fighter Pilots Association were carried in his honour in the presence of senior French Air Force and RAF officers.

Henry Lafont was married twice and had two sons and a daughter.

AIR MARSHAL SIR ALFRED BALL

Air Marshal Sir Alfred 'Freddie' Ball (who died on January 25, 2012 aged 91) was one the RAF's outstanding photographic reconnaissance pilots in the Second World War and later filled senior national and international appointments.

Ball joined No. 1 Photographic Reconnaissance Unit (PRU) in May 1941. His early targets were the Channel ports, but he was soon ordered to photograph targets deep in Germany in his single-engine, unarmed Spitfire.

In October that year he took off for the Continent but flew into a thunderstorm. At 25,000 feet the aircraft became uncontrollable and, when he attempted to bale out, the canopy jammed. Such was the turbulence that he was thrown through the canopy; recovering consciousness at 3,000 feet, he opened his parachute and landed in Norfolk.

A month later his unit was ordered to Cornwall to fly daily sorties to Brest to monitor *Scharnhorst* and *Gneisenau*. The German fighter force became familiar with the tactics of the high-flying Spitfires and set up patrols to intercept them. Ball – always prepared to be innovative – devised his own tactics to deal with the threat and on the afternoon of February 11, 1942 photographed the German capital ships at Brest – the last sighting of them before they sailed a few hours later on their audacious 'Channel Dash' home. From Cornwall he flew sorties to the Spanish border photographing the French Biscay ports. Assessed as an exceptional reconnaissance pilot, he was awarded the DFC.

On promotion to squadron leader, Ball was made commanding officer of No. 4 PRU and in October left for Gibraltar to provide support for Operation Torch. Within days his unit was flying operations from Maison Blanche in Algeria encountering the latest German high-performance aircraft. Losses to the enemy mounted and the 22-year-old Ball sought a meeting with Air Chief Marshal Sir Arthur Tedder, the Air C-in-C, to plead for the latest Spitfires. Tedder listened patiently then dismissed Ball and told him to carry on. A few days later three of the latest Spitfires arrived.

Early in 1943 Ball was sent to photograph a crucial target in Tunisia prior to a large-scale attack by the army. As he completed the task at 24,000 feet, four Focke-Wulf Fw 190s closed in on him, and he repelled eight attacks before he finally escaped. He was forced to land his damaged aircraft at a forward airfield, where he commandeered a Spitfire and flew back to base with his film. Within hours, the army mounted a successful attack.

For his work in North Africa, Ball was awarded the DSO and a US Air Medal. The DSO citation described him as a "fine leader who displayed brilliant airmanship".

The only child of Captain J.A.E. Ball MC, chief engineer of the Bengal Nagpur Railway, Alfred Henry Wynne Ball was born in Rawalpindi on January 18, 1921. He was educated at Campbell College, Belfast before gaining a cadetship to the RAF College Cranwell in 1938. Having seen his parents only rarely, he grew up self-sufficient and independent-minded – characteristics that were to be evident throughout his life.

Commissioned in December 1939, he completed his training as an army co-operation pilot before joining No. 13 Squadron in northern France. After the blitzkrieg on May 10, 1940 he flew road searches but soon realised that employing peacetime techniques in the face of intense German fighter activity was suicidal, so flew the rest of his sorties at treetop height. After heavy losses, the squadron's Lysanders were withdrawn to England, but Ball had to find his own way back. He commandeered a lorry and, with 20 airmen aboard, he drove to Cherbourg, from where they escaped by ship.

Ball volunteered for the photographic-reconnaissance role, which required experience on the Spitfire. He therefore persuaded a friend to allow him to fly three sorties, and at his interview told the squadron commander he was an "experienced Spitfire pilot". To his surprise and delight, he was accepted.

After returning from North Africa in July 1943, Ball was given command of No. 542 Squadron, equipped with Spitfires and based at Benson in Oxfordshire. His most urgent task was to photograph the building of the V-1 launch sites in the Pas de Calais. Before the Normandy invasion he photographed enemy dispositions and movements and, after the landings, identified targets ahead of the army's advance into Germany.

On his final Spitfire sortie, his engine failed when he was at 38,000 feet over Cologne. Ball was able to coax the engine into giving short bursts of power during the long glide to England, and he broke cloud at 600 feet over the Thames Estuary, scraping into the airfield at Eastchurch.

On promotion to wing commander in September 1944, he took command of No. 540 Squadron to fly Mosquitos to targets in Norway and deep inside Germany.

On October 7, 1944, Lancaster bombers attacked a vital dam on the Rhine just north of the Swiss border, and Ball was sent to photograph the damage. As he flew over the target at 200 feet he was attacked by four fighters later reporting: "We held our own to begin with, but soon things got a bit tricky. All things being fair in love and war, I decided to disappear into the Swiss mountains."

This appeared to work, so he ventured out again; but the fighters were waiting, and he ducked back into Switzerland. He then tried to give the impression of departing by flying west, using the hills to mask his route. This ruse failed, and the German pilots closed in for another attack – so Ball made his third detour into Switzerland. Eventually he managed to escape and return to base.

Ball remained with No. 540 for the rest of the war, flying into eastern Germany to photograph rail traffic and troop movements in addition to regular sorties to Norway photographing U-boat sanctuaries. At the end of the war, he was mentioned in despatches for a second time.

In January 1946 Ball left for the Middle East to take command of No. 680 Squadron (later re-numbered No. 13). Flying Mosquitos, the squadron carried out survey work over Palestine, Egypt and Iraq. Whilst at Haifa, terrorists sprayed the room he was in with machine-gun fire, but he escaped injury.

After converting to the Canberra jet in 1953, Ball commanded the reconnaissance wing at Wyton, taking a Canberra to Australia to monitor a British atomic test, and flying photographic sorties along the East German border.

After a period at HQ Bomber Command and on the British Defence Liaison Staff in Washington, he was appointed in February 1962 to command the V-bomber base at Honington in Suffolk, where he flew the Valiant and the Victor.

On promotion to air commodore in November 1964, Ball left for Aden as air officer administration. His arrival coincided with a significant increase in terrorism, which included attacks against civilians, and security issues occupied much of his time. It was also announced that British forces would leave the large base in two years' time and Ball became heavily involved in the early stages of planning a very complex operation. On his departure from Aden at the end of 1966, he was appointed CB.

After attending the Imperial Defence College, he held a series of senior appointments in the MoD. He was assistant chief of staff of the Automatic Data Processing Division at SHAPE Headquarters in Belgium.

In 1975 Ball left for Ankara to take up the post of UK representative of the Permanent Military Deputies Group at the Central Treaty Organisation (CENTO). With some member countries facing political and economic difficulties, political guidance for military planning had, for a number of years, been lacking. Ball aimed to improve this situation and they made some progress, notwithstanding the withdrawal of British forces from the region.

On his return, he was expecting to retire, but the untimely death of a senior RAF colleague resulted in his appointment for two years as deputy commander-in-chief at RAF's Strike Command, where he supervised the day-to-day activities of the many operational units. He was appointed KCB in 1976.

After retiring from the RAF in April 1979, Ball spent four years as military affairs advisor with International Computers Limited. He maintained close links with his wartime photographic-reconnaissance colleagues and rarely missed the annual reunions at Benson. He was particularly proud to be the honorary air commodore of No. 2624 (County of Oxford) Royal Auxiliary Air Force RAF Regiment Squadron.

Of slim build and always immaculately dressed, Ball was a man of great energy. Known to his staff as 'Fiery Fred', he could be a hard taskmaster – but he was equally hard on himself. He had a strong sense of humour, was good company and showed skill on the golf course and at the bridge table.

He married in October 1942 (ten weeks after they met) Nan MacDonald. She died in 2006. They had three sons, all of whom served as officers in the RAF, and a daughter.

AIR COMMODORE TED SISMORE

Air Commodore Ted Sismore (who died on March 22, 2012 aged 90) was recognised as the RAF's finest low-level navigator of the Second World War, leading 'daylight spectaculars' on targets including three separate Gestapo headquarters and on Göring and Goebbels themselves.

For the most part Sismore completed these hair-raising exploits, for which he was decorated four times, alongside Squadron Leader Reggie Reynolds. The duo teamed up in December 1942 when Sismore, recently commissioned and a veteran of a tour of operations on Blenheim bombers, joined the Mosquito-equipped No. 105 Squadron. He would see continuous action on bombing operations for the next 20 months.

On the morning of January 31, 1943, Reynolds and Sismore led a small force of Mosquitos on the RAF's first daylight bombing attack on Berlin, a round trip of 1,100 miles. The bombers were tasked to arrive at exactly 11 a.m., when Göring and Goebbels were due to address a rally commemorating the 10th anniversary celebrations of Hitler's regime.

The Mosquitos flew at low level over Germany and, as they crossed the Elbe, climbed to 25,000 feet for their attack delivered exactly on time and photographed by Sismore.

On their return, the crews were able to hear a tape recording from German radio. As the announcer introduced Göring to the crowd, bombs could be heard exploding. Göring never made the speech and his constant boasts about the security of the Fatherland were proved to be empty promises. Among those decorated was Sismore, who was awarded the DFC.

Throughout the spring of 1943, Reynolds and Sismore – who was described by a colleague as "the most brilliant navigator" – led many daylight attacks, their targets including railway workshops, steelworks and power stations, some deep inside Germany.

When Reynolds was appointed CO of No. 139 Squadron, Sismore remained as his navigator. On May 27, 1943 they led a force of six Mosquitos on the RAF's deepest-ever daylight low-level penetration of Germany from Britain. The mission was to attack the Schott glass works and Zeiss optical works at Jena near Leipzig.

Visibility was very poor as they flew at treetop height over Germany, and was reduced to 1,500 yards as they approached the target. But Sismore's navigation was perfect, and as they dodged balloons and intense anti-aircraft fire, delayed-action bombs were dropped – despite Reynolds being wounded. The aircraft was badly damaged but was nursed back to base. Reynolds was awarded a Bar to his earlier DSO and Sismore also received the DSO.

Sismore continued on operations and transferred to No. 21 Squadron as the navigation leader. In February 1944, he was instructed to plan an attack to release French Resistance leaders imprisoned in Amiens Jail in northern France.

He was to lead the attack with Air Vice-Marshal Basil Embry (the commander of No. 2 Group) but Embry's chiefs forbade him to fly because he was too valuable an asset. When Sismore said he would fly with another pilot, Embry retorted: "No you won't. If I don't go, you don't go." The operation went ahead without them, and was a complete success, except that Embry's replacement as leader, Group Captain Charles Pickard (who had three DSOs and a DFC) was shot down and killed along with his navigator.

Once again flying with Reynolds, Sismore on October 31, 1944 led a force of 24 Mosquitos in a raid on the Gestapo HQ lodged in buildings of Aarhus University in Denmark. The surprise attack, in misty weather, was delivered from low level and was a complete success. The head of the SS was killed, one of his officer's writing: "A terrible disaster

happened when our HQ was shot up by English airmen."
For their outstanding leadership, both Reynolds and Sismore
received a Bar to their DFCs.

Sismore continued to lead low-level daylight precision
raids. On March 20, 1945 he led a force to attack the Gestapo
HQ housed in the Shell House, Copenhagen. Once again, his
precise navigation resulted in a successful attack by the leading
aircraft and the building was destroyed. Tragically, a following Mosquito was shot down and crashed on a school killing
many children. However, 30 Danish patriots escaped and 150
Gestapo men were killed.

The Danish Resistance asked for one more attack to release
prisoners, this time from the Gestapo HQ in Odense. Sismore
navigated the formation of six aircraft on the last of the 'Mosquito daylight spectaculars' and the small force destroyed the
heavily camouflaged building. For his part in the two attacks,
Sismore was awarded a second Bar to his DFC.

As soon as the war was over, he joined Air Vice-Marshal
Embry and others to meet Danish resistance survivors and to
visit the damaged school. Some months later, Sismore was appointed a Knight of the Danish Order of Dannebrog. He also
received the Air Efficiency Award.

Edward Barnes Sismore was born at Kettering on June 23,
1921 and educated at Kettering County School. Barely 18,
he joined the RAF Volunteer Reserve in August 1939 and
trained as an observer.

He was posted to No. 110 Squadron operating Blenheims
and flew anti-shipping patrols and attacked ports in the Low
Countries and France at night. Returning from one night-
time operation, his Blenheim hit the sea – but his pilot managed to drag the aircraft clear and they made a safe landing.
After 30 operations he was rested before converting to the
Mosquito and joining No. 105 Squadron under Wing Commander Hughie Edwards VC.

After the war, Sismore continued his association with the
Mosquito. He was selected as the navigator for an attempt

to break the record for a flight from London to Cape Town. His pilot was Squadron Leader 'Mickey' Martin of Dambuster fame. They took off on April 30, 1947 and after refuelling stops in Libya and Kenya, completed the 6,011-mile journey in 21 hours 31 minutes and 30 seconds to establish a new point-to-point record. They were awarded the Royal Aero Club's Britannia Trophy.

In 1951, Sismore trained as a pilot, and became successful in night-fighters. In 1953 he was given command of No. 29 Squadron, the RAF's first jet night-fighter squadron and equipped with the Meteor. The squadron was busily occupied in proving this type and developing night-fighter tactics with jet aircraft and Sismore was awarded the AFC.

After commanding an advanced flying school, Sismore left for the HQ of the British Forces Middle East at the end of 1959 where he was a member of the joint planning staff. During his two years in the post he was much involved in the British counter-insurgency operations against dissident sheikhdoms.

In 1962, he was promoted to group captain and given command of the RAF's large base at Brüggen on the Dutch-German border. Responsible for two Canberra squadrons operating in the low-level bombing and reconnaissance roles, he was able to fly regularly and revisit some of his wartime targets. Both his squadrons achieved major successes in the annual NATO efficiency competitions.

After two years in Germany, Sismore converted to the Victor bomber before taking up the appointment of senior air staff officer at the Central Reconnaissance Establishment, with responsibility for the RAF's strategic photographic and electronic reconnaissance and radio intelligence gathering forces.

On promotion to air commodore in January 1971 he became the 13th commandant of the Royal Observer Corps. His final appointment was as director of the Air Defence Team, which involved planning a significant upgrade and re-equipment programme for the UK's air defence organisation – including new early warning radars and control and reporting systems.

On his retirement from the RAF in June 1976, Sismore

joined Marconi as a service advisor. During the Falklands conflict he was able to negotiate the availability of a mobile air-defence radar, something that would normally have taken a few years to procure.

Sismore, a modest man, gave up much of his time in retirement to supporting RAF charities. He also enjoyed playing golf.

Ted Sismore married his wife, Rita, in 1946 and she died in 2006. They had a son and a daughter.

SQUADRON LEADER JOE BLYTH

Squadron Leader Joe Blyth (who died on March 29, 2012 aged 86) was an outstanding RAF fighter pilot decorated five times for his post-war service, which included operations in Korea, Suez, Aden and Oman.

Blyth was an experienced instructor on the Meteor jet fighter when he left for Korea in March 1951 as one of four RAF pilots selected to assist No. 77 Squadron of the Royal Australian Air Force to convert from the piston-engine Mustang to the Meteor. Although not authorised to fly on operations, Blyth managed to persuade his Australian CO to allow him to participate in a few sorties – in the event he completed more than 100.

No. 77 was operating from Pusan, and Blyth was soon in action. On March 20, a colleague was forced to crash-land during a ground-attack mission, and Blyth remained overhead as a helicopter attempted a rescue. As he strafed advancing Chinese troops his Mustang was hit by small-arms fire, but he continued to give cover until the rescue was completed.

Blyth had flown 25 sorties, strafing and rocketing trucks, and artillery pieces when the first Meteor arrived, and he spent the next few weeks training the Australian pilots. With that task complete in September, he volunteered to remain with No. 77 and embarked on an intensive period of operations in the jet fighter.

In addition to attacking supply dumps, vehicle parks and trains, he also escorted USAF heavy bombers when MiG-15 fighters, often flown by Russian pilots, were encountered. In air-to-air combat, the MiG was superior, but Blyth engaged them on numerous occasions. On October 24 he damaged one and, a week later, he fired on another that was engaging his leader. Smoke poured from the MiG, which broke away.

On November 17, Blyth led a fighter sweep, his 105th and final operation over Korea. Shortly after returning to the UK he was awarded the DFC; the United States government awarded him the Air Medal.

Colin Ian Blyth, known throughout his life as 'Joe' was born on April 1, 1925 in Maidstone and was educated at the local county school. Aged only 15, in 1940 he volunteered for aircrew duties in the RAF having 'stolen' his sister's national insurance number, allowing him to claim that he was 18. He was accepted and started his training as a wireless operator/air gunner in November 1940. In December the following year, he joined No. 161 (Special Duties) Squadron, flying operations to drop agents and supplies into occupied Europe.

On the night of September 24, Blyth's Whitley crash-landed in the Ardennes. Some of the crew were captured but Blyth was able to head south on foot receiving help from farmers. In Lyon he was picked up by the local escape line and moved to a safe house in Marseilles. From there he was taken with other evaders to Canet Plage near Perpignan. After a nerve-wracking wait on the beach, the party was transferred to the Polish-manned felucca *Seawolf*, arriving in Gibraltar two days later.

After recovering in England, Blyth left for South Africa to train as a pilot. He was assessed as above average and became a flying instructor. After returning to Britain in January 1946, he spent two years instructing pilots on piston-engine aircraft before converting to jets and joining No. 203 Advanced Flying School to train fighter pilots. Blyth proved an innovative leader and pilot, and was awarded the AFC.

On his return from Korea, he was appointed flight commander of No. 63 Squadron flying Meteors from Waterbeach near Cambridge. His combat experience, 'press-on' attitude and professionalism ensured that the squadron was one of the most efficient in Fighter Command. At the end of his tour in August 1954 he was awarded a Bar to his AFC and left for the Middle East.

When Blyth joined No. 32 Squadron as a flight commander, the unit had just been equipped with the Venom fighter-bomber and moved to Kabrit in the Canal Zone before moving to Shaibah in Iraq. After 18 months, he left for an appointment in the headquarters in Cyprus, but he had been there only six months when the Suez crisis erupted. No. 8 Squadron, also equipped with Venoms, arrived from Habbaniya (Iraq) but without its CO who had left at short notice. As Blyth entered the operations centre his group captain spotted him and shouted: "Do you want 8 Joe?" Blyth took command that afternoon.

Operations commenced at dawn on November 1, 1956 as three Venom squadrons headed for the Egyptian Air Force (EAF) airfields. Blyth took No. 8 to Abu Sueir and Fayid and strafed lines of MiG fighters. Leading the formation, he accounted for five of the 11 destroyed. Later that morning he led a second strike, this time against his old airfield at Kabrit where he "put a few rounds through my old office". In the afternoon he took off again at the head of another section to re-attack Kabrit.

The next day, Blyth was again leading his squadron against

the EAF airfields. On one sortie he attacked a vehicle and tank park; on another, late in the day, he carried out an armed reconnaissance over Ismailia. In the first two days, No. 8 destroyed at least 43 aircraft on the ground.

Over the next three days, Blyth continued to be in the thick of the action. In preparation for the airborne assault, he led a rocket strike against gun emplacements and flew armed reconnaissance sorties to identify targets. At dawn on November 6, No. 8 joined the other two Venom squadrons, each aircraft armed with eight rockets, to attack the defence boom at Port Fouad in anticipation of the seaborne landings. The following day, a ceasefire stopped all further operational flying.

The squadron returned to its base at Khormaksar in Aden, and Blyth was soon involved in operations against rebel strongholds. In the aftermath of Suez, trouble in central Oman flared up in July 1957. No. 8 was ordered to Sharjah, and within days, Blyth was leading strikes against rebel positions in the Jebel Akhdar region. Operating in support of land forces, the Venoms attacked fortifications with rockets, and Blyth led his squadron with great dash and efficiency until returning to Britain in December that year. One of his junior pilots (who would later become an air chief marshal) observed: "He was an amazing CO. If I learnt anything about leadership, it came from Joe Blyth."

For his services in the Middle East, Blyth was awarded a Bar to his DFC, making him one of the most decorated postwar RAF officers. He spent four years as a staff officer before retiring from the RAF on his 38th birthday.

Blyth then spent 21 years as personal pilot of the banker Loel Guinness. He kept his flying licence until late in his life, and prided himself in never wearing spectacles – something he attributed to daily eye exercises.

He had an impressive singing voice, and once auditioned for the Black and White Minstrels; his voice was judged to be up to the task, but he was let down by his dancing. In recent years he lived in Acapulco, in Mexico.

Joe Blyth married Maureen Parker in July 1957 (dissolved

in 1970). They had four sons and a daughter. He had two daughters with his second wife Delia.

MAJOR NICK KNILANS

Major Nick Knilans (who died on June 1, 2012 aged 94) epitomised the contribution of RAF Bomber Command in the Allied war effort by flying a great range of missions with Nos. 619 and 617 Dambuster Squadrons, notably against *Tirpitz* and on D-Day; he was awarded the DSO and DFC.

His position with Bomber Command was particularly

special because Knilans was an American citizen. Having joined the Royal Canadian Air Force and flown with the RAF, he insisted on remaining with No. 617's Lancasters even after being nominally transferred to the USAAF.

On the night of November 26, 1943, Knilans and his crew took off to bomb Berlin. As they approached Frankfurt at 20,000 feet, a stream of cannon shells raked their Lancaster from an enemy night-fighter, which made four more attacks before the Lancaster's gunners shot it down. The bomber had been badly damaged but, though it was another 200 miles to the target, Knilans continued on three engines.

Over Berlin the anti-aircraft fire was intense but Knilans, forced to fly lower than usual, dropped his bomb load. On its return his aircraft continued to lose height and he crossed the Dutch coast at 2,000 feet. Arriving at his base, a blanket of ground fog prevented him from landing, so he flew to a near-by airfield and put down despite a damaged undercarriage.

Hubert Clarence Knilans, always known as Nick, was born on December 27, 1917 in Delevan, Wisconsin, into a family with Irish roots – his great-grandfather having emigrated from County Tyrone in 1848. On leaving the local high school, he worked on the family farm until April 1941, when he was drafted for military service.

He wanted to be a pilot but had no wish to join the US Army. So he packed a small bag, withdrew his meagre savings from the local bank, and after telling his family he was taking a few days' vacation in Chicago, left for Canada in October 1941, and enlisted as a pilot in the RCAF.

After completing his flying training in Ontario, Knilans sailed for England in the *Queen Elizabeth* and completed his training as a bomber pilot before joining No. 619 Squadron in June 1943. The squadron operated from Woodhall Spa, near Lincoln.

After two sorties with experienced captains, Knilans and his crew flew their first operation together on the night of July 24 when Bomber Command launched the Battle of Hamburg.

This devastating attack owed much of its success to the first use of 'window' – later known as 'chaff' – metal-backed strips of paper dropped to confuse the enemy radars. Bundles were dropped from Knilans' aircraft before the bombs were released.

Knilans had joined the squadron at the height of the Battle of the Ruhr and he and his crew attacked heavily defended targets in 'Happy Valley'. Against Essen, one of the four engines of his Lancaster failed but he pressed on. Shortly after receiving his commission as a pilot officer, Knilans' aircraft was attacked by a night-fighter. One of his gunners was killed and his aircraft was badly damaged but he dropped his bombs before turning for home.

In October, Knilans was informed that he was to be transferred to the USAAF. He was commissioned as a first lieutenant – with pay equivalent to an RAF group captain – but he insisted that he wanted to complete his tour with his crew on No. 619, just as the Battle of Berlin was opening.

Knilans remained with the squadron until January 1944 and made a number of attacks on the 'Big City'. On January 17 it was announced that he had been awarded the DSO.

Due for a rest, Knilans wanted to remain on operations with the RAF and his crew agreed to join him when he volunteered for No. 617 Squadron, commanded by Wing Commander Leonard Cheshire. Under Cheshire's leadership, the squadron had developed low-level target-marking techniques and precision bombing with the 12,000-lb Tallboy bomb.

During the build-up to the Normandy landings, No. 617 attacked the V-1 rocket sites, supply dumps and road and rail communications, including a spectacular attack against the Saumur railway tunnel. On the night of June 5, the eve of D-Day, Knilans flew on a successful sortie over the English Channel dropping 'window' to fool the enemy into thinking the invasion armada was heading for the Pas de Calais.

Over the next few weeks, Knilans dropped Tallboys on V-1 sites and submarine pens before setting off on his final operation with No. 617 on September 11, when he flew one of 38 Lancasters heading for north Russian airfields.

Running short of fuel, he was one of seven pilots who had to make emergency landings at various small airfields on the Kola Peninsula. His Lancaster was undamaged and he managed to re-join the main force at Yagodnik.

Four days later, 27 Lancasters took off to attack the *Tirpitz* in Kaa Fjord in north Norway. Knilans dropped his Tallboy but a smoke screen prevented accurate bombing. Although not known at the time, *Tirpitz* was hit and badly damaged.

Before leaving No. 617, Knilans had built up his hopes that the King would present his DSO; he was disappointed when it arrived in the post. A few weeks later he was awarded the DFC to add to his American DFC and several Air Medals.

Knilans had survived 50 operations and had brought six of his original seven-man crew through alive but he was the only survivor of his original pilot's course. He volunteered to fly night-fighters with the USAAF in the Pacific theatre but the war ended before he reached the region.

In addition to the losses of his friends, Knilans had witnessed the devastation of German cities and was determined post-war to devote himself to constructive public service work.

For 25 years he was a teacher, including a two-year period as a Peace Corps volunteer in Nigeria. He championed the betterment of the lives of American youths with Mexican roots and he became a counsellor within the California prison system. He finally retired in 1978, but continued to support programmes for under-privileged youths.

Nick Knilans was unmarried.

WING COMMANDER GORDON HUGHES

Wing Commander Gordon Hughes (who died on June 12, 2012 aged 94) was one of the RAF's outstanding photographic-reconnaissance pilots flying unarmed Spitfires and Mosquitos deep into enemy territory.

In February 1943, Hughes was appointed a flight commander of

the recently formed No. 540 Squadron at Benson in Oxfordshire, whose high-flying Mosquitos allowed the RAF to extend significantly its range of reconnaissance operations. His first sortie was to photograph Turin and a few days later he headed for Berlin.

Over the city he encountered heavy anti-aircraft fire but completed seven photographic runs to assess the bomb damage from a recent raid. A week later, he returned and was intercepted by two German fighters; he climbed into high cloud above 30,000 feet before speeding for home. In April, he was taking photographs over Vienna when he was again intercepted and forced to seek cloud.

Throughout the spring of 1943, the government became increasingly concerned with the activities at the German Army Research Centre at Peenemünde on the Baltic coast. Hughes and his colleagues had photographed secret weapons on earlier flights, and the site had been kept under surveillance. During a sortie on May 14, 1943, Hughes photographed the area as an A-4 ballistic missile (the V-2 rocket) was being launched, and he made two further sorties in the next few weeks.

He visited the site again on July 26, and on his return to base the photographic interpreters detected that the anti-aircraft defences had been considerably strengthened and a decoy site created.

On the night of August 17/18, 596 heavy bombers attacked the site. The following morning, Hughes took off on a 'special operation', returning five hours later with excellent photographs of the considerable damage inflicted by the crews of Bomber Command. He was awarded a Bar to a DFC he had received earlier in the war.

During these intense operations over the Baltic, the crews of No. 540 Squadron also monitored the movements of Germany's capital ships, including the construction of the Kriegsmarine's only aircraft carrier, *Graf Zeppelin*. She had vanished from her regular berth, and on June 26 Hughes relocated and photographed it near Stettin.

Flying from advanced bases in Scotland, he also flew long-range sorties over thousands of miles of coastline between Narvik, in the far north of Norway, and Gdansk in the Baltic, searching for major warships.

In September he turned his attentions to central Europe, particularly Prague, Jena and the south of France. On November 8, he carried out eight runs over the Pas de Calais photographing the construction of the V-1 launch sites. It was his last flight with No. 540 and shortly after he was awarded the DSO for his "outstanding ability, foresight and leadership".

Edward Gordon Hughes was born on May 4, 1918 at Wanstead in Essex. He was educated at Kelly College, Tavistock and Imperial College, London where he joined the university air squadron and trained as a pilot. He joined the RAF in July 1939, completed his training and went to No. 608 Squadron flying coastal patrols and anti-shipping sorties in Anson and Botha aircraft.

Having been born into a Quaker family, Hughes had an aversion to armaments and in February 1941 volunteered to join No. 1 Photographic Reconnaissance Unit (PRU). The unit's Spitfires were not armed allowing them to carry extra fuel to increase their range. Hughes became the great exponent of subtlety instead of firepower to avoid being intercepted. Once asked if he regretted not having armament in his Spitfire, he replied: "Oh no! That's the thing about PR. It's the only front-line job in this war where you aren't asked to kill. Your weapons are the cameras."

Hughes was a perfectionist, planning his sorties in great detail; his CO described him as his "finest pilot". His philosophy for survival was to make life as difficult as possible for the Luft-waffe: so he flew as high as he could enduring extreme cold, in the expectation that at least some German pilots would not venture so high. To increase his endurance, he subjected himself to a punishing fitness schedule. He also took a great interest in the assessment of his photographs, always visiting the interpreters to discuss results and new tactics.

During the spring of 1941 he flew from an airfield in Corn-wall, and in a three-month period visited Brest and the Cher-bourg Peninsula on 61 occasions to monitor the movements of the *Scharnhorst* and *Gneisenau*. He frequently encountered heavy anti-aircraft fire.

Later in the year he photographed targets on the Baltic coast and in Germany. In these sorties, which lasted more than five hours, again the principal enemy as he sat in his cramped, unheated cockpit was the cold. In August he was assessed as "exceptional and a most press-on type of pilot" and was awarded the DFC.

After his tour with No. 540 Squadron, Hughes was pro-moted to wing commander to become the operations of-ficer of No. 336 (PR) Wing at San Severo in southern Italy. There he flew Spitfires on photographic sorties into Greece, Romania and Yugoslavia before returning to England to take command of No. 34 (PR) Wing when he continued to fly operations in Spitfires. On March 24, 1945 he photographed targets in Denmark, his 192nd and final photographic recon-naissance sortie.

Two days before the end of the war in Europe, he was pilot-ing an Anson communications aircraft, which crashed. He was badly injured, and spent the next eight months in hospital. He left the RAF at the end of 1946, but joined the Royal Auxil-iary Air Force and flew Spitfires and Meteor jet fighters with No. 601 (County of London) Squadron.

Called up during the Korean War, he returned to No. 540 Squadron to carry out refresher training on the Mosquito. His service with No. 601 finished in 1952 when he received the Air Efficiency Award.

After the war, Hughes joined the family firm Kelvin Hughes as a test pilot. The company had made navigation equipment since the 18th century; early sales included a cabin clock to Captain Cook and a chronometer for Captain Bligh of *Bounty*.

Hughes settled successively in Essex, Sussex and then on to farm on Dartmoor, where he and his sons reared sheep, pigs and cattle. In retirement, he and his wife lived in France and in Cyprus before returning to Dartmoor. He was a strong supporter of the RAF Benevolent Fund.

Gordon Hughes married his wife Jayne in 1946 and she died in 1996. They had three sons.

FLIGHT LIEUTENANT KAZIMIERZ SZRAJER

Flight Lieutenant Kazimierz 'Paddy' Szrajer (who died on August 18, 2012 aged 92) played a key part in a nail-biting behind-the-lines mission to retrieve a captured rocket from the Nazi's secret V-2 terror weapon programme.

The rocket had failed on a test firing and had come down in a remote marsh area in Poland. But before the Germans had discovered its location, members of the Polish Home Army retrieved it. The trophy was taken at a time when Allied intelligence knew of the existence of very advanced Nazi weapons but had few details. So when the Poles contacted London to let them know that they had a virtually complete V-2 rocket disassembled and hidden away, immediate steps were taken to retrieve the most important components.

An RAF Dakota based at Brindisi was fitted with extra fuel tanks so that it could be flown to a rudimentary airstrip near the front line in southern Poland to collect the parts and some key personnel. But the RAF also required a Pole to act as co-pilot and interpreter. Szrajer – one of the RAF's most experienced special duties pilots – was selected for the operation, code-named Wildhorn III.

The outbound flight departed on July 25, 1944, flying over Yugoslavia and Hungary to Tarnów, 200 miles south of Warsaw, where the crew identified torch signals and landed on the airstrip, which proved to be very soft. The rocket components were loaded and five high-ranking passengers boarded the aircraft; but, as the crew attempted to taxi for take-off, the port wheel stuck in the mud. Everything had to be offloaded and Szrajer organised the partisans of the ground party in an attempt to free the aircraft. The wheel track was stuffed with straw, but a second attempt to taxi also failed. Wooden boards were then laid in the trench, but to no avail.

Szrajer discussed the problem with those on the ground and he decided that the parking brake must have locked on. To free the wheel, the hydraulic leads supplying the brake were cut but a further attempt to taxi failed. With dawn breaking, and the noise from the revving engines likely to attract uninvited guests, the partisans dug trenches under the aircraft's main wheels.

The Dakota's captain, New Zealander Flying Officer Culliford, made preparations to destroy all papers and secret equipment, and to burn the aircraft should the last attempt to move it fail. With both engines at full power, the Dakota started to move and it staggered into the air just clearing a wood. However, the crew's difficulties were not over. Because the hydraulic fluid had bled away, the undercarriage could not be retracted. The pilot's report merely stated that the reservoir was recharged "with all available fluids" until sufficient pressure was obtained to permit the undercarriage to be pumped up by hand.

On arrival at Brindisi after a five-hour flight, the aircraft had no brakes, and the two pilots had to land on an emergency runway before unloading their precious cargo for the intelligence organisation. The commanding officer of the squadron praised the four-man crew for the "courage, determination and coolness with which they carried out what must be one of the outstanding and epic flights of the war by an unarmed transport aircraft".

The valuable rocket components were later flown to England, where the Polish government in exile presented the Dakota crew with gallantry medals, Szrajer receiving the Cross of Valour.

Kazimierz Szrajer was born in Warsaw on December 30, 1919. He began flying gliders when he was 16. When the Germans invaded his homeland, he joined many of his countrymen and made the exhausting journey to freedom through Hungary and Yugoslavia, finally arriving in England from France.

After training as a pilot, he joined No. 301 (Polish) Squadron in September 1941 to fly the Wellington bomber. Over the next months he flew 22 bombing operations against some of Germany's most heavily defended targets. Three times his bomber was damaged and he was forced to crash land on his return.

In May 1942 Szrajer was transferred to No. 138 (Special Duties) Squadron where a Polish Flight was being formed. From the airfield at Tempsford he flew his Halifax to many parts of Europe to drop supplies and agents to resistance forces, including 13 to France, five to Norway, and four to Poland.

On October 29 he took off for Warsaw. But on the return flight his aircraft was badly damaged by a German night-fighter and Szrajer had to ditch the bomber in the North Sea. One dinghy was punctured, so the seven-man crew had to clamber aboard the one remaining. After a few hours in the sea, they were rescued by a launch.

At the end of his tour in July 1943, Szrajer was awarded the DFC and the Virtuti Militari, Poland's highest award for gallantry.

In January 1944 Szrajer returned to operations when he joined No. 1586 Flight at Brindisi. He flew many sorties to support Italian, Yugoslav and Greek partisans and dropped agents and supplies over Poland on six occasions before his epic flight to retrieve the V-2 parts.

Following the Polish uprising in Warsaw, seven Halifax aircraft took off on the night of August 4/5 to drop the first supplies to the beleaguered city. Szrajer was the pilot of one of the aircraft; it was his 100th and final operation.

Towards the end of the war, Szrajer flew to the Far East to repatriate survivors from the Japanese prisoner of war camps. He remained in the RAF flying transport aircraft until the end of 1948 when he embarked on a civilian flying career almost as adventurous as his wartime experiences.

He joined the Lancashire Aircraft Corporation and flew converted Halifax bombers. In July 1949 he flew to Schleswig in Germany and over the next few months made 149 sorties ferrying supplies into Berlin during the emergency airlift.

In October 1955 he and his family left for Canada where everyone knew him as 'Paddy'. He flew supplies to the Arctic to support the construction of the Distant Early Warning Radar Chain (DEW Line) that stretched from Alaska to Greenland. Over the next few years he flew long-range charter flights to destinations all over the world.

After the breakout of civil war between Nigeria and the breakaway province of Biafra, he volunteered in 1969 for a Canadian charity, Canairelief, to take food to the starving millions. Flying a four-engine Lockheed Constellation, he flew by night to an airstrip on a converted stretch of the highway in the jungle at Uli in Biafra.

Szrajer later became the chief pilot of Nordair and converted to the Boeing 737 jet airliner. He was the captain of the airline's longest-range charter when he flew to Guam in the Pacific to pick up refugees from Vietnam destined for Montreal. He flew his last flight on May 12, 1981 having amassed over 25,000 hours flying time. He retired to Barry Bay in Ontario.

Kazimierz 'Paddy' Szrajer's wife Liliana predeceased him and they had a son and daughter.

WING COMMANDER VLADIMIR NEDVED

Wing Commander Vladimir Nedved (who died on October 31, 2012 aged 95) was twice forced to flee from his native Czechoslovakia to seek his freedom; first to fight with the RAF and later to escape with his young family after the communist takeover of his country.

Following the German occupation in 1939 he left Czechoslovakia without identity papers, travelling by train and on foot through the Balkans. In Lebanon he boarded a ship for France, arriving in early 1940, and in June he managed to escape to England, where he joined the RAF Volunteer Reserve and trained as a navigator before joining No. 311 (Czech) Squadron equipped with the Wellington bomber.

On the night of December 16/17, 1940 his crew were tasked to bomb Mannheim. Shortly after take-off, one of the engines failed and caught fire and the bomber crashed into trees. Nedved survived uninjured and immediately went to the aid of the pilot, who was badly injured. Despite the flames, he was able to drag him clear. He then returned into the blazing fuselage to assist the rear gunner, who was trapped in his turret. Ammunition started to explode and the fire intensified. Even when a bomb exploded Nedved refused to leave his injured comrade.

As the flames approached the rear of the aircraft, the gunner implored Nedved to shoot him rather than let him die in the fire. Nedved refused, but the explosion of another bomb killed the gunner. Miraculously, Nedved survived but all his colleagues perished.

For his great courage in trying to save his friends in the face of extreme danger to his own life, Nedved was recommended for the George Cross. In the event he was appointed a Member of the Order of the British Empire for gallantry.

Vladimir Nedved was born in Brno, Czechoslovakia on March 27, 1917 and educated at Kyjov High School. He joined the Czech air force in October 1936 and trained as a navigator. He graduated from the military college in 1938 as a flight lieutenant.

Nedved completed 25 bombing operations with No. 311 before training as a pilot and in 1942 he returned to the Czech bomber squadron, which had recently been assigned to Coastal Command for operations against the U-boats in the Atlantic.

Flying a Wellington on September 29, 1942, Nedved was involved in a running battle with three Junkers 88 fighters over the Bay of Biscay. He jettisoned his bombs and tried to gain some cloud. His gunner shot one down before a second attacked. This was driven off with a burning engine. Nedved then escaped into cloud before returning to his base at sea level.

The squadron was re-equipped with the very long-range four-engine Liberator, giving Coastal Command the capability for the first time to close the 'Atlantic Gap' which had allowed the U-boats to operate with greater freedom. In August 1943, aged 26, Nedved was awarded the DFC for his aggressive patrolling and was also promoted to wing commander.

As the commander of No. 311 he continued to patrol the Atlantic. The Czech government in exile awarded him the Czech Gallantry Medal and the Czech War Cross with three bars.

In April 1944, Nedved left for Burma to be a staff officer at the Headquarters 3rd Tactical Air Force. Despite his ground appointment he flew a number of transport operations to drop supplies to the army garrisons surrounded at Imphal and Kohima.

After six months he returned to England to join the Czech Inspectorate with Transport Command and in January married his Czech sweetheart. In August 1945 he was repatriated to Czechoslovakia and served at the Air Force College as a tactics instructor before attending the Military Staff College in Prague on promotion to lieutenant colonel.

The communists took power in February 1948 as Nedved was completing his course. He and his RAF wartime colleagues who had returned to their homeland were persecuted and Nedved joined a group planning to escape back to England. He booked three seats on an internal flight to Bratislava piloted by a friend. After take-off, the co-pilot (a communist sympathiser) was arrested at gunpoint and the aircraft turned for Germany and flew at very low level to land at a USAF base near Munich where most of the passengers sought political refugee status.

Nedved and his family travelled to England where they were given British citizenship and he re-joined the RAF in October 1948 and for two years he flew transport aircraft with No. 31 Squadron before heading for the Middle East to take command of No. 78 Squadron flying Valetta transport aircraft. On return to Britain he converted to jets and was adjutant at the Central Gunnery School. In 1956 he was appointed to command the RAF's Selection Board for ground officers before he retired at the end of 1958 when he moved with his family to Australia. Settling in Sydney, he worked in administration for the Shell-BP oil company. He later moved to the Sunshine Coast.

Nedved spent much of his time writing and recording events of the war. A deeply religious man, he always claimed that his faith was one reason for his survival. For many years he was a lay preacher with the Uniting Church in Australia.

After the fall of communism, President Václav Havel promoted Nedved to major general in the Air Force Reserve. On October 28, 1996 he was awarded the country's highest honour, the Order of the White Lion, for outstanding service and leadership in the fight for freedom. He also received the Order of Tomáš Garrigue Masaryk, awarded to individuals who have made outstanding contributions to humanity, democracy and human rights. On May 8, 2005 Nedved was given the rank of lieutenant general.

Vladimir Nedved married his wife Luisa in January 1945 and she and their three sons survived him.

GROUP CAPTAIN MARK HOBDEN

Group Captain Mark Hobden (who died on April 7, 2013 aged 91) became in 1942 one of the founding members of the RAF Regiment; having seen considerable action in the Second World War, 20 years later he became the man to mark out the 'Green Line' that divided ethnic-Greek and Turkish communities on the island of Cyprus.

Hobden was in command of No. 3 Wing, RAF Regiment when, at Christmas in 1963, violence erupted between the Greek and Turkish communities. As festive tradition dictates, Hobden and his officers were serving lunch to their airmen; then the order suddenly came through to relocate from the base at RAF Akrotiri to Nicosia. Within two hours, the entire wing, fully armed, was on the move.

Hobden, with orders to separate the warring factions, established his headquarters in the Ledra Palace Hotel. Intensive patrols were established, though this proved a difficult task as the Cypriots were still exchanging fire with scant regard for the Union flags draped over British vehicles.

When the situation had stabilised, the commander of the British peace force, Major-General Peter Young, called a meeting with his senior operations staff. During the discussions Hobden, who had returned from the forward area, suggested where the division of the factions in the city should be and he marked it on a large-scale map with a green marker pen. Young agreed that it was a sensible and pragmatic solution and the so-called 'Green Line' was established.

Such impromptu division did not come without problems. One soon became apparent when an incandescent Greek Orthodox Archbishop Makarios visited the headquarters to point out that his Episcopal Palace had fallen firmly in the Turkish area. Yet the Green Line still exists today, and is how many refer to the United Nations buffer zone that has divided not only Nicosia, but also the whole of the rest of the island, since the Turkish parachute invasion of 1974. All subsequent peace plans aimed at uniting Cyprus have failed.

In 1964, however, Hobden faced more prosaic challenges. When he moved his HQ from the Ledra Palace Hotel, for example, he was presented with a bill for C£2.5 million – which he declined to pay on the grounds that, as the president of Cyprus had requested the British intervention, the account should be sent to the presidential palace. For his services in Cyprus, Hobden was appointed OBE and mentioned in despatches.

Mark Frederick Hobden was born at Haywards Heath on March 13, 1922 and educated at Purley County School. Just after his 18th birthday, he enlisted into the RAF as a ground gunner. With the formation of the RAF Regiment on February 5, 1942, he was transferred and commissioned before serving on a number of bomber airfields providing anti-aircraft and ground defence.

In March 1942 he was with No. 2871 Squadron in the light anti-aircraft support role with the Second Tactical Air Force (2 TAF). This moved to Normandy in September 1944 and, shortly after, Hobden was appointed to command No. 2726 Squadron, providing protection for the large RAF airfield at Eindhoven. His squadron, one of 65 RAF Regiment squadrons in 2 TAF, went forward with the Allied advance to Lübeck.

Four days before the end of the war, nine RAF Regiment task groups were tasked to occupy Schleswig-Holstein before any ceasefire was agreed and with the aim of securing Luftwaffe airfields and material. In the confused situation, Hobden's force first encountered Soviet forces east of Travemünde before being held up at the Kiel Canal near Rendsburg by an SS Panzer battalion, whose commander refused to accept that the end of the war was at hand.

Hobden had 50 men with him and after an hour of "forthright discussion", the German colonel gave way and Hobden's small force crossed the bridge to resume its advance to Flensburg, where it secured the airfield. At Flensburg, Grand Admiral Doenitz, Hitler's appointed successor, was found and arrested.

After occupying 16 airfields and securing the aircraft and equipment on them, the various regiment task groups took the surrender of 50,000 Germans. For his services with 2 TAF, Hobden was mentioned in despatches.

Post-war Hobden served with the RAF Iraq Levies, before transferring to the Canal Zone. In 1951 he took command of a light anti-aircraft (LAA) squadron and, after service at the RAF Regiment Depot at Catterick, commanded another LAA squadron providing defence for the RAF airfield at Oldenburg in north Germany.

Within two years of returning from Cyprus, Hobden headed for another trouble spot when, in January 1966, he was appointed to HQ Middle East in Aden, where he served on the HQ staff as the senior ground defence staff officer. He was also appointed to command the security wing at Khormaksar, one of the RAF's largest and busiest airfields.

With the political situation in Aden rapidly deteriorating, Khormaksar, the only reinforcement airfield in the colony, was particularly vulnerable to terrorist attack. Hobden had makeshift revetments built using water-filled oil barrels to protect the large number of aircraft on the airfield. He also organised rapid reaction teams, some of which were deployed in helicopters patrolling the immediate area around the airfield – particularly important as the date for British withdrawal approached and British families were being evacuated.

The RAF finally left Aden on November 29, 1967 after 128 years of British rule and Hobden was one of the last men to leave. For a third time he was mentioned in despatches.

After service in the MoD and at the RAF's HQ in Germany,

Hobden retired from the RAF in July 1972. He worked at British Aerospace on the Rapier air defence missile system and moved to Abu Dhabi to train the local defence force. In June 1978 he moved to Tehran but he and his wife had to be evacuated after seven months following the coup.

For 20 years he lived in Spain before returning to England in 2006 when his eyesight started to fail.

Throughout his RAF career, Hobden was faced with an unusual number of delicate political and military issues. A colleague commented: "It was mainly due to his tactful and diplomatic leadership that things ran so smoothly under very difficult conditions."

Mark Hobden was twice married and had a son and daughter from his first marriage.

AIR MARSHAL SIR REGINALD HARLAND

Air Marshal Sir Reginald Harland (who died on July 30, 2013 aged 93) was one of the RAF's most distinguished engineering officers.

Following his war service, he was one of the first RAF engineer officers to specialise in guided missiles spending two years at the Royal Aircraft Establishment at Farnborough as project officer for the Thunderbird ground-to-air missile, which was procured for the British Army. This appointment was followed by two years at the Ministry of Supply working on air-launched guided weapons.

In May 1958 he was the first British liaison officer appointed to the staff of General Bernard Schriever, of the USAF's Air Research Development Command, based in Los Angeles. Schreiver, described as the architect of USAF's space and missile programme, had established the division a few months earlier, soon after the Soviet Union had launched *Sputnik*.

Harland was thus intimately involved both in the early development of intercontinental ballistic missiles (ICBM) – such as Thor (later procured for the RAF), Atlas, Titan and Minuteman – and of Project Mercury, which put men in space.

Reginald Edward Wynyard Harland was born in Sheffield on May 30, 1920 and was educated at Stowe School and Trinity College, Cambridge where he joined the university air squadron and gained a First in Mechanical Sciences. He was mobilised in September 1940.

His first appointment after completing his engineer training was to No. 295 Squadron supporting the army's airborne forces. In late 1942 he joined No. 241 Squadron as it deployed Hurricane ground-attack aircraft to support Operation Torch, the landings in Algeria. For 18 months he was the squadron's engineering officer as it moved forward to rudimentary advanced landing grounds in support of the First British Army. This was an appointment that demanded resourcefulness, management skills and a sense of humour in the harsh terrain where supply lines were stretched and home comforts were non-existent.

When the squadron re-equipped with Spitfires, Harland moved with it to Italy. In May 1944 he joined a repair and salvage unit and, later that year, landed with it during the invasion of the South of France before finishing the war with a field maintenance HQ in Naples.

Identified as one of the few engineering officers likely to reach senior rank, he trained as a pilot and, having been awarded his wings, became the chief engineering instructor at the

RAF College, Cranwell.

On return from the United States in July 1960 he was appointed to command the RAF's central servicing and development unit, a task that stimulated his interest in the reliability and maintainability of technical equipment. Two years later he was appointed the senior technical officer at HQ No. 3 Group, which controlled all Valiant and Victor aircraft of the V-bomber force.

After a three-year spell as the air officer in charge of engineering with the Far East Air Force, Harland went to the Ministry of Technology as project director for the Harrier, playing a key role in the introduction of the aircraft into RAF service. He insisted on a number of design changes to facilitate overseas sales (in particular the United States) and to allow the Harrier to operate from aircraft carriers.

After a year at the Imperial Defence College, Harland became air officer commanding No. 24 Group, responsible for training all airmen and airwomen, including apprentices.

In June 1973 he became the air officer commanding-in-chief of Maintenance Command and when this was absorbed into the RAF's Support Command a few months later he was appointed to command this expanded organisation, which now included No. 90 (Signals) Group. Harland was responsible for providing all the logistical and maintenance support requirements of the RAF.

He retired from the RAF in August 1977 and was appointed CB (1972) and KBE (1974). He also received the Air Efficiency Award.

In retirement he became the technical director with the engineering company WS Atkins. He was also president of the Society of Environmental Engineers from 1974 to 1977 and a Fellow of the Institute of Mechanical Engineers. In the 1983 and 1987 general elections he stood as a social democrat for the constituency of Bury St Edmunds. He was very active with the Suffolk Preservation Society and in the community affairs and history of Bury St Edmunds. He was president of the Bury St Edmunds Society, a local preservation group, having been a member for over 30 years.

Harland's eye for detail extended to teaching his sons how to make airworthy paper aeroplanes; the balance had to be right, with no yaw, roll or pitch. If it didn't glide straight and true, it was immediately recalled and rectified until it conformed to his exacting standards.

At the time of his death he was working on his memoirs and on a book about his great-uncle, the shipbuilder Sir Edward Harland. He had also recently edited Lieutenant Colonel Alfred Knights' book *Singapore and the Thailand Burma Railway* and a few months before his death he published *The Complete Surgeon*, a biography of his father-in-law W.H.C. Romanis.

A competitive and highly successful sailor, Harland raced a Fireball dinghy. During his time in Singapore he was the commodore of the RAF Changi Yacht Club. He also enjoyed golf, chess, bridge and newspaper competitions.

Reggie Harland married Doreen Romanis, a VAD during the war, in October 1942. She died in November 2011. They had three sons and two daughters. A son and a daughter pre-deceased him.

LIEUTENANT GENERAL BARON MIKE DONNET

Lieutenant General Baron Mike Donnet, the distinguished airman (who died on July 31, 2013 aged 96) made a dramatic escape from his native Belgium in 1941 then served in the RAF throughout the war as a fighter pilot. He later held senior appointments in the Belgian Air Force and in NATO.

After the German invasion of his homeland, Donnet had been held in captivity for seven months. Then he and his Belgian squadron colleagues were released and returned to Brussels. Donnet and a friend, Léon Divoy, were determined to carry on the fight and they made plans to escape to Britain. They and two other patriots discovered an old Stampe SV-4b bi-plane (similar to a Tiger Moth) in a hangar in the grounds

of a heavily guarded German depot. It was intact but needed considerable attention to make it airworthy.

For three months, the four men cycled 20 miles at night to the hangar, replacing missing parts and manufacturing others before refitting them under the noses of the Germans. They also managed to acquire enough fuel for the aircraft by purchasing it on the black market from a Luftwaffe mechanic.

After a couple of false starts (due to the unsuspecting Germans changing the locks to the hangar and the engine failing to start) Donnet and Divoy crept into the hangar on the night of July 4/5, 1941 in their Belgian Air Force uniforms, wheeled out the aircraft, started the engine and took off for England.

With virtually no aircraft instruments, they climbed to 10,000 feet and crossed the English Channel intending to land in Kent. Steering by the Pole Star they eventually reached the English coast, and with their meagre supply of fuel running out, landed in a field to discover that they were near Clacton in Essex. Amongst those who met them at the local police station was the immigration officer from Harwich. Like Donnet, the vintage aircraft was pressed into RAF service for the duration of the war before being returned to its Belgian owner.

Michel 'Mike' Gilbert Libert Marie Donnet was born on April 1, 1917 in London where his Belgian parents had married in 1914. On the outbreak of the First World War, Donnet's father signed up with the Belgian engineer corps. At the conclusion of the conflict the family returned to Brussels, where Donnet was educated at the College St Michel before joining the Aviation Militaire Belge in 1938 and training as a pilot.

He joined the 9th Squadron at Bierset flying the outdated Renard R-31 aircraft. Following the German invasion of the Low Countries on May 10, 1940, Donnet flew reconnaissance missions in support of the retreating armies until he was captured on June 1 following the capitulation of Belgium.

After his arrival in England, he was commissioned in the RAFVR and trained on Spitfires before joining No. 64 Squadron in November 1941. His first success came in March 1942 when he damaged two Focke-Wulf Fw 190s over Ostend. A few days later his aircraft collided with another Spitfire and he was forced to bale out. His friend Divoy was shot down to spend the rest of the war as a POW.

On July 30 Donnet shot down a Focke-Wulf Fw 190 over St Omer and in the space of a few days damaged three more. He was awarded the Belgian Croix de Guerre. After completing 100 operations, many over enemy territory at low level attacking trains, armed ships and gun posts, he was awarded the DFC for his "great courage and devotion to duty". During the celebrations that followed, 17 of his friends piled into one taxi and headed for London.

In February Donnet shot down a Focke-Wulf Fw 190 over Dunkirk and a month later he was given command of No. 64 when the squadron was used to escort bomber forces and Beaufighter formations attacking enemy convoys off the Dutch coast. After a period as a fighter instructor, Donnet was given command of No. 350 Squadron, the first all-Belgian squadron to be formed in the RAF.

On D-Day, Donnet led his squadron providing cover over the beachhead. He was in action against the V-1 flying bombs and the retreating German forces when he shot down a Focke-Wulf Fw 190. The day after learning that Belgium had been liberated, he led a formation of 12 Spitfires over Brussels in celebration. He provided cover for the Arnhem operation and, on promotion to wing commander in October, he took command of the Hawkinge Wing of Spitfires escorting bomber formations.

In February 1945 Donnet commanded the Bentwaters Wing flying the long-range Mustang. During the Allied airborne landings on the River Rhine, he led his squadrons to attack trains and road convoys being used to support the beleaguered German forces. On March 22 he and his squadron pilots provided an escort for a force of Mosquitos carrying out a pinpoint attack on the Gestapo HQ in Copenhagen. Then, on May 6, he escorted a formation of Beaufighters seeking out German naval units in the Skagerrak. It was his 375th and final operation.

After attending the RAF Staff College, Donnet returned to Belgium to re-organise the air force. Later he was head of the fighter force when he flew the Mcteor jet and in December 1952 was assigned as the senior air staff officer of the 83rd (Anglo-Belgian) Tactical Group. In August 1959 he was appointed deputy co-ordinator of the Air Defence of Central Europe at HQ SHAPE at Fontainbleau before taking up the appointment as chief of staff of NATO's Second Allied Tactical Air Force, with its headquarters in Germany and with squadrons from the RAF and the air forces of the Netherlands, Belgium and West Germany assigned.

After a senior appointment as the deputy to the Belgian chief of air staff, he returned to NATO to chair the Air Defence Ground Environment Committee, which was addressing the upgrade of the radar early warning and reporting system in the Central Region of NATO. In 1970 he was appointed Belgium's defence attaché in London and two years later he became the Belgian military representative of the NATO Military Committee. He retired in July 1975 having flown over 5,000 hours.

He was appointed a Companion of the Royal Victorian

Order and in Belgium, a Grand Officer of the Order of the Crown. The French government appointed him as a Chevalier de la Légion d'Honneur. He was also elected as a Fellow of the Royal Aeronautical Society.

He wrote several books including *Flight to Freedom* (1974), an account of his escape and wartime experiences.

Mike Donnet married Jacqueline 'Kiki' Gautier and they had one son and four daughters.

FLIGHT LIEUTENANT TONY SNELL

Flight Lieutenant Tony Snell (who died on August 4, 2013 aged 91) was shot down in his Spitfire over Sicily and escaped from a German firing squad. Recaptured, he leapt from a train and finally escaped over the Alps into neutral Switzerland.

On July 10, 1943 Snell was patrolling over the beachhead after the Sicily landings when a force of Messerschmitt fighters attacked him. His Spitfire was hit and he had to make a forced-landing on enemy territory. He avoided capture and tried to return to the beachhead after dark, managing to convince a group of Italian soldiers that he was a Vichy Frenchman. Later he was challenged by a German patrol that ordered him to put his hands up. Without warning they rolled a hand grenade towards him but he jumped clear and ran off, followed by more grenades.

He hid in scrub and realised that he was in a minefield, which he picked his way out of towards a track. There he blundered into a German airfield very near the battle area, and was captured. The Germans decided to execute him as a spy, marched him to an open space and ordered him to kneel down. Realising that he was about to be shot, he leapt up and ran off as the Germans fired. He was badly wounded, his right shoulder being smashed, but he managed to escape.

He tried to make the Allied lines but, owing to extreme weakness, his attempt failed. Re-captured at dawn he was again threatened with execution but managed to prove his identity. He was taken to hospital and later transferred by ship to Lucca in Tuscany where he remained for two months being treated for his wounds.

The Germans decided to transfer him to Germany by train. Although not fully recovered, he made plans to escape en route. In company with an American officer, he jumped from the train as it slowed at a junction and the two headed south. For the next week they had several narrow escapes before joining up with Italian partisans. With their help, they reached Modena, where families sheltered them for several months. When they were fit, the two decided that they should head for the Swiss border.

They made a long and risky train journey, accompanied by their Italian friends, to a small village near the frontier where they were introduced to two guides. After a very long and steep climb over the mountains, they crossed the frontier into Switzerland. They were interned until October 1944 when the American advance from the south of France reached the Swiss border.

Snell was awarded the DSO, one of very few awarded exclusively for escaping from the enemy.

Anthony Noel Snell was born in Tunbridge Wells on March 19, 1922 and educated at Cheltenham College. He joined the RAF in November 1940 and trained in the United States as a pilot under the US/UK bilateral Arnold Scheme.

In July 1942 he joined No. 242 Squadron flying Spitfires. Three months later he headed for North Africa where the squadron covered the landings of Operation Torch. Over the next few months the squadron provided support for the First British Army as it headed eastwards to Tunis. Snell flew air interception sorties and convoy patrols. With German air activity reducing, bomber escort and ground-attack strafing operations predominated until the final Axis collapse on that front in May 1943.

The squadron moved to Malta to prepare for the invasion of Sicily. As the Allies launched their amphibious and airborne landings on July 10, Snell took off to provide cover over the beachhead.

On his return to Britain, he spent time in hospital before returning to flying duties. He converted to the Meteor jet fighter and flew with No. 504 Squadron (later re-numbered No. 245), which moved to Germany just after the war finished. Snell remained with the squadron until August 1946 and was discharged from the RAF shortly after.

For twenty years Snell was an actor and songwriter. He toured a one-man show around Africa and, with his wife Jackie, travelled around the United States and Mexico in a Volkswagen bus. In New York he recorded an album of his songs, 'Englishman Abroad', half of which were written by him, with the others by his friend, Donald Cotton, the author of early Doctor Who scripts.

In 1966, he returned to England, bought a catamaran, sailed it with his wife to Spain and set up a business giving day charters out of Ibiza. In 1969 he moved to the British Virgin Islands (BVI) and established Virgin Voyages with three boats; but this was not a success and he and his wife opened a restaurant, The Last Resort, on Jost Van Dyke. After a year the restaurant was burnt down and they returned to Ibiza to sell their catamaran before heading back to BVI to reopen The Last Resort on Bellamy Cay, a tiny island in Trellis Bay, Tortola. While living on a houseboat, they built the restaurant from scratch on the ruins of a derelict building.

Snell co-owned the restaurant and bar and provided most of the entertainment, playing the guitar, the piano and the chromatic harmonica, singing songs (many of his own composition) and never fully grasping the meaning of political correctness; Jackie was chief cook.

The restaurant was just one product of a buccaneering business spirit. During their three decades in the Caribbean they also bought a large derelict hotel in New Hampshire that now houses 12 apartments, travelled to Bali to buy furniture for the hotel, bought a cottage in Sussex and an investment property in Brighton.

Although his family eventually took over The Last Resort, Tony Snell – relentlessly energetic – was still entertaining just a few weeks before his death. One colleague remarked: "You haven't seen energy in action until you have met Tony Snell."

Tony Snell's wife Jackie died in 2001. They had a son and a daughter.

AIR MARSHAL SIR JOHN CURTISS

Air Marshal Sir John Curtiss (who died on September 14, 2013 aged 88) had an unusual breadth of operational flying experience, which proved invaluable when, in 1982, he was appointed as the air commander for Operation Corporate, the recovery of the Falkland Islands.

He had flown as a navigator with Bomber Command in the Second World War, flew with the air transport force and later specialised as a night-fighter navigator. He served on a strategic nuclear V-bomber base and later commanded a large RAF air base in Germany at the height of the Cold War. After serving in a senior appointment at No. 11 (Fighter) Group, he was appointed as the air officer commanding (AOC) No. 18 Group where he led the RAF's maritime air assets.

Curtiss had his headquarters at Northwood, west of London co-located with C-in-C Fleet, Admiral Sir John Fieldhouse. The two men struck up a strong rapport and friendship and both knew how to mix humour with determination and the attention to detail. As soon as the government authorised the formation of a naval task force to reclaim the Falklands following the Argentinian invasion in April 1982, Fieldhouse was appointed commander Task Force 317 and Curtiss was made his air commander.

He commanded a large range of operational aircraft but much of the RAF's activity was covert. Nimrods carried out maritime surveillance sorties and patrols in support of the Fleet as it sailed south and Hercules transport aircraft began carrying supplies to Ascension Island, the only staging airfield, lying almost exactly halfway along the 8,000 miles that separated Britain from the Falklands. Without the island's single long runway, the RAF's capability to support the task force would have been minimal.

With such prodigious distances involved, the need for in-flight refuelling became paramount. Nimrods, Hercules and Vulcan bombers, and their crews, were hastily converted to the role and the large force of Victor tankers at Ascension became pivotal in support of all air operations. This capability allowed Nimrods, and the Victor tankers, to carry out reconnaissance sorties deep into the vast regions of the South Atlantic and Hercules aircraft were able to support the task force as it approached the area of operations.

Crucially it allowed Vulcan bombers to attack Port Stanley airfield and its defences. As operations increased, RAF Harrier ground-attack aircraft flew direct from Ascension to reinforce the naval squadrons on the aircraft carriers in the combat area.

The limitations at Ascension made the need to identify priorities essential and Fieldhouse and Curtiss decided these in consultation with the task force commander. Once the conflict started, it was Curtiss' task to keep Ascension re-supplied, in addition to mounting the long-range missions to support the force in the operational area. He also recognised the possibility of an attack against the island base and he deployed Phantoms and Harriers to provide an air-defence capability and RAF Regiment squadrons for ground defence.

Once the conflict was over, much remained to be done. Ascension had to be maintained and, within two weeks of the surrender, Curtiss flew to the Falklands where the runway at Stanley had to be repaired and equipped with landing aids to allow RAF Phantoms to deploy to provide air defence cover. He also identified sites for permanent radar and air defence missile units.

Curtiss recognised that the RAF's part was largely kept from public gaze because of the need to keep Ascension Island secure but he considered the campaign to be a fine example of close inter-service co-operation at all levels. He was loud in his praise of the remarkable efforts of the engineers and support staff in the military and in industry. In particular, he singled out the vital importance of in-flight refuelling and commented that "without it, the RAF was impotent at long range". For his services as air commander he was appointed KBE.

John Bagot Curtiss was born on December 6, 1924. He was educated at Radley College and Wanganui Collegiate School in New Zealand before attending Worcester College, Oxford. He joined the RAF in 1942 and trained as a navigator.

He flew bombing operations over Germany with Nos. 578 and 158 Squadrons flying the Halifax. He joined the air transport force and in 1949 was promoted to be a flight commander on a York squadron, completing 263 return trips flying supplies into Berlin during the Soviet blockade of the city.

In 1953, Curtiss converted to the night-fighter role and flew in Meteor and Javelin aircraft with Nos. 29 and 5 Squadrons, the latter providing a quick reaction alert force in Germany.

After commanding the operations wing at RAF Wittering, the home of Victor bomber squadrons equipped with the Blue Steel nuclear missile, he returned to Germany as the station commander at Brüggen, the RAF's largest operational base. Curtiss managed the introduction of four Phantom strike/ attack squadrons to the base where he flew with the units, often electing to fly with a junior pilot. He and his wife were popular with all ranks and as a 'people person', he was recognised as an excellent station commander who ran a happy and efficient base.

In 1974 he was appointed senior air staff officer at HQ 11 (Fighter) Group at a time when the UK's air defence organisation was undergoing a major upgrade. In 1977 he became commandant of the RAF Staff College at Bracknell where the RAF's high-grade junior officers, joined by international air force officers, were trained to fill higher command and staff appointments.

Three years later, in 1980, he was promoted to air marshal and appointed AOC No. 18 Group and NATO commander Maritime Air Forces, Eastern Atlantic and the Channel, not expecting to find himself commanding air operations 'out of area' during his final appointment in the RAF. He retired in 1983.

Curtiss' career was a great inspiration to the navigators of the RAF. During his time, pilots dominated command appointments, but the abilities and experience of Curtiss (and one other), could not be ignored and they paved the way for a later generation of navigators to assume higher command.

On leaving the RAF he was appointed chief executive of the Society of British Aerospace Companies. His services were in great demand by charities and associations, with Curtiss, no mere figurehead, taking a lively and direct interest in their aims and work. For 11 years he was a member of the executive committee of the Air League and was president of the Aircrew Association and of the Berlin Airlift Association. He had a great affection for New Zealand where some of his family lived.

Curtiss was universally admired. He could be outspoken when needed and he would vigorously defend his views but his smiling demeanour, humane and friendly personality endeared him to all ranks. He was able to touch all levels of society and always be at complete ease.

He had a wide range of interests, the most important being his family. He was a member of MCC, a fisherman and sailor and enjoyed cycling.

Curtiss was appointed CB (1979) and KCB (1981) and was elected a Fellow of the Royal Aeronautical Society.

John Curtiss married Peggy Bowie and they had three sons and a daughter.

SQUADRON LEADER ULRIC CROSS

Ulric Cross (who died on October 3, 2013 aged 96) is thought to have been the most decorated Caribbean airmen of the Second World War: he went on to enjoy a distinguished career in Trinidad as a judge and diplomat.

Cross was working for Trinidad Railways when the war broke out, and was anxious to play his part. "The world was drowning in Fascism and America was not yet in the war," he later recalled. "So I decided to do something about it and volunteered to fight in the RAF."

Philip Louis Ulric Cross was born on May 1, 1917 in Port of Spain, Trinidad where he gained a government scholarship to St Mary's College. His first job was with the *Trinidad Guardian* before he spent four years working in a solicitor's office. In 1941, after three years working for the railway, he joined the RAF and sailed for England.

After training as a navigator at Cranwell, Cross joined No. 139 (Jamaica) Squadron equipped with the Mosquito – many of the aircraft were paid for by donations made by the citizens

of Jamaica. Cross was in fact then the only West Indian on the squadron, where his friends gave him the fond nickname 'The Black Hornet'.

He made a number of precision daylight attacks at low level over France and Germany before the squadron converted to night operations with Bomber Command's Pathfinder Force. The squadron supported the main bomber force dropping 'window' electronic countermeasures to confuse German radars, before embarking on a number of 'spoof' raids on other targets with the aim of drawing the Luftwaffe night-fighter force away from the main target to be attacked by the heavy bombers.

On the night of August 18, 1943, Cross and his pilot, Roy Crampton, took part in a diversionary raid against Berlin as the main force attacked the German rocket-testing facility at Peenemünde. Over Berlin, the starboard engine of their Mosquito was hit by flak when they were flying at 30,000 feet and it had to be shut down. The two men then flew their damaged aircraft 500 miles back to base on one engine, all the time steadily losing height. They landed at the first available airfield in Norfolk where the aircraft careered across the airfield and stopped on the edge of a quarry.

November 1943 saw the start of the Battle of Berlin, and Cross made 22 sorties to the 'Big City' in the high-flying Mosquito. The squadron became part of the Light Night Striking

Force, identifying targets for the main bomber force with the new marking aid 'Oboe'. Having completed 30 operations, Cross was eligible for a rest but he volunteered to carry on. He also declined to be rested after 50 operations when he was awarded the DFC.

During April 1944 he attacked targets in the Ruhr, and when Bomber Command's heavy bomber squadrons were diverted to support the D-Day offensive, Cross and his colleagues continued to mount 'nuisance raids' over German cities with the aim of denying sleep to the factory workers and forcing the German military to retain thousands of men on air defence duties.

Finally, after completing 80 operations over enemy-occupied territory, Cross was rested at the end of 1944. Shortly afterwards he was awarded the DSO in recognition of his "fine example of keenness and devotion to duty" and his "exceptional navigation ability".

He was then seconded to the Colonial Office as the liaison officer for colonial forces in the RAF. He left the service as a squadron leader in 1947 to study law at Middle Temple and was called to the Bar in 1949.

For four years, Cross was the legal adviser to the controller of imports and exports in Trinidad and Tobago before becoming a lecturer at the University of West Indies located in Trinidad.

After four years in London working with the BBC, in 1958 he went to Africa to practise law. In Ghana, he became a Senior Crown Counsel and lecturer at the Ghana School of Law. From 1960 to 1966 he was in Cameroon as Senior Crown Counsel and Attorney General. The Cameroon government awarded him the Order of Merit and Order of Valour.

In 1967 Cross became a High Court judge in Tanzania and chaired the Permanent Labour Tribunal. Four years later he returned to Trinidad, where he served as a judge of the High Court and, from 1979, of the Court of Appeal. His work as chairman of the Law Reform Commission of Trinidad was acknowledged by the country's prime minister, who observed:

"Some of his judgements changed the landscape of Trinidad and Tobago."

In 1990 Cross became his country's High Commissioner in London, a post he held for three years; he combined this appointment with those of ambassador to Germany and to France.

On his return to Trinidad, Cross was active in a number of charitable causes, including the Cotton Tree Foundation to aid the deprived communities in Port of Spain, and in 2011 he received his nation's highest award, the Order of the Republic of Trinidad and Tobago. In the same year the local military air base at Piarco was renamed the Ulric Cross Air Station. One commentator on hearing of his death said: "Cross will be remembered for his brilliant legal mind, but most of all for his service to humanity."

The thriller writer Ken Follett based the character of the black squadron leader, Charles Ford, on Ulric Cross in his book *Hornet Flight*, published in 2002.

Ulrich Cross's wife Ann predeceased him. They had a son and two daughters.

WING COMMANDER JIMMY FLINT

Wing Commander Jimmy Flint (who died on December 16, 2013 aged 100) had the unique distinction of receiving two gallantry awards for separate actions during the same flight.

On the night of July 5/6, 1941 Flint and his all-sergeant crew took off in their twin-engine Hampden bomber to attack Osnabrück. Shortly after crossing the Dutch coast at 10,000 feet, the aircraft was caught and held in enemy searchlights. Flint took violent evasive action, but a night-fighter attacked, causing extensive damage to the aircraft. As Flint dived away the fighter inflicted further damage. Eventually, after 10 minutes, and by descending to 500 feet, Flint was able to shake off the fighter and escape.

Unperturbed, he climbed back to bombing height and

headed for the target. But the aircraft was again caught by searchlights and was unable to shake them off until Flint had jettisoned the bombs. He finally escaped at 1,000 feet when he turned and headed for the North Sea.

The Hampden was 50 miles from the English coast when two Messerschmitt Bf 110 fighters appeared and set up a series of devastating co-ordinated attacks. Flares were ignited in the cockpit and the aircraft's radio and internal communication system was damaged making it impossible for the crew to contact each other. The fighters made three more attacks, and the port engine of the bomber was set on fire and some of the crew were wounded. Flint turned off the petrol to the damaged engine and flew a few feet above the sea before the fighters finally broke away.

As he approached the coast near Cromer, Flint realised that he would be unable to climb over the cliffs. He turned away and ditched the bomber 800 yards from the shore.

Two of the crew were able to evacuate the aircraft, only to discover that the dinghy had been holed. Flint also escaped but immediately realised that the navigator was missing. He crawled back into the sinking bomber, where he found his badly wounded comrade. As the aircraft began to go down, Flint hauled the helpless navigator through the escape hatch. With no dinghy, Flint supported the unconscious navigator as he swam and dragged him towards the shore. Fifty yards short of the beach, a soldier appeared to help, allowing Flint to scramble ashore. There was no sign of the air gunner and he asked for boats to search for the missing man.

Flint refused to leave the beach until it was clear that the air gunner had been lost. He then walked a mile to a waiting ambulance and was taken to hospital.

He was awarded an immediate DFM for "his cool courage and determination to strike at the enemy". When the full extent of his gallant efforts to save his crew became clear, he was awarded the George Medal, the citation concluding: "This airman displayed great gallantry, fortitude and disregard of personal safety in his efforts to save his helpless navigator." Sadly, the navigator succumbed to his wounds.

James Flint was born on May 24, 1913 at Nottingham and educated at the Trent Bridge Central School, which he left at 14. The company he worked for soon went out of business, but the liquidators were so impressed with his work and attitude they offered him a job. He joined the RAF in August 1938 and trained as a pilot.

He went to No. 49 Squadron at Scampton near Lincoln in February 1941 and flew his first operations as second pilot and navigator. These included attacks against targets in Germany and mine-laying operations off the Brest Peninsula and the German coast.

When Flint became the captain of his own aircraft, Bomber Command was concentrating on attacks against the U-boat ports and the *Scharnhorst* and *Gneisenau* battle cruisers in Brest. Minelaying also remained a priority task and, during April, Berlin was attacked. On one occasion Flint's Hampden was badly damaged but he managed to nurse the aircraft back to Lincolnshire where he was forced to crash-land in a field. Shortly after scrambling from the wreck they were met by a farmer's wife carrying a tray on which she had laid out a breakfast for the four men. When Flint took off on his eventful flight in July, it was his 32nd operation against the enemy.

Flint was rested and commissioned and spent the next two years as an instructor at a bomber-training unit. In April 1944 he returned to operations, flying the Lancaster. He was appointed the commanding officer (CO) of No. 50 Squadron.

The squadron flew in support of the Allied landings in

Normandy before returning to the strategic bomber offensive over Germany in August 1944. The CO of a Lancaster squadron was expected to fly only occasionally on operations but Flint completed 20 bombing sorties before relinquishing command in the spring of 1945. He was awarded the DFC and received the Air Efficiency Award.

Flint returned to Nottingham where he spent the rest of his life. During his youth he had been an outstanding sportsman excelling at cricket and football. After his demobilisation, he was immediately offered a job with the large sports outfitters and suppliers, Redmayne & Todd Ltd.

Always immaculately dressed, Flint was a great supporter of activities in Nottingham. For many years he was the president of the Nottingham Club (formerly the Nottingham and Notts United Services Club), where a room was named after him.

He was also a stalwart of RAF associations and was a long-time vice president of No. 50/61 Squadron's Association, rarely missing an annual reunion. In July 2012 he attended the unveiling of the Bomber Command Memorial in London, which he described as "a great token to men who have done everything to save this country". His portrait hangs in the officers' mess at the RAF's HQ Air Command at High Wycombe.

Jimmy Flint was an excellent golfer, playing to a handicap of seven and a fine fly fisherman.

He married his wife Joyce in June 1944 and she died in 2003.

WING COMMANDER CLIFF ALABASTER

Wing Commander Cliff Alabaster (who died on February 17, 2014 aged 95) was a highly decorated bomber captain who flew more than 100 raids with Bomber Command and the Pathfinder Force before embarking on a distinguished career in civil aviation.

After completing his training as an air observer, Alabaster joined No. 51 Squadron operating the twin-engine Whitley

bomber. He made his first operational raid on August 5, 1940 against a flying boat base on the Baltic and over the next few months he attacked targets in Germany and France. On the night of April 3, 1941 he took off to bomb the German battle cruisers *Scharnhorst* and *Gneisenau* at Brest. On the outward route over Dorset, his Whitley was hit by machine-gun fire, which inflicted heavy damage, and the crew were forced to bale out. It was later established that the attack came from an RAF Hurricane, which had been hunting for German bombers returning to France from a raid on Swansea.

After completing 30 operations, Alabaster was awarded the DFC. He had been identified as an outstanding navigator and was sent to Canada to complete a specialist course before returning to Bomber Command. He applied to train as a pilot but his services as a navigator were considered too valuable.

Soon after the formation of the Pathfinder Force, Alabaster was asked by its leader Group Captain (later Air Vice-Marshal) Don Bennett to be the force's navigation officer as an acting wing commander. Six months later, in June 1943, he was appointed a flight commander on No. 97 Squadron equipped with the Lancaster. Unusually for a navigator, he was appointed as a captain of his aircraft.

He attacked targets deep in Germany and on the night of August 17/18 his was one of the lead Pathfinder crews on the raid against the secret German V-1 and V-2 Research and Production Station at Peenemünde.

During an attack on Cologne, his Lancaster was severely damaged by a night-fighter and some of his crew were wounded but Alabaster was determined to press on to the target. After a successful attack, the aircraft became difficult to control and an engine caught fire. The pilot made a brilliant landing at a coastal airfield. He was awarded the DFC and Alabaster added a Bar to his earlier award for his "masterly captaincy".

After completing a further 30 operations, Alabaster was awarded the DSO. The citation noted: "His fearlessness and skill have been an important factor in the many successes obtained. He is a most excellent flight commander." Finally, his repeated requests to train as a pilot were granted and he completed his training in May 1944, when, at Bennett's insistence, he returned to the Pathfinder Force, initially on Lancasters before converting to the Mosquito.

In November 1944 he assumed command of No. 608 Squadron, part of the Light Night Striking Force, and he made attacks against Berlin and other major cities. After completing his 100th operation he was awarded a Bar to his DSO. He was one of only 27 men to be awarded the DSO and Bar and DFC and Bar. He also received the Air Efficiency Award.

Robert Clifford Alabaster was born on March 11, 1918 at Willesden, Middlesex. He won a county scholarship and was educated at Willesden County School. On leaving school he worked in the legal department of London Transport but seeing the war clouds gathering he enlisted in the Royal Air Force Volunteer Reserve in May 1939.

At the war's end, Alabaster was offered a permanent commission with the RAF but he chose to join Don Bennett who had just established British South American Airways (BSAA) operating Lancastrians (converted wartime Lancasters). On January 1, 1946, Bennett and Alabaster flew the first international service out of 'Heath Row' en route to Buenos Aires in the Lancastrian 'Starlight'.

BSAA merged with BOAC in 1949 and Alabaster began flying Argonauts. During a flight from London to Rio via Lisbon and Dakar, the aircraft was well past the point of no return over the South Atlantic when it suffered a double engine failure. Alabaster set course for the nearest landing strip, on Fernando de Noronha, part of a remote archipelago 400 miles east of the Brazilian coast where there was an emergency airstrip. It was very close to the side of a mountain and had been rarely used since the war. In Alabaster's words: "We landed at night amongst the sheep." All on board survived. For his airmanship he was awarded the King's Commendation for Valuable Service in the Air.

He was posted to BOAC's Comet Development Flight in 1951 and flew many proving flights between London and Beirut. On May 2, 1952 he was in command on the world's first jet passenger service on the Khartoum to Johannesburg leg from London. When the Comets were grounded following disastrous crashes due to metal fatigue, he flew Constellations but was happy to return to the Comet fleet, of which he was appointed flight manager, when BOAC brought back the redesigned version, the Comet 4, in 1958.

In February 1959 he took the then prime minister, Sir Harold MacMillan on a state visit to Russia for meetings with Nikita Khrushchev.

Later in 1959 he was in command of the first ever jet service between London and New York. Eventually the Comet was withdrawn from service and, appropriately, Alabaster operated the final flight, which touched down at London Heathrow in November 1965 ending 13 years of aviation history. He then converted to the Vickers VC10, the aircraft he was still flying in 1973 as a route check captain when he retired from BOAC.

Alabaster worked for British Caledonian Airways as flight safety advisor before joining Gulf Air in Bahrain flying ex-BOAC VC10s until 1978.

Following his final retirement he became treasurer for the Association of British Airways Pensioners (ABAP) and spent much time defending their cause. He also enjoyed his hobbies of sailing, furniture making, astronomy, playing the piano and gardening.

Cliff Alabaster and his wife Valerie were married for 52 years, and they had two sons and two daughters.

LETTICE CURTIS

Lettice Curtis (who died on July 21, 2014 aged 99) was arguably the most remarkable woman pilot of the Second World War, flying a wide range of military combat aircraft with the Air Transport Auxiliary (ATA) and being the first woman to qualify to fly a four-engine bomber.

She had qualified as a commercial pilot in April 1938, and was working for the Ordnance Survey when, in June 1940, she was approached by the ATA. There was an urgent need for more pilots to ferry aircraft and, with most men joining the RAF, it was decided to form a women's pool to bolster the number of pilots. Curtis was amongst the first to join.

With a small group of other young women, she began flying light training and communications aircraft at Hatfield. She soon graduated to fly more advanced trainers and also the twin-engine Oxford. ATA pilots often flew alone and with no navigation aids – they had to rely almost entirely on map reading as they ferried aircraft from factories and airfields to

RAF units around the United Kingdom. Weather conditions were often difficult.

Until the spring of 1941 there was a government ruling that women could not fly operational aircraft, but everything changed that summer. Without any extra tuition, and just a printed pre-flight checklist, Curtis ferried a Hurricane to Prestwick. Soon she was flying the fighter regularly, and it was not long before she was also delivering Spitfires to front-line squadrons.

In September 1941, the role of women pilots was extended further, and Curtis quickly graduated to the more advanced aircraft, and started to ferry light bombers including the Blenheim and the Hampden. She then converted to the more demanding Wellington. Later observing: "Before flying (the Wellington) it was simply a question of reading Pilot's Notes."

At the end of September 1942, Curtis left for an RAF bomber airfield, where she was trained to fly the Halifax bomber. On October 27, Mrs Eleanor Roosevelt, accompanied by Mrs Churchill, visited the ATA to meet the women pilots. Curtis stood under the wing of a Halifax in the pouring rain and was introduced to the American president's wife as the first woman to fly a four-engine bomber. The encounter prompted a field day in the national press, one headline reading: "Mrs Roosevelt meets Halifax girl pilot".

During 1943, she was authorised to ferry more types of heavy bombers, including the US B-17 Flying Fortress. The following year she was the first woman pilot to deliver a Lancaster. By the end of the war, when the ATA closed down, Curtis had flown over 400 heavy bombers, 150 Mosquitos and hundreds of Hurricanes and Spitfires.

Eleanor Lettice Curtis was born in Denbury, Devon on February 1, 1915 and educated at Benenden School and St Hilda's College, Oxford, where she read Mathematics and captained the women's lawn tennis and fencing teams; she also represented the university at lacrosse, and was a county tennis and squash player.

She learned to fly at Yapton Flying Club near Chichester in the summer of 1937. After her initial training, she continued to fly a further 100 hours solo in order to gain her commercial B licence. She did not expect to get a flying job, but in the event was taken on by C.L. Aerial Surveys, which she joined in May 1938.

Flying a Puss Moth fitted with a survey camera, she photographed specified areas of England for the Ordnance Survey. On the outbreak of war she transferred to the research department of the Ordnance Survey and later she joined the ATA.

Post-war, Curtis worked as a technician and flight test observer at the Aeroplane and Armament Experimental Establishment before becoming the senior flight development engineer with Fairey Aviation in 1953. She also flew as a test observer in the Royal Navy's Gannet anti-submarine aircraft and regularly flew Fairey's communication aircraft.

Her love of flying never diminished, and she regularly took part in the National Air Races organised by the Royal Aero Club, piloting a variety of competitive aircraft, including a Spitfire belonging to the American civil air attaché in London. In this Spitfire she raced against the country's top test pilots, and achieved a number of high placings. She later bought her own aircraft (a Wicko) in which she competed in a number of *Daily Express* air races.

In the early 1960s, Curtis left Fairey for the Ministry of Aviation, working for a number of years on the initial planning of the joint Military and Civil Air Traffic Control Centre at West Drayton. After a spell in the Flight Operations Inspectorate of the Civil Aviation Authority, in 1976 she took a job as an engineer with Sperry Aviation.

A strong supporter of Concorde (her club number was 151), she made two flights in the famous airliner. In 1992 she gained her helicopter licence, but three years later decided that at the age of 80, her flying days were over.

A strong-willed, determined individual, Curtis always felt that the ATA did not receive the recognition it deserved and in 1971 she published *The Forgotten Pilots*. Her autobiography,

Lettice Curtis, came out in 2004.

Lettice Curtis, who was unmarried, was in great demand on the lecture circuit and as a guest on RAF stations. She was one of the first patrons and supporters of the Yorkshire Air Museum.

SQUADRON LEADER TERRY BULLOCH

Squadron Leader Terry Bulloch (who died on November 13, 2014 aged 98) was a pilot in Coastal Command who made the greatest number of sightings and attacks against German U-boats during the Battle of the Atlantic. By the end of the war he had been credited with sinking four, twice the number by any other pilot.

Due to the lack of long-range aircraft in 1941 and early 1942, sinking of Allied shipping by German U-boats in the mid-Atlantic had reached alarming proportions. The introduction into RAF service of the American-built B-24 Liberator finally helped close this 'Atlantic Gap' and gave added protection to the essential convoys sailing from North American ports to the UK.

In December 1942, Bulloch, known throughout Coastal Command as 'The Bull', was in charge of a small detachment of No. 120 Squadron in Iceland and had already developed a reputation as one of the most determined and successful

U-boat hunters. On December 8, he and his crew took off from Reykjavik in their Liberator to fly a convoy patrol; 16 hours later they landed after one of the most remarkable operational wartime flights by an RAF aircraft. Its like would never be repeated.

Two large convoys had left Halifax in Nova Scotia and were approaching an area where naval intelligence estimated that a U-boat 'Wolf Pack' of 14 submarines was lurking in wait (post-war analysis established that there were 22). Bulloch intercepted convoy HX 217 and took up a position astern to counter a known U-boat tactic of shadowing a convoy whilst others from the pack converged.

The weather was poor but Bulloch's amazing eyesight picked up the wake of a surfaced U-boat and dived to attack. The submarine commenced a crash-dive but it was too late and Bulloch straddled it with six depth charges. There was a great upheaval of water and oil; wreckage and bodies soon floated to the surface. A Norwegian Navy corvette escorting the convoy investigated and confirmed the sinking.

Soon after this success, Bulloch spotted two more U-boats and he attacked one with his two remaining depth charges forcing the submarine to dive. This was Bulloch's 22nd sighting of a U-boat (he had attacked 12) – far more than most squadrons had achieved, or ever did. However, this unique flight was not over.

Before it was time for him to depart, Bulloch and his crew sighted another five submarines. With no depth charges remaining, he dived and attacked each with his four Hispano 20-mm cannons. On every occasion he forced the submarines to dive and abandon their attacks.

A second Liberator arrived to relieve Bulloch and it continued the attacks forcing five more U-boats to dive. The attackers had been thrown into disarray and their positions revealed to the escorting naval forces who engaged them. Just two of the 90 ships were lost from the convoys.

Bulloch was awarded a Bar to a DSO that had been gazetted four weeks earlier. Some of his outstanding crew were also decorated including a DSO to his navigator and a DFM to his flight engineer.

The national press in the UK and in Canada gave extensive cover to the events with headlines of "The Bull gets a U-boat" and "Sub smashers win 5 awards in big convoy fight". An official Coastal Command report concluded: "The convoys were brought safely to port in the face of the most determined opposition yet encountered."

Terence Malcolm Bulloch was born on February 19, 1916 in Lisburn, County Antrim and he attended Campbell College Belfast where he was the piper sergeant major in the Officer Training Corps and an excellent rugby player.

He joined the RAF on a short-service commission in 1936 and trained as a pilot before flying Ansons in Coastal Command. By early 1940 he had transferred to No. 206 Squadron to fly the twin-engine Hudson patrolling the French, Dutch and Belgian coastal areas, including a number of hazardous trips during the evacuation of the BEF from Dunkirk. He attacked and damaged a German floatplane, forcing it to land on the sea, where he then bombed it. He also bombed the Channel ports being used in Hitler's preparations to invade England in September 1940. At the end of the year, he was awarded the DFC, which was soon followed by a mention in despatches.

Rather than have a rest, Bulloch joined the RAF's Ferry Command in Canada and flew four-engine bombers across the Atlantic to British airfields. On one occasion, flying a B-17 Fortress, he took just over eight hours to reach Prestwick in Scotland, a record flight across the Atlantic at that time.

With the arrival of the B-24 Liberators, some of which Bulloch had delivered, No. 120 Squadron was formed at Nutts Corner, Belfast and Bulloch joined as a flight commander.

On October 21, 1941, he made the squadron's first attack against a U-boat but abandoned it briefly to attack a Focke-Wulf 200 Condor aircraft that was shadowing the convoy he was protecting. The Condor left the area rapidly and Bulloch resumed his hunt for the submarine. He spotted a periscope and dived to attack with three depth charges. The attack was inconclusive and he was credited with a 'damaged'.

Over the next nine months of patient patrolling, Bulloch made six more U-boat sightings. He damaged U-59 as it returned to Brest and, two days later, he seriously damaged U-653 forcing it to return to Brest where it spent six months being repaired.

In September he was in Iceland and on October 12 he achieved his, and the squadron's, first confirmed 'kill'. His depth charges virtually blew U-597 out of the water and it was last seen tipping vertically before disappearing.

Over the next two weeks he sighted and attacked four more submarines and on November 5 he sighted another two. Attacking one of them from bow to stern, his aim was accurate and his depth charges destroyed U-132. He was awarded a Bar to his DFC, the citation commenting, "his power of leadership is outstanding".

After his memorable sortie of December 8, he became an instructor but took the opportunity to test new equipment including a battery of eight rockets fitted to the nose of his aircraft. He was attached to No. 224 Squadron and, on July 8, 1943, he was on patrol near Cape Finisterre when he spotted the conning tower of a submarine in the wake of a fishing boat. He attacked and fired his eight rockets in pairs from 50 feet. He pulled up and re-attacked with his depth charges. U-514 outbound to South African waters was destroyed with all hands.

At the end of his tour, Bulloch refused to be rested and he joined a long-range transport squadron flying converted Liberators across the Atlantic. Later he flew with a special RAF transport squadron on routes across the Pacific. Towards the end of the war, he was seconded to BOAC and after his release from the RAF in July 1946 he joined the airline as a captain.

Bulloch flew BOAC's prestigious Trans-Atlantic service and was to spend almost all his long career with BOAC and British Airways (BA) flying over the ocean he knew so well. Initially he flew converted bombers and progressed to the elegant

Constellation and the less elegant Stratocruiser. He shunned all offers to be a training captain or to take on managerial duties. He simply wanted to keep flying, and he spent many hours at the controls of the jet-powered Boeing 707 before moving to the Boeing 747.

On reaching BA's retirement age, he had flown across the Atlantic 1,113 times. His passion for flying had not diminished, so he joined the Portuguese National Airline (TAP) and took command of a Boeing 707 and continued to fly routes across the Atlantic. He finally retired in 1974.

Bulloch was a man of few words, but he had a great determination to attack the enemy and, when not flying, which was rare, he spent many hours studying the enemy's tactics and capabilities. He insisted on total dedication and professionalism from his crew and he was an inspiring captain. Some thought him too forthright and terse, but his knowledge, courage and skill, not to mention his unique record, were greatly admired. He had little time for authority and less for paperwork and bureaucracy, but he was a man of compelling honesty and integrity.

After so much travelling for almost 40 years, in retirement he devoted himself to his garden and to his local golf club at Denham. A colleague wrote his biography *Coastal Ace* in 1986.

Terry Bulloch's first wife Joan died in 1969. He married his second wife Linda, a Canadian, in 1974.

SQUADRON LEADER H.G. 'JIMMY' JAMES

Squadron Leader H.G. 'Jimmy' James (who died on January 7, 2015 aged 92) was the pilot of the RAF transport aircraft shot down in the Western Desert, resulting in the death of Lieutenant General William 'Strafer' Gott.

On August 7, 1942, 19-year-old Sergeant James flew his pre-war Bombay transport aircraft on a re-supply mission to an advanced landing ground at Burgh-el-Arab near El Alamein.

After the cargo was unloaded, wounded soldiers were brought to the aircraft to be flown back to hospital in Cairo.

Instead of taking off immediately, in accordance with normal procedures, James was ordered to wait for two special passengers who had been summoned to meet Winston Churchill in Cairo. One was Lieutenant General Gott, who was to replace General Sir Claude Auchinleck as the commander of the British Eighth Army.

With all 21 personnel on board, James took off and flew eastwards at 50 feet, to avoid German fighters. But 20 minutes into the flight, the Bombay's starboard engine exploded and stopped as tracer from two Messerschmitt Bf 109 fighters hit the aircraft. Two others then attacked the lumbering transport and set the port engine on fire.

James was forced to find a place to land but after coming to a stop, a third pair of enemy fighters strafed the Bombay; the fuel tanks exploded, setting the whole aircraft ablaze. Although wounded in the shoulder and arm, James managed to struggle out of the cockpit just before tracer wrecked the area where he had been sitting. He was horrified to see the fuselage burning; just four of his 21 passengers lay injured by the wrecked aircraft.

Despite his wounds and severe burns to his hands and feet, James decided to seek help, and he set off alone to trek north. He had covered two miles when a friendly Bedouin gave him a camel to ride, and not long afterwards he spotted a

British Army vehicle and waved his blood-soaked shirt to attract attention. He was taken to an advanced army post where it took him some time to persuade the officers of the truth of his story.

Despite lapsing out of consciousness, James insisted in making the 20-mile journey into the desert to direct the rescue party. The wreckage was located, and it was found that 17 men, among them Gott, had been killed.

James had to undergo three operations at a field hospital before being transferred to Cairo where he underwent a further four months' treatment. He was awarded an immediate DFM, the citation concluding: "In a crisis he completely ignored his own personal safety and welfare and acted in a clear-headed and very courageous manner."

For many years there was intense speculation about the circumstances of Gott's death. James was always convinced that he was assassinated since the six German fighters had ambushed his aircraft over Allied territory and did not leave the scene until the Bombay had been completely destroyed on the ground – an unusual tactic in the desert war.

In 2005, James met one of the German fighter pilots involved, who confirmed that shortly after they had landed after this mission, their commander congratulated them "for killing General Gott"; this had been several hours before James had reached the British post to report the loss of the Bombay. As a result of Gott's death, Lieutenant General Bernard Montgomery was appointed to command the Eighth Army.

Hugh Glanffrwd James (always known as Jimmy) was born on October 3, 1922 at Cilfynydd in the Rhondda and educated at Pontypridd Grammar School where he excelled at singing and rugby (he would later represent the RAF at the sport).

The minimum age for joining the RAF was 18 but James 'adjusted' his birthday when he started training as a pilot as a 17-year-old. His ambition was to be a fighter pilot, but he was sent to the Middle East to join No. 216 Squadron to fly transport aircraft.

After recovering from his wounds, James re-joined No. 216 and, for the next two years, he flew Dakotas in support of the army in North Africa and on re-supply flights to Malta. He parachuted supplies to the beleaguered garrison on Leros in the Aegean during the ill-fated Dodecanese campaign. Later he flew from airfields in Italy to re-supply the partisans in Yugoslavia and Greece.

On return to Britain at the end of the war, James joined No. 24 (Commonwealth) Squadron based initially at Hendon. Flying Dakotas, he served as a training captain and flew VIPs. At the end of 1946 he was awarded the AFC.

James was one of very few captains allowed to fly royalty. He was the pilot on Princess Margaret's first solo official visit (to Northern Ireland). Prime Minister Clement Attlee was a regular passenger and James also flew Commonwealth leaders, among them Field Marshal Jan Smuts who he considered to be one of his most gracious and appreciative passengers.

Because such people had to arrive at their destinations on time to meet crucial deadlines, James often had to fly in very difficult weather conditions: but he established a reputation as one of the best and most reliable captains. During the Berlin Airlift, he was a training captain and monitored pilots who had to fly in bad weather along the designated corridors into and out of Berlin. In January 1950 he was awarded a Bar to his AFC.

In 1952 James finally achieved his ambition of becoming a fighter pilot converting to the Mosquito night-fighter and joining No. 25 Squadron. The squadron re-equipped with the Vampire jet, and after two years, he went to Alaska to join the USAF's 10th Air Division. He was appointed the chief training officer for the night-fighter wing, which guarded the routes from eastern Russia and those over the North Pole. The wing flew the F.89D Scorpion, an aircraft that did not impress James – and he was not afraid to say so.

In late 1956, he was appointed the senior flight commander of No. 46 Squadron flying the Javelin, an aircraft he rated highly. After a period testing the latest air-to-air missiles and a staff tour at a headquarters, he left the RAF in July 1965, a decision he later regretted.

He worked for a number of years for an electronics company in Bracknell before retiring to Chobham in Surrey. He was immensely popular in the village and was a long-serving churchwarden. He was also a very supportive member of the Woking branch of the Aircrew Association.

Hugh 'Jimmy' James was married first to Beth Jones and they had three sons and a daughter before the marriage was dissolved. In 1964 he married Juliet Laughton (née Chapman) and they had a son and a daughter.

SQUADRON LEADER LES MUNRO

Squadron Leader Les Munro (who died on August 4, 2015 aged 96) was the last-surviving pilot to have taken part in the Dambusters raid, which attacked the Ruhr dams in May 1943.

Munro's Lancaster was one of the first to take off on the night of May 16/17. Its target was the Sorpe Dam. Flying at very low level over the Dutch island of Vlieland, their Lancaster was badly damaged by anti-aircraft fire. The radios and electrical system were disabled but, crucially, so was the intercommunication system between the members of the crew. Without this it was impossible to carry out the precise attack from a height of 60 feet. With great reluctance, Munro turned for his home base, still with his 'bouncing bomb' on board.

The raid against the Ruhr dams was successful, with the main targets, the Mohne and Eder Dams, both breached. But the cost was high with eight of the 19 Lancasters failing to return with the loss of 53 airmen. The leader of the operation, Wing Commander Guy Gibson, was awarded the Victoria Cross.

John Leslie Munro was born at Gisborne, New Zealand on April 5, 1919 where his Scottish father had emigrated to in 1903. He worked as a farmer before joining the Royal New Zealand Air Force in July 1941.

He trained initially in New Zealand and then in Canada where he qualified as a pilot. On arrival in England he trained on bombers before joining No. 97 Squadron, which had recently been re-equipped with the Lancaster.

After an operation to drop mines in the sea-lanes to German occupied ports, Munro attacked industrial cities in Germany during the so-called 'Battle of the Ruhr' when Essen, Düsseldorf and Cologne were amongst his targets. He also flew on two raids to Berlin and attacked targets in Italy. Munro and his crew were approaching the end of their tour of operations when volunteers were called for to form a new squadron for a 'special operation'. Munro discussed it with his crew and they agreed to apply. A few days later, on March 25, they arrived at Scampton in Lincolnshire to join 'X' Squadron on its formation, later to become No. 617.

Soon after leaving No. 97 Squadron, Munro was awarded the DFC for "pressing home his attacks with great courage and determination".

Within days of arriving at Scampton, all the crews were practising intensive low-level flying involving routes that included runs over lakes and reservoirs when high-tension cables, barrage balloons and birds were an ever-present hazard. During a trial flight with the 'Upkeep' bouncing bomb designed by Barnes Wallis, Munro was flying below the prescribed height of 60 feet when a great plume of water made by the bomb as it made its first bounce damaged the tailplane of his Lancaster.

After the Dams Raid, No. 617 suffered further heavy losses and morale was badly affected. Under the leadership of its new commanding officer, Wing Commander Leonard Cheshire, Munro was made a flight commander, along with Dave Shannon, an Australian, and the American Joe McCarthy and these three, under Cheshire's inspiring leadership, created one of the most effective squadrons to serve in Bomber Command. Cheshire described his three flight commanders as "the backbone of the squadron". Of the three, the taciturn New Zealander was the least flamboyant but his rock steady dependability and utter reliability were an inspiration to his young crews.

Cheshire was dissatisfied with the marking of targets by the Pathfinder Force and he developed his own low-level marking technique that proved highly successful. Munro dropped flares from high level and Cheshire dived beneath them to accurately mark the targets for the following bombers.

On the eve of D-Day on June 5, 1944, No. 617 flew Operation Taxable, a complex flight requiring extremely accurate flying, navigation and timing. Munro, with Cheshire as his co-pilot, flew one of the lead aircraft in a series of orbits as it advanced across the English Channel towards the Pas de Calais dropping 'window' (reflective metal strips) to simulate an amphibious landing force approaching the area. This deception plan created doubt in the Germans' minds as to where the Allied landing was taking place and delayed the despatch of reinforcements to Normandy.

After the landings, the squadron flew in support of establishing the bridgehead. On the night of June 8, it had a spectacular success when Munro dropped one of the new 12,000-lb Tallboy bombs, which completely destroyed the Saumur railway tunnel.

On the following nights he dropped Tallboys on the E-boat pens at Le Havre and Boulogne before attacking the V-weapon sites at Wizernes and Mimoyecques. After this latter raid, his 55th, he and his fellow flight commanders were 'retired'.

He had recently been awarded the DSO.

Munro finished the war in command of a Bomber Defence Training Flight. He returned to New Zealand and left the RNZAF in February 1946 as a squadron leader.

Munro made a major contribution to community life in New Zealand and was mayor of Te Kuiti from 1978 to 1995. He was awarded the Queen's Service Order (1981) and appointed Commander of the New Zealand Order of Merit (1997) for "services to local government and community".

Munro retained strong links with his old squadron and made a number of trips to Britain. He was present when the Queen dedicated the Bomber Command Memorial in Green Park in 2012. Earlier this year he placed his medals with an auction house to raise money for the maintenance of the memorial. At the last minute, Lord Ashcroft stepped in, offering to donate £75,000 to the memorial's upkeep if Munro gifted his medals to the Museum of Transport and Technology in Auckland.

Les Munro's wife Betty predeceased him. They had five children.

AIR VICE-MARSHAL SIR JOHN SEVERNE

Air Vice-Marshal Sir John Severne (who died on October 4, 2015 aged 90) was a Cold War fighter pilot before becoming the equerry to HRH the Duke of Edinburgh. After a series of senior command posts in the RAF he was appointed captain of the Queen's Flight.

Ever since he was a small boy building model aeroplanes, Severne had been passionate about flying. His career in the RAF ranged from post-war fighters and jet trainers to the Nimrod maritime patrol aircraft. He won the King's Cup Air Race in 1960 and became the British Air Racing Champion the same year, flying a Turbulent aircraft entered by the Duke of Edinburgh. In addition to the 32 service aircraft types, he flew 39 different civilian light aircraft.

The son of a Royal Flying Corps observer and doctor, John de Milt Severne was born in London on August 15, 1925 and educated at Marlborough School. He joined the RAF in April 1944 and completed his training as a pilot in October 1945.

He first flew the Mosquito night-fighter with No. 264 Squadron for two years, before leaving for the Central Flying School (CFS), an organisation he would become very familiar with in later years. He trained as a flying instructor and spent the next few years teaching student pilots before returning to CFS to train instructors. In 1952, while serving at CFS, Severne was able to participate for the first time in the King's Cup Air Race, an annual event that had fascinated him from his school days.

In January 1954, he joined No. 98 Squadron flying Venom

day-fighter/ground-attack aircraft based in northern Germany close to the Iron Curtain. He was soon appointed a flight commander. On November 1, 1954 he was carrying out a looping manoeuvre when the engine of his Venom caught fire.

A few days earlier, a colleague had suffered the same failure and had died when he tried to land the aircraft. Severne would have been justified in ejecting from his single-engine fighter but elected to crash-land in order that investigations into the incident could be carried out. He landed alongside the runway with the wheels retracted as the fire continued to burn and he scrambled clear. For his gallantry he was awarded the AFC.

He converted to the Hunter fighter and in January 1956 took command of No. 26 Squadron, also based in northern Germany. Following the infamous Sandys' 1957 Defence White Paper, which stated that air-defence missiles would replace manned fighters, Severne had the distasteful task of telling his men that their squadron was to be disbanded.

After a year in the personnel department of the Air Ministry, he was appointed to be equerry to the Duke of Edinburgh. Among other duties Severne was responsible for making all travel arrangements for the Duke and accompanying him on many trips, which included flying with the Queen's Flight. This also gave him the opportunity to learn to fly helicopters.

In 1959 Severne entered the King's Cup Air Race flying a Turbulent painted in Prince Philip's colours. After a creditable performance, the aircraft was entered again the following year. A number of modifications were made, which resulted in Severne winning the coveted King's Cup while wearing his daughter's riding hat as a crash helmet. After two years, and promotion to wing commander, he was appointed Lieutenant of the Royal Victorian Order (LVO) and returned to RAF service.

After completing the RAF Staff College course, he flew Javelin and Lightning fighters during his appointment as wing commander flying at RAF Middleton St. George (now Teesside Airport). With the closure of the RAF airfield, he became the chief instructor of the Lightning Operational Conversion Unit at Coltishall in Norfolk.

Severne's next appointment was a very different affair. He left for Aden in January 1966 as the political situation in the Protectorate worsened. He was responsible for the operations of fighter, maritime-reconnaissance and helicopters working in close co-operation with the army. Hunter aircraft, which he flew on operations, were kept very busy patrolling the Yemen border and attacking dissidents. The Shackleton maritime patrol aircraft were heavily engaged in the Beira Patrol, the implementation of the Rhodesian oil embargo.

As the dissident and terrorism activity increased, Severne was also heavily involved with the planning for the withdrawal from Aden of British Forces scheduled for November 1967. On 28 November, the day before the final withdrawal, Severne was one of the last RAF officers to leave Aden. For his services he was appointed OBE.

Severne's already varied flying career took another turn in January 1971 when he was appointed to command the RAF's largest maritime base at Kinloss in Scotland. His three squadrons of Nimrods patrolled the North Atlantic shadowing Soviet submarines and powerful surface fleets. He accumulated almost 500 hours flying time in two years and once commented:"Flying low over the sea at 200 feet, at night, in bad weather, 1,000 miles over the North Atlantic, concentrates the mind no end." He also flew the Shackleton in the airborne early warning role. During his command of Kinloss, the station was awarded the Wilkinson Sword of Peace for 1971, which he accepted from the Duke of Edinburgh. In 1972 he was appointed as an ADC to the Queen.

After attending the Royal College of Defence Studies, Severne returned to the Central Flying School as commandant. This provided him with a wide variety of flying opportunities, including having the Red Arrows under his command.

After leaving CFS in February 1976 he spent two years responsible for all flying training in the RAF before taking over as commander, Southern Maritime Region, a role that also carried two senior NATO war appointments. He controlled all UK and NATO maritime aircraft, when operating out of British bases, south of a line from southern Ireland to Greenland. He also controlled the Rescue Co-ordination Centre, which included air-sea rescue helicopters. His last flight in the RAF was piloting a Whirlwind helicopter during a training air-sea rescue sortie. He retired from the RAF in 1980.

In 1982 he was recalled to be captain of the Queen's Flight and a member of the Royal Household. Severne travelled worldwide with members of the Royal Family. After seven years, he finally retired, at which point he was advanced to KCVO.

Severne and his family had always had a close interest in the horse world and in 1973 he was president of the RAF Equitation Association and later chairman of the Combined Services Equitation Association.

His retirement to Somerset was almost as busy as his service life. He served as a deputy lieutenant of the county from 1991 to 2001 and was honorary air commodore of No. 3 Maritime Headquarters of the Royal Auxiliary Air Force. He was president of the SW Region of the Royal Air Force Association and also president of the Queen's Flight Association and of the Central Flying School Association.

A man of great charm, he was a keen photographer and took a close interest in local affairs. He was chapel warden at Ditcheat Church and raised £25,000 for the restoration of the church's Alhampton Chapel, a project completed in 2011. He wrote his autobiography *Silvered Wings* in 2007. He never lost his love of flying and a week before his 90th birthday, and 80 years after his first flight in a Gypsy Moth, he took the controls of a Tiger Moth.

John Severne married Katharine Kemball in November 1951 and they had three daughters.

MARSHAL OF THE RAF SIR MICHAEL BEETHAM

Marshal of the RAF Sir Michael Beetham (who died on October 25, 2015 aged 92) was, with the exception of the RAF's founder, MRAF the Lord Trenchard, the longest-serving chief of the air staff (CAS) and was the RAF's senior surviving marshal on his death.

In a career that took him from flying bombing raids to Berlin during the Second World War to overseeing the RAF's successful role in the Falkland's War he was never less than personally courageous and a tenacious champion of the force.

Beetham became CAS on August 1, 1977 after Sir Neil Cameron had been promoted to be chief of the Defence Staff following the untimely death of Marshal of the RAF Sir Andrew Humphrey.

He inherited the appointment at a difficult time and at a relatively young age. Recognising the seriously impaired morale of the service following the heavy cuts his predecessors had been compelled to accept, he set about restoring some stability and the further improvement of the terms of service of RAF personnel. Along with his fellow chiefs, he had to address the severe problems of service pay, which were seriously hindering recruitment and causing an exodus of skilled people. The need for the military to meet the demands of the fireman's strike at the end of 1977 brought the issue into the public domain. By the middle of April 1978, the Labour government had not addressed the matter, so the four chiefs released details to the national press.

The story was covered in considerable detail and it attracted much public support but it earned the chiefs a very sharp public reprimand from the prime minister. Within a few weeks the Armed Forces Pay Review Board recommended a significant pay increase. On his first visit to an RAF station after this result, Beetham earned a spontaneous round of applause.

Soon after the election of Margaret Thatcher's government in 1979 he faced further serious challenges when it was decided to carry out a major defence review. Beetham had ensured that the senior appointments in the air staff were filled by the brightest men of that RAF generation. Thus he was well equipped to fight the RAF's corner, which he did with considerable skill, tenacity and resolve, during the Nott Review.

While major issues such as the purchase of Trident and the deployment of cruise missiles were being debated at chiefs of staff level, there were many RAF matters also engaging his attention. The Tornado had just entered service and he had to defend it against much unjustified criticism in the early days. The RAF's air defence posture was also far from satisfactory and the purchase of helicopters and development of the transport force were other important issues. He was also determined to build up the RAF Regiment and the revived Royal Auxiliary Air Force, which had been cut in the 1957 Defence White Paper.

He was nearing retirement when the Argentinians invaded the Falkland Islands on April 2, 1982. As Admiral Sir Terence Lewin was in Australia for defence talks, Beetham was acting chief of defence staff. He was undoubtedly vexed by the direct approach made by Admiral Leach, the First Sea Lord, to the prime minister, without any prior consultation with his fellow chiefs, during which he convinced her that the islands could be retaken by an amphibious-led assault.

He put this episode aside, however, and set about energetically drawing up plans on how the RAF could be involved most effectively. At the heart of this was Beetham's concern that the RAF should make a direct operational contribution and not be confined solely to the re-supply of men and materials. He put the whole of the RAF's transport fleet on standby, despatched Nimrods to Ascension Island and pressed successfully for the employment of RAF Harriers from the navy's aircraft carriers.

With his knowledge of strategic bombing and his expertise on air-to-air refuelling, he instructed his staffs to assess if a bombing attack against Port Stanley Airfield was feasible. He appreciated that there was little prospect of inflicting lasting, or major, damage but he believed such an attack, mounted at extreme range – the longest bombing operation in history at the time – would send a clear message to the Argentinians that air power based on Ascension Island could pose a major threat to mainland Argentina, in addition to boosting the morale of the islanders. He realised that such an attack was an especially demanding undertaking for his Vulcan bomber and Victor tanker crews but he pushed for it in the face of some scepticism in Whitehall.

For Beetham, the operation was a potent illustration of the case for the strategic impact and flexibility of air power which he had argued for during the previous year's defence review, and a confirmation that the qualities of daring and courage which he had experienced in Bomber Command during his time as a Lancaster pilot in the Second World War were still present in the service which he led. His personal staffs later recalled that at the moment he learned of the success of the operation, his eyes moistened and he beat his hand with his fist, a rare display of emotion.

A few months after the end of the Falkland's conflict, Beetham handed over the reins to his successor and retired from the service.

The son of Major G.C. Beetham MC, Michael James Beetham was born on May 17, 1923 in London and educated at St Marylebone Grammar School. He volunteered for the RAF in 1941 and trained as a pilot in the USA under the US/UK bi-lateral Arnold Scheme.

On his return to England, Beetham trained on Lancasters,

an aircraft he would describe later in his life as the one for which he had the greatest affection. He joined Bomber Command's No. 50 Squadron in November 1943 just as the Battle of Berlin had got underway and Beetham flew his Lancaster to the 'Big City' no fewer than 10 times. He also flew on the disastrous raid to Nuremberg on the night of March 30/31, 1944 when 96 of the bomber force failed to return. Such losses had a profound effect on the 20-year-old Beetham.

Although his bomber was damaged by anti-aircraft fire on a number of occasions, he faced his greatest danger on a training flight when he and his crew were forced to bale out of their burning Lancaster. He went on to survive 30 operations over Germany when the losses were at their highest. Assessed as an outstanding pilot, he was awarded the DFC for his gallantry and leadership.

After a period training bomber crews, he returned to operations as the war ended and dropped food supplies to the starving Dutch population during April and May 1945.

Offered a permanent commission in the peacetime RAF, Beetham served at HQ Bomber Command. In August 1949 he assumed command of No. 82 Squadron flying Lancasters on photographic survey and aerial mapping for the Colonial Office in East and West Africa.

In 1953 he moved to the operational requirements branch in the Air Ministry where the issues of bringing the three V-bombers into service took up much of his time. He was closely involved in drafting the specification for the TSR-2 aircraft, and its subsequent cancellation was, in his view, a grave mistake. During this period he attended the atomic weapons trials at Maralinga, Australia in 1956 where he witnessed the four tests. This experience had a major influence on his later strategic thinking and the employment of nuclear weapons.

Beetham joined the V-force in 1958 when he was given command of No. 214 Squadron operating the Valiant. The squadron was about to embark on air-to-air refuelling trials. He recognised the strategic significance this capability afforded for projecting air power at extreme range and he strove to perfect the flying techniques and procedures. A year later he felt ready to demonstrate the value of this additional capability with a number of special long-distance flights.

On July 9, 1959 he and his crew took off from Marham in Norfolk and headed for South Africa. Refuelling in the air twice, they arrived over Cape Town after a flight of 11 hours 28 minutes. A few days later they returned in just over 12 hours. These two non-stop flights broke the speed record for the distance and provided a convincing demonstration of the feasibility and potential of air-to-air refuelling. For his work, Beetham was awarded the AFC.

Then almost totally a Bomber Command man, Beetham spent the next four years in senior staff appointments working for some of the command's most dedicated and forthright commanders. These challenging times included the Cuban missile crisis and the shooting down of Gary Powers over the Soviet Union, an incident which exposed the vulnerability of the high-flying tactics of the V-force. The cancellation of Skybolt and the acquisition of Polaris, which led to the transfer of the UK's strategic nuclear deterrent capability to the Royal Navy, had major implications for Bomber Command and he was deeply involved in the staff work.

Identified as heading for the top of his service, there was a need to broaden his experience. So, in 1964, he was sent to Aden to command Khormaksar, then the RAF's largest operational base, operating a wide variety of tactical and transport aircraft, but no bombers. His arrival coincided with the start of a major terrorist campaign against British forces and his squadrons were in action over Radfan and in support of ground forces throughout the troubled colony.

After two years as the director of strike operations in MoD, Beetham took command of the RAF's Staff College at Bracknell. In August 1972, he became assistant chief of staff (Plans and Policy) at SHAPE, an appointment that over a number of years attracted the RAF's most capable senior officers. He worked under the charismatic and bullish American General Al Haig and his work was at the heart of NATO policy making, in particular the nuclear planning aspects. This unique opportunity to work in the international arena was to prove a great asset in his future appointments.

After a period as the deputy C-in-C at Strike Command, he left in January 1976 to be the C-in-C of RAF Germany and commander Second Allied Tactical Air Force. His RAF squadrons were in the midst of a major aircraft re-equipment programme and there was great emphasis on the ability of his airbases to survive any pre-emptive attack.

This exposure to tactical operations and integrating his squadrons' capabilities with those of other Allied air and land forces was invaluable when he took up his appointment as CAS. Beetham always maintained that his time in Germany was one of his most challenging and satisfying.

Throughout his career, Beetham was determined to keep flying and remain abreast of current capabilities and tactics. He was a very determined man who dominated his service during his time as CAS giving it strong leadership. He fought tenaciously for the RAF's cause and was unafraid of taking a combative stance if he felt it necessary. No detail escaped his attention, and he was always the master of his brief.

At heart, and more privately, he was an intensely loyal and compassionate man. He was, however, a product of his generation in not overtly displaying that latter quality. Indeed, he was seen by some as an authoritarian figure, not a natural communicator, and he never sought popularity but he was considered by many to be one of the RAF's strongest and most influential Cold War chiefs.

After retiring from the RAF, Beetham's services and experience were much in demand. For four years he was chairman of GEC Avionics Ltd but the RAF remained his greatest love. For many years he continued to have an influence on numerous service issues, all with a view to improving its capabilities and public image.

He joined the board of the RAF Museum at Hendon in 1984 at a time when it was emerging from the growing pains of early expansion. The addition of the Battle of Britain and the Bomber Command Halls had over-extended the finances. Beetham was determined to ensure the debts incurred were covered but the fundraising strategy he inherited was fatally flawed. In characteristically vigorous style, and with the help of key trustees, he negotiated for the debt to be paid through a loan agreement with HM Treasury.

With the survival of the museum in question, Beetham's consistent support of the organisational changes introduced by a new director secured its future. With confidence restored and the foundations laid for its financial future, he retired in 2000 after 15 years as chairman. In recognition of his significant service the trustees named their new conservation centre at RAF Cosford after him in 2002.

Determined to put the RAF's history on a formal footing, he was a leading instigator in the formation of the RAF Historical Society in 1986 and remained the society's president until his death. He also gave immense support to the RAF Club in Piccadilly and was a long-serving president who always took the closest interest in the club's affairs.

For many years he was president of the Bomber Command Association. He was instrumental in the erection of a statue to his wartime chief, Sir Arthur Harris, at the RAF Church of St Clement Danes in London. After it became apparent that successive governments would not sanction a Bomber Command medal, he poured his energy and influence into the creation of a major memorial to all the lost aircrew of the Command. Despite failing health, he was determined to see the culmination of his efforts and he was able to attend the dedication of the memorial by HM the Queen in Green Park in July 2012.

Beetham never forgot his lost colleagues. In 1981 he unveiled a memorial on the site of his old airfield at Skellingthorpe near Lincoln, which commemorates the 1,984 men killed flying from the airfield. He was assiduous at attending annual reunions, on one occasion meeting up with four men of his old crew who had not seen each other since the end of the war.

A keen golfer and tennis player in his younger days, and in retirement a captain of the Royal Norfolk Golf Club, Beetham was appointed CBE (1967), KCB (1976) and GCB (1978). He was a deputy lieutenant of Norfolk, was elected as a Fellow of the Royal Aeronautical Society (1982), and was an Honorary Liveryman of the Guild of Air Pilots and Air Navigators. He was awarded the Polish Order of Merit in 1998.

Michael Beetham married Patricia Lane in 1956 and they had a son and daughter.

SQUADRON LEADER KEITH THIELE

Squadron Leader Keith Thiele (who died on January 5, 2016 aged 94) was decorated four times as a bomber and a fighter pilot and was one of only four New Zealand-born airmen to earn three DFCs; he also won a DSO.

His career as a bomber pilot began in October 1941 when he flew Wellingtons with No. 405 Squadron. Returning from a raid on Cherbourg in January 1942 he had to make a crash-landing in his damaged aircraft.

After converting to the four-engine Halifax, Thiele flew on the first 1,000-Bomber Raid to Cologne and the second to Essen a few days later. His Halifax came under heavy attack but he successfully weaved his way through the searchlights and anti-aircraft fire.

After completing 32 operations, 11 on the Halifax, Thiele was rested and awarded the first of his DFCs. His obvious leadership qualities were soon recognised and he was promoted directly from flying officer to squadron leader. Instead of completing the customary six months' rest, he volunteered to return to operations after just two months when he was posted to No. 467 Squadron to fly Lancasters.

En route to attack Berlin he pressed on to the target despite two of his crew having to attend to a sick colleague. On another occasion he returned from a target at low level to allow his gunners to engage the enemy searchlights and anti-aircraft defences.

In March 1943 he attacked Nuremberg. An engine caught fire on the outward journey but he continued to the target. A month later he attacked Stuttgart when his Lancaster was badly damaged and he had to make a forced-landing on two engines and one main wheel at an airfield on the south coast. He was awarded the DSO for his "outstanding courage".

On his 56th operation he attacked Duisburg on the night of May 12, 1943. As he approached the target, his Lancaster was badly damaged but he pressed on and held the bomber steady for the bombing run. Over the target, the aircraft was hit again, destroying an engine.

He had just stabilised the aircraft when another shell disabled a second engine, damaged the cockpit and wounded Thiele and another crew member. He regained control and headed for England steadily losing height. He made a crash-landing at an airfield in Norfolk without injury to his crew, an action which resulted in the award of an immediate Bar to his DFC. The citation highlighted his "exceptional valour and skill".

At the end of his tour, he was offered command of No. 617 Squadron to replace Guy Gibson but Thiele, the thrice-decorated 22-year-old squadron leader, turned down the opportunity because he was determined to fly fighters.

Keith Frederick Thiele was born in Christchurch, New Zealand on February 21, 1921 and educated at Christchurch High School for Boys. He spent a brief time as a reporter on the *Christchurch Star-Sun* before joining the RNZAF to train as a pilot. In June 1941 he travelled to Britain to complete his training as a bomber pilot.

For a period after finishing his tour on No. 467 Squadron, he ferried Canadian-built bombers across the Atlantic. In February 1944 he achieved his ambition to be a fighter pilot when he converted to Spitfires, then joined No. 41 Squadron based in southern England.

Over the next six months he flew 100 operations escorting light bombers and on cross-Channel sweeps to attack ground targets including operations on D-Day. As the V-1 flying bomb campaign opened, he flew 'anti-diver' patrols and shot down one of the terror weapons.

In October he converted to the Typhoon and completed another 50 operations with No. 486 Squadron attacking enemy transports in the Netherlands and Germany. During ground-strafing operations, he destroyed two Luftwaffe transport aircraft and damaged 14 locomotives, numerous barges and motor transports. He was also successful in the air and in December shot down a Messerschmitt Bf 109 over Malmédy and on December 29 he shot down another over Münster when the enemy pilot baled out.

In early January 1945 he was given command of No. 3 Squadron flying the RAF's most powerful piston-engine fighter, the Tempest. He continued to attack ground targets but on February 10 during an armed-reconnaissance sortie he was hit by ground fire over Paderborn and was forced to bale out.

Slightly wounded, he was taken prisoner, and received some rough treatment, but he was only held captive for a few weeks before escaping from a transit POW camp near Frankfurt. On March 31, he and a colleague slipped away on bicycles and later 'acquired' a motorcycle. They crossed the Rhine on the bridge at Remagen before reaching US ground forces. He returned to his squadron but he was not medically fit for further operational service. A few weeks later, he was awarded a Second Bar to his DFC, one of only 50 awarded during the Second World War.

Thiele returned to New Zealand and, after a brief spell as a journalist, he commenced a long career as an airline pilot. He moved to Australia and became a senior captain with Qantas.

An avid adventurer, Thiele twice had his tiny yacht *Spitfire* smashed by mountainous waves, during sailing excursions on the notorious Tasman Sea, yet managed to sail home.

He later built and operated a marina in Sydney and, aged 80 years, he sailed his own yacht across the Tasman Sea to see New Zealand's first America's Cup defence.

Keith Thiele was survived by his daughter.

AIR VICE-MARSHAL JOHN HOWE

Air Vice-Marshal John Howe (who died on January 27, 2016 aged 85) was one of the RAF's most experienced and capable Cold War fighter pilots, whose flying career spanned Second World War piston-engine aircraft to the supersonic Lightning and Phantom.

In early 1960, Howe was appointed to command the RAF's first Lightning squadron, No. 74 'Tiger' Squadron, based in Norfolk. The aircraft provided a great advance in technology and performance, with a remarkable rate of climb to heights in excess of 60,000 feet and was able to fly at twice the speed of sound.

With no simulator or two-seat training version of the aircraft, Howe made his, and the squadron's, first flight on June 14, 1960. A few weeks later he was tasked to provide a four-aircraft formation for the annual Farnborough Air Show.

Despite the inevitable early teething troubles with the complex aircraft, Howe and his pilots flew on all but one day of the show. The squadron was made the RAF's official aerobatic team for 1961 and it was in demand to appear at British and European shows. For the 1961 show at Farnborough, Howe trained and led a 'diamond nine' formation.

Howe realised that air shows were good for publicity and potential international sales, but it hindered the development in achieving a full operational capability. He drove himself, and others, hard, but he was a highly respected leader. The squadron's high morale helped it to reach operational status within the first 10 months despite the many problems that had to be overcome.

He said of the Lightning: "It was one of the most exhilarating aeroplanes, even by today's standards." At the end of his tour, Howe was awarded the AFC.

John Frederick George Howe was born in East London, South Africa on March 26, 1930 and educated at St Andrew's College, Grahamstown. As soon as he left school, he joined the South African Air Force and trained as a pilot. In early 1951 he joined No. 2 Squadron, known as the Flying Cheetahs, which was based in South Korea as part of the United Nations forces.

The squadron, equipped with the piston-engine Mustang, was heavily engaged in the ground-attack role in support of the army. On June 24, Howe took off with three others. They responded to an emergency call for air support by a surrounded ground force. In the face of intense anti-aircraft fire, the four Mustangs attacked gun emplacements a number of times. Howe did not expect to survive but the four aircraft returned to base. All four pilots received US gallantry awards. A month later, Howe was forced to crash-land and was rescued by a helicopter.

In September, as a 21-year-old second lieutenant, he was

the leader of four aircraft tasked to attack enemy troops threatening friendly forces. Fierce enemy fire damaged Howe's aircraft but he continued to lead his formation in further attacks on the target. The US authorities awarded him an immediate DFC, the citation recording: "He displayed a standard of leadership above and beyond that normally expected."

After completing his flying tour, Howe remained in Korea as a forward air controller before returning to South Africa. At the end of 1954 he travelled to Britain to join the RAF.

In April 1956 he joined No. 222 (Natal) Squadron flying the Hunter. When a volunteer was required for forward air controller duties with No. 3 Commando Brigade in late 1956, Howe's experience in Korea helped land him the job. He sailed with the brigade for the ill-fated Suez campaign and, at dawn on November 6, he landed on the beaches at Port Said with No. 40 Commando, to direct aircraft on to targets in the area. In the event, the campaign was short lived.

Howe returned to his squadron before joining No. 43 Squadron as a flight commander, still flying the Hunter. He was awarded a Queen's Commendation for Valuable Service in the Air, receiving a second two years later. In June 1959 he started training to take command of his Lightning squadron.

Howe remained in the fighter business, including a tour of duty with the USAF, which gave him an opportunity to fly the latest American fighters including the Phantom. In 1968 he was appointed to command the RAF's operational conversion unit that saw the introduction of the Phantom into RAF service, his unit being responsible for the conversion of the first squadron crews.

After a staff tour he became the station commander of RAF Gütersloh, the home of two Lightning squadrons and a support helicopter squadron. His fighter squadrons, based a few minutes flying time from the border with Warsaw Pact forces, mounted a continuous quick reaction capability. He rarely missed an opportunity to maintain his fighter pilot proficiency.

After attending the Royal College of Defence Studies, he served at HQ 11 (Fighter) Group, and on promotion to air commodore, was appointed the commandant of the Royal Observer Corps (ROC). The organisation had a fine record but Howe justifiably believed that it was in need of modernisation and a more robust attitude. With his usual, not always popular, vigour, he set about applying the same exacting standards and tight discipline to the ROC as he did to his flying. By the time he left in 1980, the efficiency of the corps had risen sharply.

In May 1980 he was appointed the air officer commanding the Southern Maritime Region, a departure from his previous fighter experience and where his usual forceful approach was much in evidence.

His final appointment in the RAF was the dual role of commandant general RAF Regiment and Provost Marshal of the RAF. He retired in November 1985. He was appointed CB (1985) and CBE (1978).

In his younger days, Howe was a high-spirited officer who knew how to enjoy life and trouble was no stranger to him following some of his more extreme escapades – his 'Zulu war dance' at social functions was a speciality. But on duty he was utterly professional and he set himself and those around him difficult goals.

In retirement he was a sheep farmer in Norfolk, where he was known as the 'supersonic shepherd'; he retired in 2004. He was a very capable skier and a devoted chairman of the Combined Services Skiing Association. He was a sailor and a keen follower of rugby. His biography, *Upward and Onward* was published in 2008.

John Howe married Annabelle Gowing in March 1961 and they had three daughters.

WING COMMANDER ARTHUR ALDRIDGE

Wing Commander Arthur Aldridge (who died on December 20, 2015 aged 95) was one of the RAF's most successful torpedo-bomber pilots and his attacks on enemy shipping earned him two DFCs.

Aldridge was a Beaufort pilot with No. 217 Squadron, which arrived at Malta in early June 1942. On June 15, reports were received that the Italian Fleet was positioning to attack a crucial re-supply convoy heading for the island. Eight aircraft, armed with torpedoes, were ordered to attack. Aldridge was delayed before finally taking off and, to make up time, he chose not to follow the dog-leg route of the others but to fly direct to the estimated position of the enemy fleet.

He arrived at sunrise ahead of the rest of the squadron and immediately spotted a large naval force. He was well positioned and decided to attack immediately. He picked out a heavy cruiser and positioned to drop his torpedo from 800 yards. It struck the 10,500-ton *Trento* causing severe damage. A Royal Navy submarine, *Umbra* had seen the action and closed in to fire another torpedo. The Italian cruiser sank.

Six days later the squadron was again involved in a major action. Two Axis merchant ships, escorted by Italian destroyers, were carrying valuable cargo to Rommel's army in North Africa. Nine Beauforts took off, with Aldridge leading one section. He attacked the 7,700-ton *Reichenfels* in the face of withering anti-aircraft fire. He dropped his torpedo from 750 yards at a height of 80 feet. As he released his weapon his aircraft was hit, wounding him and a member of his crew. The aircraft was badly damaged.

While his gunner was tending Aldridge's wound, a German fighter was seen about to attack another Beaufort. Aldridge immediately flew to his colleague's aid, positioned his aircraft close and engaged the fighter, which broke away. The two aircraft staggered back to Malta.

The *Reichenfels* was hit, caught fire and had to be abandoned. Aldridge was awarded a Bar to his earlier DFC.

The son of a clergyman, Arthur Harold Aldridge was born on August 23, 1920 near Florence, Italy being partly of Italian descent. His first nine years were spent in Italy before he attended St Lawrence College, Ramsgate. In 1939 he went up to St Edmund College, Oxford to read Modern Languages and after a year he interrupted his studies and volunteered to be a pilot.

He completed his training in Canada and in August 1941 joined No. 217 Squadron, a torpedo-bomber squadron operating the Beaufort aircraft from St Eval in Cornwall.

His early sorties were into the Bay of Biscay and to lay mines off the French ports of Brest and Lorient. Early in December some of the squadron's Beauforts, including Aldridge, were sent to Manston in Kent for attacks off the Dutch coast.

On December 9, 1941, Aldridge and his crew took off with two other aircraft to head for the Hook of Holland where a convoy had been reported. The water was too shallow for the use of torpedoes so each Beaufort carried four 500-lb bombs. Flying at 50 feet, the formation of three aircraft spotted the convoy, which was escorted by two armed vessels. Attacking in line, the leader's bombs hit the 8,777-ton U-boat depot ship *Madrid*. The anti-aircraft defences were intense and the second aircraft, flown by his closest friend, was shot down immediately in front of Aldridge.

Flying below mast height, Aldridge approached, pulling up slightly to drop his bombs, which hit the bows of the ship. As he climbed away, his port wing hit a bracing wire on the ship's mast and six feet of the Beaufort's wing was sheared off. With great difficulty he managed to maintain control and head for the nearest airfield in Kent. With the light fading, he landed the badly damaged aircraft.

At the time Aldridge left the scene of the action the ship was on fire and later reports confirmed that the *Madrid* had sunk. Aldridge won an immediate DFC, the citation concluding, "he showed great courage, combined with rare skill and judgement".

Early in February 1942 intelligence indicated that the German battlecruisers *Scharnhorst* and *Gneisenau*, together with the heavy cruiser *Prinz Eugen*, were preparing to leave Brest. No. 217 moved to Thorney Island near Portsmouth in anticipation that the fleet would sail up the English Channel. The Germans took advantage of very bad weather on February 12 and made a dash up the Channel. They remained undetected until near the Straits of Dover before the British launched attacks.

Six Beauforts took off from Thorney Island, including Aldridge and his crew, and attempted to locate the fast-moving fleet. In the murk, Aldridge saw a huge ship at close range and launched his torpedo before breaking away to safety. He never identified the ship and later he learned that his torpedo had missed as the three ships escaped.

On June 3, the squadron departed for Ceylon but on arrival at the beleaguered island of Malta, the plan was changed and it was tasked to attack enemy shipping in the Mediterranean.

The squadron suffered heavy losses in Malta and finally headed for Ceylon in August. Aldridge was rested and served on the staff before returning to No. 217 as a flight commander in April 1944 when the squadron was operating the Beaufighter.

Aldridge left the RAF in early 1946 and resumed his studies at St Edmund College before teaching French and German at Glasgow Academy. In 1954 he took up an appointment at King's School, Worcester where he spent the next 26 years.

During his time at King's School he formed the air section of the Combined Cadet Force (CCF), which he led for 20 years, assuming command of the whole cadet force section in later years.

A cultured man, Aldridge enjoyed the music of Beethoven, Mozart and Schubert, as well as the art of the Italian Renaissance. He was also a keen tennis player in his early years and cricket remained a lifelong interest. He wrote of his war experience in *The Last Torpedo Flyers* (2013).

Arthur Aldridge married Beryl Jones in 1948; she died in December 2011. They had two sons and a daughter.

WING COMMANDER LEN RATCLIFF

Wing Commander Len Ratcliff (who died on April 1, 2016 aged 96) flew agents into occupied Europe and was one of the RAF's most decorated special duties pilots.

He was an experienced bomber pilot and instructor when he joined No. 161 Squadron at the secret RAF airfield at Tempsford in June 1943. Initially he flew the four-engine Halifax dropping supplies and agents into France, Denmark and Norway at night. On one occasion he was crossing the French coast when one of the aircraft's engines failed but he decided to press on. He found the dropping zone near Mâcon, north of Lyon, and dropped two agents and two packages from a height of 600 feet. With daylight approaching, he headed for Algeria where the dead engine was replaced before he returned to his base.

Later in the year, Ratcliff flew to a field east of Bordeaux and dropped Yvonne Cormeau, code name 'Annette', one of SOE's most successful wireless operators whose exploits were immortalised in the 2001 film *Charlotte Grey*.

In December 1943 Ratcliff was awarded a Bar to an earlier DFC for his "unfailing devotion to duty" and a month later took command of the squadron's new Hudson Flight. He flew his first sortie almost immediately and landed in a field near Angers with an SOE officer who was to bring back Henri Déricourt – suspected of being a double agent – for interrogation. Déricourt became suspicious and persuaded the SOE officer that he had to secure a new landing ground and Ratcliff returned with eight agents but not with Déricourt. A Lysander picked him up a week later.

When landing fields were unavailable, agents were parachuted from the Hudson. In February Ratcliff dropped Wing Commander F. Yeo-Thomas (known to the Gestapo as the White Rabbit) who was later captured but survived and was subsequently awarded the George Cross.

In April, Ratcliff took command of the Lysander flight. The single-engine, black painted aircraft was capable of very short take-offs and landings making it ideal for the hazardous operations. Flying alone, the pilot had to carry out precise navigation in order to find the small fields lit only by a handful of torches held by the reception party.

On the night of April 28/29 he took three agents to a field near Chartres and on May 9 he flew one of three Lysanders to a field near Touraine taking in two agents and returning with three. The three aircraft flew independently to a landmark on the River Cher, arriving within three minutes of each other. Ratcliff headed for the rough airstrip, identified the coded flashing signal and landed. He was airborne again within five minutes allowing the second aircraft to land. After almost six hours he landed back in England.

A month later, Ratcliff had completed 40 special duties flights and was rested when he was awarded the DSO. The sensitive nature of his work prevented a detailed citation being published.

Leonard Fitch Ratcliff was born in Maldon, Essex on July 27, 1919. He joined the RAF Volunteer Reserve in June 1939 and trained as a pilot.

In July 1941 he was posted to fly the Hampden. New pilots flew their first sorties in the twin-engine bomber as the navigator so Ratcliff attended a brief navigation course, which was to stand him in good stead later when he flew his clandestine operations over France alone.

He joined No. 49 Squadron at Scampton near Lincoln in July 1941. Over the next six months he flew 30 operations, the majority to industrial targets in the Ruhr and to Hamburg. He also flew operations to drop mines in the entrances to occupied ports and river estuaries in Germany, the Netherlands and France.

On the night of December 28 night-fighters intercepted his aircraft as he headed for the synthetic rubber plant at Hüls. He skilfully evaded the attackers and went on to the target. A few weeks later he was attacking the German capital ships at Brest when he was again intercepted but his evasive action allowed his gunners to frustrate the attacks of the two enemy fighters. At the end of his tour he was awarded the DFC for "setting a very valuable example".

After leaving No. 49 Squadron Ratcliff spent a year as a bombing instructor when his service was recognised with the award of the AFC.

Ratcliff's long tour with No. 161 Squadron came to an end in October 1944 when he was posted to the Air Ministry's Directorate of Intelligence where he dealt with the clandestine activities carried out in occupied Europe.

In February 1945, he returned to Tempsford as a wing commander in charge of operations but, following the loss of No. 161's commanding officer on operations, he assumed command of the squadron until the end of the war when there was no further requirement for such a unit. He left the RAF in December 1945.

The French government awarded him the Croix de Guerre (with Palm) and later he was invested as a Chevalier de la

Légion d'Honneur. He also added the Air Efficiency Award to his British decorations.

After the war, Ratcliff settled in Essex. He was a successful grain merchant gradually expanding his business before becoming a director of Spillers.

He was appointed High Sheriff of Essex in 1988 and he made a major contribution to the life of Halstead. In 1948 he was a founder member of the Halstead Rotary Club, which he supported all his life. In 1985 he became chairman of the League of Friends of Halstead Hospital. In recognition of his long service and fundraising activities, a rehabilitation centre at the hospital was named the Leonard Ratcliff Building in 2015.

A modest, unassuming man, Ratcliff maintained close contact with his fellow RAF special duties colleagues. In 2010 he was invited by the French authorities to help dedicate the Musée de la Resistance et de la Deportation in the town of Bourges close to where he had once landed agents. In May 2015 he was a special guest at a Tempsford commemoration where he spoke of his wartime experiences.

Leonard Ratcliff married Betty Stewart in August 1939 and she predeceased him. They had three sons and a daughter. His second wife Dorothy survived him.

EILEEN YOUNGHUSBAND

Eileen Younghusband (who died on September 2, 2016 aged 95) served in Fighter Command during the Second World War and helped plot the launching points of the V-2 rockets that threatened to devastate London.

By late 1944, the second of Hitler's 'terror weapons', the V-2 ('Vengeance 2') ballistic missile, was being launched against London and also Antwerp, the Allies major port during the advance into the Netherlands and Germany. The V-2 could be launched almost anywhere from specially adapted lorries, making it highly mobile and hence very difficult to detect.

It was impossible to intercept once airborne so it was essential to destroy the missile before it was launched – or destroy the launcher.

In December 1944, and with the threat to Antwerp becoming acute, Eileen and a number of her Women's Auxiliary Air Force (WAAF) colleagues travelled to Mechelen in Belgium to join a team aiming to identify the launch points of the missile. Their only tools were their knowledge of mathematics and a slide rule. Knowing the landing spot and the trajectory of the missile it was possible to calculate the position of the launch point.

Time was of the essence since the launchers could move within 10-15 minutes after a launch. Patrolling fighter-bombers were briefed in the air and attacked the sites with bombs or rockets. By early March most of the launchers had been destroyed.

The daughter of a Royal Flying Corps pilot, Eileen Muriel Le Croisette was born in London on July 4, 1921 and educated at Southgate County School.

As a young au pair in France, she was sent home during the Munich crisis, sharing her railway carriage with Jews escaping Nazi persecution. Only weeks before the outbreak of war, she was in Germany, experiencing the menace of Hitler's regime. She later provided tea and sympathy for trainloads of British soldiers returning from Dunkirk, and she witnessed the Blitz on London.

Aged just 19, she volunteered to serve in the WAAF and

was trained as a plotter to work in Fighter Command's control rooms. She was commissioned in 1941 and worked at No. 10 (Fighter) Group HQ at RAF Rudloe Manor near Bath before moving to the Headquarters of Fighter Command at Bentley Priory.

There she worked in the filter room, the key element of the air defence operations room. It was the job of her section to filter the many reports received from radar sites, observation posts, radio-intercept posts, and other intelligence sources sent to the centre and then present a coherent picture of the air situation to the plotting room and the fighter controllers. This 'air picture' then had to be constantly updated.

She was on duty during the D-Day landings, the launching of the V-1 flying bomb campaign and she received the first 'Big Ben' (code name for a V-2 attack) warning of the V-2 rocket, which landed in Staveley Road, Chiswick on September 8, 1944 and was the first to land in London.

At the end of the war, Eileen Younghusband, who was fluent in French, worked as a translator at the Breendonk concentration camp in Belgium, a time she found particularly harrowing. She left the WAAF in December 1945.

She spent most of her post-war career in the hospitality industry, working in hotels and catering, taking on the male establishment in the industry.

She moved to Wales in 1984 and became an advocate for health and education issues and in 2012 was awarded the British Empire Medal for services to lifelong learning.

At the age of 87 she completed a degree from the Open University and was named as one of the students of the year. She published her autobiography *Not An Ordinary Life* in 2009. "The girls who worked in that section," she wrote, "many of them nearly 90 years old, have never felt that the work they did has been recognised, so this is one of the reasons that made me write this book." A second book, *One Woman's War*, was awarded the People's Book Prize in 2013. A children's book *Eileen's War* was published shortly before her death.

In 2014 she made an emotional return to the Belgian

concentration camp, in the company of two teenage RAF cadets from Wales, to lay to rest an experience she said had haunted her all her life. She has been described as "a remarkable woman, an inspirational figure, who was tireless in promoting the work of the women who helped to defeat Nazi Germany".

A life-size statue of Eileen Younghusband as a young WAAF officer stands in a replica filter room at the Battle of Britain Museum at Bentley Priory.

She married Peter Younghusband in 1944. He and their son predeceased her.

LIEUTENANT GENERAL WILHELM MOHR

Lieutenant General Wilhelm Mohr (who died on September 26, 2016 aged 99) escaped from his native Norway following the German occupation to fly fighters with the RAF rising to become the chief of the Royal Norwegian Air Force (RNoAF) and to hold senior NATO appointments.

When the Germans invaded Norway on April 9, 1940, Mohr was the deputy commander of a reconnaissance squadron based near Trondheim. It was soon apparent that the airfield would become untenable so skis were fitted to the aircraft and Mohr and his men headed to an army unit further south, where he took command of the squadron.

Mohr and his pilots flew reconnaissance sorties to identify German advances but by the end of the month it was clear that south Norway would have to be surrendered. Mohr headed for the west coast when his aircraft was attacked and damaged en route, but he reached the HQ for the remnants of the Norwegian Army Air Arm on a frozen lake. He met the commanding general of the Norwegian Forces, who gave him permission to escape to Britain.

Mohr left the small port of Molde on May 2 with other Air Arm personnel, but their fishing boat was attacked and sunk. Undaunted, they commandeered another and headed for the Shetlands.

Wilhelm Mohr was born on June 27, 1917 in Fana on the west coast of Norway near the city of Bergen. In 1936 he joined the Norwegian Army Air Arm and trained as a pilot. A year later he started his officer studies at the Norwegian Army's Military Academy. He was selected to attend the Massachusetts Institute for Technology, but with war threatening he returned to flying duties.

Mohr soon demonstrated his courage and tenacity. In late 1938 an emergency call came to evacuate a pregnant woman from a remote farm. Owing to the bad weather, overland travel was impossible, so Mohr flew his bi-plane to the area and with the woman sitting on his lap, he took off and she was safely taken to a hospital.

After reaching England, Mohr soon left for Canada. Following the successful escape to England of the Norwegian royal family and government, it was decided to establish a training base for all Norwegian military personnel and a site near Toronto was chosen. Mohr was one of the first flying instructors and he played a key role in establishing what became known as 'Little Norway'.

He returned to the UK in May 1941 and joined No. 615 Squadron to gain combat experience on the Hurricane. He was soon made a flight commander and took part in attacks over northern France. He provided fighter escort to a force of heavy bombers on a daylight attack against German capital ships in Brest.

In January 1942 Mohr became a founder member of No. 332 Squadron, the second Norwegian fighter squadron equipped with the Spitfire. After a brief spell as the deputy commander, he assumed command in April. Operating from RAF North Weald, just north of London, Mohr led his squadron in attacks over France. During one operation he was in combat with a Focke-Wulf Fw 190 when he was wounded in the face but he continued to fly on operations.

On August 19, the two Norwegian Spitfire squadrons provided fighter support for the ill-fated raid on Dieppe. Mohr was involved in dogfights with Luftwaffe fighters and was wounded in the leg but continued his patrol for a further 30 minutes; his squadron accounted for seven of the enemy. On landing he refused treatment until he had organised a further operation by his squadron. Shortly afterwards he was awarded the DFC for his actions over Dieppe.

In September, King Haakon VII and his family visited North Weald and Mohr, with his foot in plaster, was presented with the Norwegian War Cross with Swords. A few weeks later he married his fiancée Jonna who had served as a courier with the Norwegian Resistance but had been forced to flee to Sweden in late 1941 where she worked for a year as a secretary for the Norwegian defence attaché before leaving for England.

Mohr continued to fly on operations before being rested in April 1943. Six months later he joined No. 132 (Norwegian) Wing as the wing commander plans. On the morning of D-Day he flew a patrol over the beachhead in his Spitfire and later commented, "the impression stays overwhelming".

Within weeks, Mohr and his wing moved to a makeshift airstrip in Normandy to provide close support for the Allied ground forces. Over the next few months the Norwegians moved eastwards to Belgium and the Netherlands, attacking lines of communication, trains and enemy formations. Two weeks after the German surrender he landed back in Norway.

For three years he was the aide-de-camp to King Haakon and he played an important role in establishing the RNoAF. After a series of appointments in Norway he spent three years in Washington as Norway's representative on NATO's Military Committee. In 1960 he was appointed chief of staff of the RNoAF and three years later became its commander-in-chief, a post he held for six years.

In 1969 he was appointed deputy commander-in-chief of NATO's Allied Forces Northern Europe and later was the director of the National Defence College in Oslo, before retiring in 1975. He was leader of the Norwegian Civil Aviation Accident Commission from 1977 to 1989.

A modest man, Mohr was reluctant to emphasise his own role in the Second World War or his service in the RNoAF. He retained a deep interest in air force doctrine, contributed numerous articles to Norwegian military publications and lectured to air force cadets. He was recognised as one of the most influential officers in the history of the RNoAF and was often described as "the grand old man of the air force".

In October 2010 aged 94, he flew in a Vampire jet of the RNoAF's Historical Squadron, more than 50 years since his last flight in the fighter.

Mohr was appointed a Commander of the Order of St Olav (Norway) and a Knight of the Order of Danneborg (Denmark). He was also awarded the Legion of Merit (USA).

Wilhelm Mohr's wife predeceased him and they had a son and two daughters.

MOLLY ROSE

Molly Rose (who died on October 16, 2016 aged 95) was a pilot in the wartime Air Transport Auxiliary (ATA) and became one of the 'Spitfire Women' when she delivered 273 of the fighters from aircraft factories to RAF units.

Already a qualified pilot, she joined the ATA in September 1942 and initially flew light aircraft such as the Tiger Moth before advancing to more powerful single-engine aircraft. As her experience increased she started flying the Hurricane fighter

and then progressed to the Spitfire, which she described as "a thrilling moment".

For much of her service she flew from Hamble airfield, an all-female unit near Southampton. On some days she flew three or four different types of aircraft. Before flying a new type, the pilots read aircraft notes and used a detailed checklist prior to starting up the aircraft and taking off. They flew without a radio, and many airfields were camouflaged and difficult to find. On one occasion she had to interrupt a cricket match being played so that she could land on one airfield and, as she taxied away, the game was resumed.

She also delivered twin-engine aircraft such as the Anson and the Hudson, before she started flying the Wellington bomber, which she found "nice to fly". She mastered the Beaufighter and Mosquito, aircraft that could develop a pronounced swing on take-off and which many RAF pilots found a handful. As the war progressed she transferred to the more advanced Spitfire variants, the Typhoon and the powerful Tempest fighter-bomber.

While at Hamble she saw the forces assembling for the forthcoming invasion of Europe in June 1944. Her husband

Bernard, a captain in the 4th City of London Yeomanry (Sharpshooters), was embarked in a tank landing craft. A week later it was reported in a national newspaper that he had been killed in action. But she continued with her flying duties and six weeks later learnt that he had survived and was a prisoner of war.

That was her busiest year and during it she delivered 253 aircraft. She added a further 94 the following year, which included the Mustang, before leaving the ATA in May 1945 as a first officer. Altogether she delivered 486 aircraft and flew 38 different types. She never flew again as a pilot.

The daughter of David Marshall, the founder of Marshall Aviation of Cambridge, Molly was born on November 26, 1920 and educated at a school near Cambridge before spending a year at a finishing school in Paris.

In 1937 she joined the family business as an apprentice engineer, working in the hangars and maintaining aircraft engines. Her older brother kept a Tiger Moth in a field behind the family home and she persuaded him to teach her to fly. She gained her pilot's licence when she was aged 17; the same year she got her driver's licence and in 1939 she married Bernard Rose.

In 1942, just after her husband had left for North Africa with his armoured regiment, she received a call inviting her to join the ATA. She travelled to London in her new uniform to have a formal photograph taken and sent a copy to her husband with a note: "I hope you don't mind darling, I've just joined up!"

After completing her training she was based at Luton before moving to the ferry pool at White Waltham and then, in September 1943 to Hamble close to the Supermarine factory where many Spitfires were built.

Post-war she settled in Oxford where her husband became a lecturer in music at The Queen's College; he was later appointed Informator Choristarum and a fellow in music at Magdalen College where he was to spend the rest of his distinguished musical career.

Molly Rose sat as a magistrate for the Bullingdon circuit and was later the chairman of the bench. She was a dedicated charity fundraiser in the county and was appointed a deputy lieutenant for the county of Oxfordshire in 1983, and in 1990 was appointed OBE for "services to Oxfordshire". She was for many years a parish councillor for Appleton-with-Eaton.

Molly Rose was a generous hostess and many music scholars and choristers enjoyed tea and dinner parties at their home. After the death of her husband in 1996 she continued to lead a very busy social life and on September 11, 2016, shortly before her death, former musical protégés were invited to celebrate what would have been her husband's 100th birthday. After lunch and a tea, a concert of Bernard Rose's music, conducted by one of their sons, was performed to a full St Mary's Church in Bampton.

In September 2008 the service of the 'Forgotten Pilots' of the ATA was finally formally recognised and Molly attended a ceremony at 10 Downing Street, where Prime Minister Gordon Brown presented her and other survivors with the ATA Veteran's Badge.

In 2014 she was one of the veteran guest judges at *The Great British Menu, the D-Day Banquet* on BBC television.

Molly and Bernard Rose had three sons.

WING COMMANDER BRANSE BURBRIDGE

Wing Commander Branse Burbridge (who died on November 1, 2016 aged 95) was the RAF's most successful night-fighter pilot, being credited with the destruction of 21 enemy aircraft, including four during one patrol.

Teamed up with Flying Officer 'Bill' Skelton, he achieved the first of his successes on the night of February 23, 1944, during the Luftwaffe's Operation Steinbeck, known as the 'baby blitz', a series of lightning hit-and-run bombing attacks on southern England.

Flying a Mosquito of No. 85 Squadron, Skelton gained a contact on his radar set near Beachy Head and directed Burbridge behind an enemy night-fighter. After a long burst of cannon fire, one of the crew baled out and the fighter crashed into the sea.

Over the next few weeks, the two men accounted for a further four aircraft and each was awarded an immediate DFC. They achieved further successes during the summer, including the destruction of three V-1 flying bombs.

Having flown in support of the D-Day landings, Burbridge and Skelton began operating over occupied France. On the night of June 14/15 they intercepted a Junkers 88, flown by the Luftwaffe *Experten* (ace) Major Wilhelm Herget, and shot the aircraft down – Herget survived. Ten days later Burbridge claimed another Junkers 88, but debris from the enemy aircraft hit his radiator forcing him to return to base on one engine.

By September, flying a more advanced Mosquito, the pair were to achieve an astonishing run of success over Germany. It began on September 11 when they shot down an enemy night-fighter. A month later they were supporting a Bomber Command raid on Brunswick when two more fell to their guns, from one of which a parachute was deployed.

On the night of November 4, the two men, by now dubbed by the national press as the 'night hawk partners', took off to provide support for a bombing raid on Bochum. Over the Bonn area, Skelton picked up on his radar tube a stream of contacts and he directed Burbridge on to them. They soon identified a Junkers 88 night-fighter and shot it down. Continuing their patrol, Skelton obtained another contact and after a brief engagement, a second Junkers was destroyed.

The two now joined the homeward bound bomber stream to protect it from attack. Within minutes they saw an enemy fighter, pursued it and shot it down. This was not the end of their night's work; they destroyed a fourth.

Bill Rawnsley, another night-fighter ace, later described this remarkable sortie as "the most extraordinary of all long-range escort patrols ever accomplished". Both Burbridge and Skelton received a Bar to their DFCs and a few weeks later they were awarded the DSO.

Their success continued and they downed a Messerschmitt Bf 110 over Mannheim on the night of November 21 when return fire damaged their cockpit. Flying in support of RAF bombers attacking targets in Germany, they accounted for four more enemy fighters before the end of the year.

On January 2, 1945 the two men took off to support a bombing raid on Ludwigshafen in Bavaria. Skelton gained a contact and Burbridge closed in on a Junkers 88. A short burst sent it crashing to the ground. It was the crew's 21st and final success. The following morning, Group Captain John 'Cat's Eyes' Cunningham, their former CO, telephoned his congratulations on their having surpassed his total of 20 to become the most successful British and Commonwealth night-fighter partnership of the war.

The crew were gazetted for a Bar to their DSOs and in March they left No. 85. Burbridge was later awarded an American DFC.

The son of a Wesleyan preacher, Bransome Arthur Burbridge was born on February 4, 1921 in East Dulwich, London and educated at Alleyne's Grammar School. He was working in the City of London on the outbreak of hostilities in September

1939. As a committed Christian and pacifist, he initially registered as a conscientious objector, but he later felt an increasing unease about his position and in September 1940 he joined the RAF. By October 1941 he had completed his training as a night-fighter pilot and joined No. 85 Squadron, commanded by the Battle of Britain ace, Peter Townsend.

Flying the Havoc, an aircraft not ideally suited to operating as a night-fighter, he had to wait until the following June to achieve his first success, when he was credited with probably destroying a German bomber near Ipswich. The squadron re-equipped with the Mosquito in August but further success eluded him and at the end of the year he became an instructor at a night-fighter training unit. In July 1943 he returned to No. 85 Squadron where he teamed up with 'Bill' Skelton.

In Skelton, Burbridge had found an ideal partner. Both were committed Christians (Skelton was later ordained an Anglican priest) and they made every effort not to aim at the cockpit of their targets in the hope that the crew could escape, as a number of them did. Burbridge claimed that successful night fighting was based on teamwork and he described his navigator as "magnificent". They maintained a lifelong friend-ship until Skelton's death in 2003.

After leaving No. 85 in March 1945, Burbridge became the commanding officer of the Night-Fighter Leader's School. In May he met Major Herget, whom he had shot down a year earlier, and invited him to be a guest speaker at his unit. He took him for a flight in a Mosquito and, before departing, Herget countersigned his host's flying logbook acknowledg-ing the victory.

Burbridge left the RAF in December 1945 to read History at St Peter's College, Oxford. He considered entering the Church but in 1948 he joined the staff of Scripture Union (SU), pi-oneering the work of the Inter-School Christian Fellowship. His goal was to create and support extra-curricular Christian groups in secondary schools, where young people could meet to encourage one another in the pursuit of their faith.

Burbridge gained the respect of many head teachers across

the country who acknowledged the value of SU's ministry in schools. Christian groups mushroomed as a consequence. A gifted artist and musician, he used creative methods of communication to engage with the youth culture of the 1960s and, under his leadership, SU produced a range of multi-media educational resources for young people.

In addition Burbridge developed holiday activities for young people and launched residential courses for sixth-formers, in a wide variety of academic disciplines, exploring the relevance of Christian faith to science and arts-based studies.

By the mid 1970s, by which time he had taken up a part-time role with the Oxford Pastorate, an Anglican chaplaincy serving the university, his work took on a global focus. Often travelling with his wife, he continued his ministry to school pupils and students in many countries.

The last phase of Burbridge's life was deeply affected by worsening dementia, but despite this he taught his family and friends much about living gracefully and patiently with a declining body and mind. After the death of his wife Barbara (née Copper) in 2012 – they had been married since 1949 – he needed specialist care and to provide the necessary funds for this his family reluctantly decided to sell his medals. His son commented at the time, "we value him more than the medals". The money raised allowed Burbridge to live the rest of his life in comfort.

Branse Burbridge was survived by a son and a daughter.

AIR VICE-MARSHAL PETER LATHAM

Air Vice-Marshal Peter Latham (who died on December 5, 2016 aged 91) flew fighter aircraft throughout the Cold War and was the leader of the Black Arrows formation aerobatic team, one of the predecessors of today's RAF Red Arrows.

No. 111 Squadron, always known as 'Treble One', had formed an aerobatic team under the leadership of Squadron Leader

Roger Topp. Flying all-black Hunter aircraft, and supplemented by aircraft from other squadrons, they had grabbed the headlines when they performed a 22-aircraft formation loop at the 1958 Farnborough Air Show; the first time such a manoeuvre had been flown.

Latham assumed command of Treble One in October 1958, a few weeks after the Farnborough event. Having flown in other formation teams during his earlier career as a fighter pilot, he brought with him the same enthusiasm for formation aerobatics as his predecessor.

By this time, the Black Arrows had become the RAF's official aerobatic team and Latham realised that more was required than just a perfect display of precision flying. As one of his pilots commented: "We were now in the world of entertainment."

Latham introduced bolder manoeuvres and new sequences for the nine-aircraft team. He also brought in innovative formations and gave them attractive names such as the 'wine glass' in addition to the more traditional such as 'diamond nine'. He ended each display with a 'bomb burst', when each aircraft disappeared in different directions. The added attraction of smoke trails made the team's performance even more compelling. On occasions he used all 16 of his squadron aircraft flying in tight formation and the squadron's flypast opened the 1959 Farnborough Air Show in spectacular fashion.

The team was in great demand at air shows at home and abroad throughout 1959 and their superb performances resulted in the award of the Royal Aero Club's Britannia Challenge Trophy, the first time it had been awarded to an RAF squadron. It was presented to Treble One by the Duke of Edinburgh.

Fittingly, the Black Arrows completed their final display over the squadron's home base at RAF Wattisham in November 1960. Since its formation, the team had displayed over 150 times, often at overseas venues including the Paris Air Show.

In June 1960, Latham was awarded the AFC "in recognition of his leadership of the Black Arrows and the international esteem in which its work is held".

The son of a master plumber, Peter Anthony Latham was born in Birmingham on June 18, 1925 and educated at St Phillips Grammar School, Birmingham. He grew up immersed in his father's workshop learning engineering skills, which developed throughout his life.

He enlisted in the RAFVR in March 1943, but it was almost a year before he was called up. In the meantime, he attended a short course at Cambridge University where he studied mechanical engineering. With a surplus of pilots in the later stages of the war, he spent a few months as a motor transport driver.

He completed his flying training in August 1946 and joined No. 26 Squadron flying the powerful piston-engine Tempest from an RAF base in Germany. This heralded the beginning of a long career as a fighter pilot.

In 1949 he converted to jets and flew the Meteor with No. 263 Squadron. Here he had his first experience of formation aerobatic flying as a member of the squadron team, which performed at the Farnborough Air Show in 1950. After a spell as the adjutant of No. 614 (Auxiliary) Squadron, flying Vampire fighters, he returned to No. 263 Squadron to be a flight commander. He was awarded a Queen's Commendation for Valuable Service in the Air (the first of two) and was sent to be an instructor at Fighter Command's Day Fighter Leader's School, where he converted to the Hunter. After a spell in the Air Ministry he took command of No. 111 Squadron.

After attending the RAF Staff College in 1961 he served in MoD before being posted to RAF Akrotiri in Cyprus where he commanded the Strike Wing of four Canberra bomber squadrons and a reconnaissance squadron.

On promotion to group captain he joined the air staff at HQ No. 38 Group, the RAF's mobile tactical force which included transport aircraft, helicopters and the Harrier, which operated from dispersed sites at various European locations. Always keen to fly, Latham added the army's Auster observation aircraft to his list of aircraft flown.

In April 1969 he moved to Singapore to take command of Tengah, the RAF's largest operational airfield in the Far East, where he had RAF, RAAF and RNZAF fighter and bomber squadrons equipped with Canberra, Hunter and the supersonic Lightning fighters. Latham remained current as a pilot flying all these types. He remained in command until September 1971, when he handed over the base to the new Singapore Air Force. He was a very popular station commander and he and his wife Barbara were described by one of his squadron commanders as "a great team", a description that would be used in later appointments.

On returning to Britain he joined the operational requirements staff in the MoD, and two years later was appointed commandant of the Officers and Aircrew Selection Centre at RAF Biggin Hill. He returned to No. 38 Group as the senior air staff officer, an appointment giving him further opportunities to fly operational aircraft.

After two years in MoD, Latham was appointed in September 1977 as the air officer commanding (AOC), No. 11 (Fighter) Group responsible for the air defence of the UK. The mainstays of his force were the Phantom and Lightning squadrons together with the Bloodhound surface-to-air missile squadrons. He was also responsible for implementing a major upgrade of the UK's air-defence radar and reporting system and its integration into NATO control systems.

Shortly before relinquishing his post as the AOC, Latham made valedictory visits to his stations including RAF Coningsby, home to two Phantom squadrons and the Battle of Britain Memorial Flight. On the morning after a formal farewell dinner there he was offered a final flight in a Phantom. He declined, saying he would prefer to fly the Hurricane. The station commander could hardly refuse the request, but waited with bated breath to see the precious aircraft return safely – which it did.

Latham was greatly admired throughout the RAF. Personable and with a well-developed sense of humour, he was protective of his staff and his ability to take everything in his stride helped create a happy and effective organisation. He was appointed CB (1980).

On retirement from the RAF he was for five years the principal of Oxford Air Training School before becoming the director of CSE Aviation. He was the senior service advisor of Short Brothers until 1990, and he joined the International Air Tattoo, retiring as honorary president in 1999.

Latham's greatest passions after flying and his family were sailing and horology. He was commodore of the RAF Sailing Association for six years and president of the Association of Service Yacht Clubs. He discovered horology by accident. Knowing that he was a good engineer, a friend asked if he could repair her clock. He tried, and ultimately became an expert repairing antique clocks. Later he was elected as a liveryman of the Clockmakers Company and a member of the court of assistants. In 1996 he was appointed master.

Peter Latham married his childhood sweetheart, Barbara Caswell, in September 1953 with whom he had two sons and six daughters.

SQUADRON LEADER DENNIS BARRY

Squadron Leader Dennis Barry (who died on March 10, 2017 aged 95) was one of the first RAF pilots to convert to the Meteor jet fighter before flying against the V-1 flying bomb and operations over Germany in the final weeks of the Second World War.

Barry was an experienced flight commander on No. 616 (South Yorkshire) Squadron who led offensive patrols over northern France in the build up to D-Day. Shortly after providing support for the Allied landings in their Spitfires in June 1944, the pilots left for Farnborough to convert to the Meteor.

After two flights in a training aircraft to practise twin-engine flying, the pilots clustered round the cockpit of the Meteor, were shown the instruments, briefed on the drills and the flying characteristics and then told to take off on their first familiarisation sorties. After five flights, they were deemed 'qualified on jets'. Barry described this conversion from single-engine piston aircraft with a tail wheel to a twin-engine jet with a tricycle undercarriage as "rudimentary, not least since there were so few Meteors available".

Barry returned to the squadron when his flight continued to operate the Spitfire over the Normandy bridgehead but by the middle of August, the squadron had a full complement of 14 Meteors.

The aircraft had been rushed into service to help combat the V-1 flying bomb menace and was sent to Manston to operate over Kent. The squadron enjoyed modest success against the terror weapon before the Allied armies overran the launch sites in the Pas de Calais region.

Dennis Albert Barry was born in London on August 26, 1921 and educated at Haberdashers School. He joined the RAF in October 1940 and trained as a pilot before joining No. 504 Squadron to fly Hurricanes. Shortly after his arrival the squadron converted to the Spitfire.

He flew many offensive patrols over France before attending a fighter leader's course. In September 1943 he joined No. 616 Squadron as a flight commander and continued to fly bomber escort and intruder operations before converting to the Meteor jet.

With the demise of the V-1, Barry took four aircraft to a USAAF base where they provided jet 'opposition' for the long-range American fighters, which flew in support of the USAAF 8th Air Force's bomber force. Tactics to combat the Luftwaffe's new Messerschmitt Me 262 jet fighter were developed when the US commanding general described the exercises as being "of inestimable value".

In mid-January, No. 616 was assigned to the Second Tactical Air Force and on February 4, 1945 Barry led four aircraft to Melsbroek airfield near Brussels, the first RAF jets to be deployed to the continent. The aircraft were painted white to enable Allied troops to distinguish the Meteor from the German jet fighters.

On March 26, Barry moved his flight to the Netherlands when the Meteors were used in the ground-attack role attacking motor transports, aircraft on the ground and troop concentrations. The squadron ended the war at Lübeck attacking targets on the Danish border.

The pilots flew in a number of victory air shows, the biggest near Copenhagen held in the presence of Queen Ingrid, when Barry led a low-level flypast by 12 Meteors. This was a spectacular success, as was the final departure from Copenhagen a few days later. Barry later wrote: "The local population was well informed of our departure since I was able to look up at the spire of the city hall as I led the formation of 12 aircraft through the city."

At the end of July it was announced that he had been

awarded the French Croix de Guerre with Palm.

Barry returned to civilian life in Sheffield but with the reformation of the Auxiliary Air Force squadrons in June 1946 he re-joined No. 616, initially to fly the Mosquito before Meteor jets arrived.

During a flight on January 8, 1950 both engines of his Meteor failed at 25,000 feet. He descended in a glide but was still in cloud at 1,500 feet. With no ejector seats fitted to the early Meteors, he had no option but to bale out breaking his leg as he hit the frozen ground. His was one of very few successful manual escapes from a jet fighter. Shortly afterwards, he left the Royal Auxiliary Air Force.

Barry spent many years in the motor trade establishing Central Motors in Sheffield, his own dealership for Daimlers, Jaguars and the Alvis. He played squash and golf until late in his life and was a keen supporter of the 616 Squadron Association.

Dennis Barry married Brenda Nelson in 1947 and she died in December 2015. They had a son and a daughter.

WING COMMANDER PETER ISAACSON

Wing Commander Peter Isaacson (who died on April 7, 2017 aged 96) was a highly decorated Royal Australian Air Force Pathfinder pilot who later had a distinguished career in publishing in Australia.

Isaacson had completed one tour of operations as a bomber pilot when he joined No. 156 Squadron in late November 1942. The squadron was re-equipping with the Lancaster and had just been selected as one of the first five squadrons to form the nucleus of the new Pathfinder Force. Using new navigation aids and dropping flares and target indicators, Isaacson and his fellow crews marked the target for the main bomber force following behind.

Over the next few months Isaacson attacked industrial targets in Germany during the Battle of the Ruhr. On one of his

early raids as a Pathfinder, his Lancaster was damaged when a German night-fighter attacked it and he escaped into cloud before pressing on to the target. On the night of March 1, 1943 he had dropped his target markers over Berlin flying at 17,000 feet when his aircraft was hit by anti-aircraft fire and severely damaged.

The controls to the tail plane had been badly disabled, a gun turret was put out of action and the aircraft lost a great deal of height but, with the aid of two of his crew, he was able to regain control and level out at 4,000 feet. On the return flight, a cone of searchlights illuminated the Lancaster for 15 minutes before Isaacson escaped. At this stage his aircraft had lost more height and was flying at 900 feet. Still over enemy territory, and in a perilous situation, he managed to get the bomber back to base. He was awarded an immediate DFC, the citation commenting that he was "an outstanding captain". Two of his crew were also decorated.

The son of an Australian soldier who had fought in World War One and an Austrian mother, Peter Stuart Isaacson was born on July 31, 1920 in London. When he was six his family moved to Melbourne in Australia where he was educated at Brighton Grammar School. Aged 16, he became a messenger boy for the *The Age* newspaper.

In December 1940 he started training as a pilot, initially in Australia and then in Canada before returning to England to convert to bombers. Nearing the completion of his course

Bomber Command launched a series of 1,000-Bomber Raids. To make up the numbers, some Wellingtons were flown by instructors and students from the bomber training units and Isaacson flew on the first two raids against Cologne and Essen in May and June 1942. He then joined the recently formed No. 460 (RAAF) Squadron.

Soon after joining the squadron, Issacson and his all-Australian crew attacked Kassel. An enemy night-fighter damaged their Wellington as they were leaving but Isaacson managed to escape. On a raid to Turin, they were one of only two crews to bomb despite bad weather. In November, the squadron sent seven aircraft to Mannheim when severe icing was encountered; Isaacson's crew was the only one to bomb the target successfully. A week later, returning from Munich, they were attacked over Belgium and the two gunners beat off the night-fighter.

When Isaacson had completed 22 operations he was awarded the DFM. His CO described him as "exceptional and an ideal leader". He was commissioned and he and his crew volunteered for the Pathfinder Force and joined No. 156 Squadron in late November 1942.

On completion of their tour with No. 156 Squadron, having flown 45 operations, they were selected to fly their Lancaster 'Q for Queenie' to Australia. They set off on May 21, 1943 and, after a 15-hour flight over the Atlantic, they flew over Canada and the USA before heading across the Pacific. On arrival at Sydney, as the first Lancaster to reach Australia, large crowds including the prime minister and the governor general met them. For this first east to west flight from the UK to Australia by the RAF, Isaacson was awarded the AFC.

Over the next few months, the crew flew the bomber around Australia and New Zealand to encourage people to buy war bonds – £250 bought a flight and £5 a look around the aircraft. The tour offered the crew the opportunity to 'beat up' cities, towns and RAAF bases. On October 22 they were demonstrating the aircraft at Sydney when Isaacson dropped down to 100 feet over the harbour and then, on impulse, flew under the Sydney Harbour Bridge. This was captured on film and reinvigorated the war bond campaign.

Isaacson left the RAAF in February 1946 and began a career in publishing that lasted for almost 50 years. He launched his first newspaper in 1947 before he established Peter Isaacson Publications. When he sold off his group of companies he was the largest independent publisher in Australia.

He built a stable of suburban papers, which transformed the Australian newspaper business. Among his 60 Australian titles were dozens of industry publications and the *Sunday Observer*. He also started a company in Singapore, which published 14 titles. In 1969 he founded the Pacific Area Newspaper Publishing Association and was made an honorary life member in 1987. In 1991 he was appointed a member of the Australian Order for his services "to the print media and the community".

For 60 years he served in support of the Victorian Shrine of Remembrance first as a trustee, then chairman and finally as a life governor.

His guiding principle in life was: "When in doubt, do the courageous thing."

Peter Isaacson married Anne McIntyre in 1950 and she died in 2016. They had two sons.

AIR VICE-MARSHAL PETER COLLINS

Air Vice-Marshal Peter Collins (who died on April 17, 2017 aged 87) had a long career as a Cold War fighter pilot, which included many years associated with the Lightning aircraft.

Collins was already an experienced day and night-fighter pilot when he became a member of a five-man team tasked with the introduction into RAF service of the Lightning. The single-seat twin-engine aircraft, with its spectacular rate of climb and performance, offered a major advance in capability compared to previous fighters. Equipped with the latest air

intercept radar it was capable of operations in all weathers.

Collins and his four colleagues joined the Air Fighting Development Squadron based at the Central Fighter Establishment (CFE) in Norfolk in September 1959. This proved to be the beginning of a long association with the fighter capable of flying at almost twice the speed of sound. He commented: "It was one of those life-changing experiences, which would determine much of my future career in the RAF." For the next two years he was involved in the development of the Lightning and its weapon system. At the end of his tour he was awarded the AFC.

His next appointment was to the RAF Handling Squadron at Boscombe Down where he was responsible for producing pilot's notes for a number of RAF aircraft including the first aircrew manual for the Lightning.

After a brief tour at the MoD and attendance at the RAF Staff College, Collins resumed his connection with the Lightning when he became the flight commander on No. 23 Squadron at RAF Leuchars in September 1966. The aircraft mounted quick reaction alert (QRA) at 15 minutes readiness and aircraft were scrambled on numerous occasions to intercept and escort Soviet bombers entering UK airspace.

In February 1967, Collins was tasked to reform No. 11 Squadron with the latest version of the Lightning. During his time as the acting CO, the squadron made the first trial flights with external fuel tanks mounted on top of the wing; on one occasion he completed a sortie of eight hours.

After a tour at HQ Strike Command as wing commander air defence, Collins was appointed to command No. 111

'Treble One' Squadron, operating the Lightning from RAF Wattisham in Suffolk. At the end of his tour he was assessed as "an exceptional flyer and squadron commander".

Peter Spencer Collins was born in Dover on March 19, 1930 and educated at the Royal Grammar School, High Wycombe and Birmingham University where he read History. He began his flying career with the university air squadron in 1948 before doing his National Service in 1951 at the height of the Korean War.

After completing his training as a pilot, he elected to remain in the RAF and flew Meteor day-fighters with No. 63 Squadron before converting to Venom night-fighters. He joined No. 141 Squadron at Coltishall and in 1957 the squadron became the second to convert to the Javelin.

In April 1958 he joined the All-Weather Development Squadron at the CFE as a trials pilot where he was involved in the tactical development of the air-to-air missile-armed Javelin. In 1959, he transferred to the Air Fighting Development Squadron to introduce the Lightning into service.

At the end of his time in command of No. 111 Squadron in July 1972 he was promoted to group captain and returned to HQ Strike Command, responsible for air defence. His role was to review the potential vulnerability of the Linesman-Mediator air defence ground environment. The report of his team led to the implementation of a new organisation for the UK Air Defence Ground Environment.

In the spring of 1974, Collins was appointed the station commander at RAF Gütersloh in Germany, the home of two Lightning squadrons, two helicopter squadrons and two squadrons of the RAF Regiment. Situated near to the Inner German Border with the Warsaw Pact, the Lightning squadrons were tasked with QRA and the air defence of the region with other NATO allies.

After attending the year-long course at the Royal College of Defence Studies, Collins was appointed the senior air staff officer at No. 11 (Fighter) Group in March 1981. The Lightning was still in squadron service but it shared its UK air defence role with Phantom squadrons. Collins was also able to see how his proposals for the air defence ground environment had been implemented and developed.

His final tour before retiring in 1985 was as director general Communications, Information and Organisation in the MoD. He was appointed CB in December 1984.

After leaving the RAF, Collins worked for Marconi Defence Systems in a number of senior consultant and director appointments. He maintained a close link with his squadron associations and was the honorary president of the Essex Wing of the Air Training Corps and vice president of the Chelmsford Branch of the Royal Air Force Association.

Collins was a strong, kind, thoughtful man with unshakeable integrity whose concern was for those around him rather than himself. He listed his interests as golf, music and gardening but his greatest love was his family.

Peter Collins married Sheila Perks in 1953 and she died in 2000. They had three sons and a daughter.

WING COMMANDER REX SANDERS

Wing Commander Rex Sanders (who died on May 10, 2017 aged 94) was the lead navigator of a select nine-man RAF team that flew USAF reconnaissance aircraft on a series of top secret, and highly risky, spy flights deep into the Soviet Union in the early 1950s.

In August 1951, three RAF bomber crews flew to a USAF base in Louisiana to train on the North American RB-45C four-engine jet reconnaissance aircraft. The leader of the team was Squadron Leader John Crampton and Sanders was his navigator. The following February the crews were briefed on the operation code named Ju-Jitsu.

Four RB-45Cs were flown to an RAF base in north Norfolk, where they were shorn of their USAF markings and

repainted with RAF roundels (one aircraft was to act as a spare).

After Crampton and Sanders had flown a practice flight – a high-speed, high-altitude sortie along the Berlin Air Corridor to test the Soviet reaction (there was none) – Prime Minister Winston Churchill gave approval for the top-secret flights. Sanders recalled: "We went at full throttle...to try and stir things up. We were like ferrets going into a rabbit warren."

The three aircraft took off on April 27, 1952 and headed over Denmark where they refuelled from airborne tankers. Crampton then turned south-east for Russia flying at 36,000 feet. Electronic intelligence was gathered and photographs taken of the targets; the aircraft landed back at base after an uneventful 10-hour flight.

The three crews returned to normal duties, but the special unit was reformed in April 1954 for another series of flights. On the 28th, Crampton and Sanders headed for Kiev; the longest of the three flights. Sanders had just taken some photographs when the RB-45C came under anti-aircraft fire. Realising that his aircraft had been identified and was being tracked by ground radars, Crampton applied full power and turned west towards Germany, some 1,000 miles away.

General Vladimir Abramov, commander of the Kiev region, revealed in later years that he had ordered MiG fighter pilots to try and ram the spy aircraft but they were unable to reach the 36,000 ft to intercept the RB-45C.

This highly clandestine Cold War episode remained a closely guarded secret until 1994 when the BBC and the

Daily Telegraph disclosed some details. Sanders was among retired RAF personnel interviewed on the BBC's *Timewatch*
programme a few years later. When asked for his views, he responded: "I think it was an amazing decision and very much
reflects the character of Churchill. Had we gone down, there
would have been quite a furore."

The RAF and USAF commanders considered the flights
valuable and Crampton and his crews were decorated, Sanders
receiving the AFC, adding a Bar for the second flight.

The eldest of five children of a civil servant, Rex Southern
Sanders was born on December 14, 1922 at Bridlington and
brought up in Wandsworth, south-west London, where he attended the Central School. No great academic, he was a good
sportsman and he ended up as the swimming captain. He left
school at 15 and took a job as a draughtsman; he was working
at an ordnance factory at Wrexham when war broke out.

In April 1941 he enlisted in the RAFVR, training as a navigator in Canada under the British Commonwealth Air Training Plan. On his return to Britain he completed a bombing
course and in October 1943 joined No. 78 Squadron based in
Yorkshire, operating the four-engine Halifax.

Within a few weeks of his arrival, Bomber Command
embarked on its most intensive period of operations with
the start of what became known as the Battle of Berlin.
Sanders made a number of sorties to the 'Big City', which he
described as "quite difficult".

Nevertheless, before the first operation he had told the crew
he was happy to bomb Berlin because his parents had been
bombed out of their home in London. "We didn't have any
reservations," he remembered. He also attacked other major
cities before the bombers were switched to targets in France
in preparation for the D-Day landings.

On the night of June 5, 1944 he attacked gun batteries on
the Channel coast, unaware that the air and sea invasion was
about to begin. He recalled: "Coming back my radar showed the
Channel chock-a-block with ships. I told the crew: 'This is it'."

Sanders was rested after completing 33 operations. In 11 months his crew were only the third in their squadron to complete a full tour of duty. More than half had been lost. He was awarded the DFC.

Having been a religious person before the war, by the end of it Sanders had lost his faith, and in later years he reflected: "When I look back on it now it weighs very heavily on me…I feel badly about dropping bombs on civilians but it just had to be I suppose. I've closed my mind to so much."

He went to India in April 1945 but the war against Japan came to an end before he flew on operations.

On his return to Britain he specialised in navigation before his clandestine flights and in August 1953 he assumed command of No. 35 Squadron flying the US-built B-29 Washington bomber, before the squadron converted to the Canberra twin-engine jet bomber.

After completing the RAF Flying College Course, when he made a hazardous flight to the North Pole in a Canberra, Sanders specialised in guided weapons before he served on a Thor Intercontinental Ballistic Missile Site in Norfolk.

After two years as the air adviser to the Pakistan Air Force he assumed command of RAF Aberporth on the Welsh coast from where air-defence missiles, including the Bloodhound surface-to-air guided missile, were tested. His final appointment was a five-year tour in the MoD operational requirements directorate. His secret work resulted in him being appointed OBE.

He retired in December 1977, after which he took up painting and lived quietly in Norfolk before eventually settling on the west Wales coast. He had no children himself but became something of a mentor to his autistic step-grandson Tommy, patiently encouraging the boy in his considerable practical skills.

Rex Sanders' first wife Gloria died in 1986. He later married his second wife Rhiannon who had a son.

AIR VICE-MARSHAL GEORGE CHESWORTH

Air Vice-Marshal George Chesworth (who died on May 24, 2017 aged 86) specialised in maritime air patrol and anti-submarine operations and was one of the RAF's most experienced officers in this role, first as a pilot and then as a senior commander.

His first tour as a junior pilot involved flying operations during the Korean War and in his last appointment, he had a key role in the Falklands air campaign. In the intervening years, he tracked the Soviet Navy's formidable surface and submarine fleets and was involved in the 'Cod Wars' with Iceland.

As the chief of staff at HQ No. 18 Group located at Northwood, the Joint Force Headquarters for Operation Corporate, Chesworth was responsible for co-ordinating the flying in support of the task force in the South Atlantic. Following the decision to re-take the islands, his Nimrod squadrons were soon in action flying surveillance operations and in support of the fleet before it was decided that the opening shot of the war would be a bombing attack on the runway at Stanley airfield on East Falkland.

The air commander (Air Marshal Sir John Curtiss) immediately sent Chesworth to Ascension Island where he arrived on April 29, 1982 to oversee the operation (Black Buck). The following day he received the message to mount the ambitious plan and then watched two Vulcan bombers (one a reserve) and the fleet of 15 Victor tankers take off. All that he and the planning team could do was wait anxiously for their return. After 14 hours the final Victor returned very short of fuel. Two hours later the Vulcan (XM 607) and a Nimrod, which had provided rescue cover, finally landed after a successful mission, which was then the longest-ever bombing raid.

Fuel margins for all three aircraft were critical and Chesworth had anticipated the possible loss of all of them. He drafted a signal ready to send to Curtiss should the aircraft fail to return, but as the Vulcan of Flight Lieutenant Martin Withers landed he was able to telephone his chief with the news that the attack had been a success. Almost immediately he was asked to prepare for a similar operation the following day but he insisted that an in-depth analysis of the raid had to be completed before a further one could be contemplated.

Chesworth returned to Northwood to continue with his key role at the headquarters. In the post-war honours list he was appointed CB.

George Arthur Chesworth was born in Beckenham, Kent on June 4, 1930 and educated at Wimbledon Technical College. He was called up for National Service in July 1948 and served in the RAF, training as a pilot. He was commissioned and decided to remain in the service.

After converting to the Sunderland flying boat he was posted to Singapore to join No. 205 Squadron, one of three that formed the Far East Flying Boat Wing. Over the next two-and-a-half years he flew operations during the Malayan Emergency but much of his time was spent on detachments to Japan, flying anti-submarine patrols and weather reconnaissance flights during the Korean War. He flew 53 operational sorties, some in extreme weather and sea conditions, and was awarded the DFC for "gallant and distinguished service in Korea".

After tours as a flying instructor and at the Second Tactical Air Force in Germany, he returned to the maritime role and converted to the Shackleton before serving as the flight commander of No. 201 Squadron based in Cornwall when his squadron was placed on standby during the Cuban missile crisis. After attending the RN Staff College, he served as a wing commander in the operational requirements branch at the

MoD where he wrote the air staff requirement for the Nimrod maritime patrol aircraft, the Shackleton's replacement.

This appointment marked the beginning of his long association with the Nimrod. He took command of No. 201 Squadron at Kinloss in Morayshire, initially flying the Shackleton, but in early 1970 the squadron converted to the Nimrod, the first in the RAF to do so. At the time, the Soviet Navy was expanding into a formidable force and making regular forays into the North Atlantic, the Norwegian Sea and transiting to Cuba. His Nimrods tracked them and gathered valuable intelligence. For his services in command of No. 201 he was appointed OBE.

After a short tour as a staff officer with the US Navy in San Diego he returned to command RAF Kinloss in August 1972, by which time there were three resident Nimrod squadrons and a Shackleton airborne early warning squadron. The Nimrods provided support for the Royal Navy's submarines tasked with maintaining the British strategic nuclear deterrent. His squadrons also flew surveillance patrols during the fishing disputes with Iceland in addition to monitoring Soviet Navy movements; they also provided an immediate air-sea rescue capability.

On promotion to air commodore, Chesworth took charge of the Central Trials and Tactics Organisation. In April 1979 he became chief of staff at HQ 18 Group until he retired in 1984.

Chesworth settled in Morayshire where he was active in local affairs and with RAF charities in Scotland. From 1985 to 1988 he was chief executive of the Glasgow Garden Festival. He was appointed a JP in 1992 and served as Lord Lieutenant of Morayshire (1994–2005). He was vice president for the charity Houses for Heroes.

He was a great supporter of reserve military units in Scotland. These included being Honorary Air Commodore of No. 2622 (Highland) Squadron Royal Auxiliary Air Force, RAF Regiment; Honorary Colonel of No. 76 Engineer Regiment (Volunteers), and chairman of the Air Training Corps Council for Scotland and Northern Ireland.

Chesworth remained devoted to the RAF and was deeply upset at the cancellation of the Nimrod MRA 4 aircraft and, with it, the loss of the important maritime air patrol capability at which the RAF excelled. One of his staff described him as a "wise leader and perfect gentleman".

George Chesworth's wife Betty, to whom he was married for 65 years, died in 2016. Their two daughters survived him. Their son was killed whilst serving with the army in Germany.

SQUADRON LEADER WALLY LASHBROOK

Squadron Leader Wally Lashbrook (who died on June 6, 2017 aged 104) piloted one of the aircraft on the first commando raid made by British airborne forces in 1941; he was later shot down over France and evaded capture to cross the Pyrenees into Spain with the aid of the Comet Escape Line.

Lashbrook had completed 29 bombing raids over Germany when he and his crew were selected to join a force of eight aircraft for Operation Colossus, a daring airborne assault to destroy the fresh-water aqueduct at Tragino in Southern Italy. Six of the Whitley bombers were converted to drop paratroopers, the other two to drop supplies.

After a period of training, the aircraft set off on a 10-hour flight to Malta. The operation was mounted on the night of

February 10/11, 1941. Lashbrook flew in the first formation
of three aircraft, led by Squadron Leader J.B. Tait (who would
lead the raid that finally sank the *Tirpitz* to earn his fourth
DSO). The three aircraft reached the valley at low level and
as soon as Lashbrook saw the aqueduct in the moonlight, he
alerted the men of 'X' Troop of the 11th Special Air Service
Battalion and they dropped, landing close to the target. Four
of the other crews landed near the target, which was destroyed.

The withdrawal plan for the troops failed, however, and
they were all captured. Although the raid was a strategic failure, it demonstrated that the Allies could strike deep into enemy territory and it forced the Italians to divert manpower to
guard other major assets. The raid completed Lashbrook's tour
on operations and he was awarded the DFM.

Wallace Ivor Lashbrook was born at Chilsworthy, Devon
on January 3, 1913 and educated at Okehampton Grammar
School. He joined the RAF in January 1929 as an aircraft
apprentice: he excelled at his trade and at sport. He graduated
in the top 20 of an entry of 500 and was awarded first prize
for the best aero-engine fitter. He boxed for the RAF as a
bantamweight.

After three years at RAF Halton he joined No. 204 Squadron
operating flying boats from Mountbatten near Plymouth. He
became friendly with an Aircraftman Ross (an assumed name of
Lawrence of Arabia) and they worked together servicing their
respective Brough Superior motorcycles. In 1934 Lashbrook
left for the Far East and served in Singapore for three years.

In August 1936 he trained as a sergeant pilot. After a spell
flying Hendon bombers with No. 38 Squadron, he spent
three years as a ferry pilot and amassed 2,000 hours' flying
time on a variety of aircraft. As war clouds gathered he joined
No. 51 Squadron to fly Whitley bombers based at Dishforth
in Yorkshire.

He flew his first raid on September 9, 1940 as a co-pilot; a
flight that almost ended in disaster when the crew became lost
over the sea. Over the next six months he flew a further 28

operations including raids on Milan and Turin in addition to targets in Germany.

After the commando raid in Italy, Lashbrook joined No. 35 Squadron, the first RAF squadron to be equipped with the four-engine Halifax. After a brief demonstration flight on the new aircraft, he flew his first raid. Returning from Kiel, the aircraft suffered a major fuel failure, which resulted in all four engines stopping. In the darkness, Lashbrook managed to crash-land the aircraft into a field with the seven-man crew suffering only minor injuries.

After 18 months as a bombing instructor, Lashbrook was promoted to squadron leader and joined No. 102 Squadron, also flying the Halifax. His second operation was to bomb the Skoda Works at Pilsen in Czechoslovakia. On the return flight his Halifax was attacked near the French-Belgian border by a German night-fighter and set on fire. The rear gunner was killed but the rest of the crew baled out. Lashbrook landed seconds after his parachute opened. It was 4 a.m. on April 17, 1943.

After three days of walking into France, he called at a remote farmhouse where he was fed and sheltered. He was hidden for six days before being moved, unaware that he was in the hands of the Belgian-run Comet Line. He was led to a safe house in Paris before a courier arrived to take him by train to the south-west via Bordeaux. At Gare du Sud he was astonished to meet up with his bomb aimer who was with an American pilot.

The three were taken to Dax before cycling to St Jean-de-Luz near the Spanish border. They were hidden in the last house at Urrugne, where the veteran Basque guide Florentino met them and took them overnight across the mountains into Spain; after the war Florentino was awarded the George Medal.

Once in Spain, the team were taken to San Sebastian then to Madrid and Gibraltar before flying home. Lashbrook had been on the run for two months and shortly after his return was awarded the DFC. He was also mentioned in despatches for his successful evasion.

It was policy that escaping aircrew would not fly over occupied Europe again so Lashbrook became a test pilot at the Central Flying School. He flew many different types including the new jet fighter, the Meteor. On one flight both engines failed and he had to glide the crippled aircraft to a safe landing. Shortly afterwards he was awarded the AFC.

He was released from the RAF in September 1946 when he became a civilian test pilot before joining the airline Skyways as its chief pilot. He stopped flying in 1953.

For 20 years he was an officer with the Ayrshire Army Cadet Force retiring in 1966 when he was appointed MBE.

Lashbrook was a devoted member of the RAF Escaping Society and its successor the Escape Lines Memorial Society, attending annual reunions until late in his life. He made a number of visits to France to meet those who had helped him and they and their relatives remain in close contact with his family. On his 100th birthday he was presented with his Bomber Command clasp to add to his wartime medals.

Wally Lashbrook married Betty Young in 1938 and she pre-deceased him. They had two daughters.

AIR VICE-MARSHAL TED HAWKINS

Air Vice-Marshal Ted Hawkins, (who died on October 22, 2017 aged 97) was twice awarded the DFC for maritime patrol and anti-submarine operations during the Second World War.

After a winter of flying Catalina flying boats on Atlantic patrols and anti-U-boat sorties with No. 240 Squadron, Hawkins was tasked to carry out a top-secret reconnaissance to obtain information about the sea ice between Jan

Mayen Island and Spitsbergen Island in the high Arctic. He was also to report on the state of ice conditions in the fjords of West Spitsbergen and to determine if enemy forces were on the island.

Two passengers accompanied him and his crew when the aircraft left the Shetland Islands on April 4, 1942. One was the Norwegian Captain Einar Sverdrup, who knew the area well, and the second was Lieutenant Commander Alexander Glen, an experienced Arctic explorer who would later land on the island to conduct clandestine operations.

Flying through severe weather en route, they were greeted by brilliant sunshine when they reached the edge of the ice to complete their reconnaissance before heading for Spitsbergen. They saw no evidence of the enemy and were able to confirm that sea conditions were suitable for flying boat operations. On return to the Shetlands after a flight of 2,000 miles the crew had been airborne for over 24 hours. Hawkins and his navigator were both awarded the DFC. The citation concluded: "These officers showed great powers of endurance and their outstanding performance is worthy of the highest praise."

The son of a master mariner in both sail and steam, Desmond Ernest Hawkins, always known as Ted, was born on December 12, 1919 at Loughton in Essex and was educated at Bancroft's School.

Leaving school in 1937, he started work as an insurance clerk, but resigned after three weeks. Walking home, he chanced to meet an MP who was also the colonel of the 3rd Battalion of the London Irish Rifles of the Territorial Army. Inviting him to join as a rifleman, the colonel recruited him to undertake an undercover intelligence-gathering mission in Germany, Austria and Czechoslovakia during the winter months of 1937-38. The mission was to infiltrate the Hitler Youth Movement, which could be achieved quite openly by joining the British Youth Hostel organisation, which was affiliated to the Wanderschaft of the Hitler Movement. After formal briefings, Hawkins was taken to Aachen to begin his 'long walk' of almost 2,000 miles to Austria, Czechoslovakia and on to Berlin, using German youth hostels and fraternising with the Hitler Youth organisation along the way.

His adventures included sketching Krupps armament works by moonlight, attending a mass rally in Cologne addressed by Hitler himself, being questioned by the suspicious Gestapo (who failed to find the drawings in the lining of his rucksack) and being entertained and debriefed by British ambassadors in Innsbruck and Berlin. He was then taken by car to Hamburg to join a British cargo ship arriving in London to be debriefed at the end of January 1938.

Two months later he joined the RAF on a short-service commission and trained as a pilot before being assigned to No. 1 Anti-Aircraft Co-operation Unit flying a variety of aircraft acting as targets for anti-aircraft units. After attending a specialist reconnaissance course, he converted to flying boats before joining No. 240 Squadron based in Northern Ireland in September 1941.

After the Arctic sortie the squadron was ordered to Madras to open up a new base. Four aircraft, including Hawkins', were detained at Gibraltar in June 1942 to carry out anti-submarine patrols in support of the convoys sailing to Malta.

On June 6 he spotted a surfaced U-boat near the Balearic Islands and he dived to attack. Avoiding heavy anti-aircraft fire he dropped four depth charges. The submarine submerged leaving a large pool of oil on the sea. It soon resurfaced and was observed settling by the stern. Its crew began to arrive on deck as others jumped into the sea. Shortly after, the Italian U-boat *Zaffiro* sank. Hawkins decided to land to pick up survivors and leave life-saving equipment but the heavy swell damaged the Catalina's hull and he was forced to abandon his rescue attempt and return to Gibraltar. For this attack he was awarded a Bar to his DFC.

Having returned the patched-up aircraft to the UK for repair, Hawkins and his crew were sent to assist the scattered Archangel convoy PQ 17, going on to alight at Murmansk. From there they joined the hunt for survivors and for the *Tirpitz* and its escorts – a task he regarded as near suicidal in an aircraft as slow as the Catalina.

A month later, he set off to re-join his squadron in Madras. From August 1942 to October 1944 he flew on convoy escort duties, anti-submarine patrols and special duty operations including dropping agents along the coasts of Burma and Malaya. He was mentioned in despatches.

After a spell on the air staff in Ceylon, he took command of No. 230 Squadron in Singapore flying the Sunderland on relief operations to isolated garrisons in New Guinea and to repatriate sick POWs and Dutch internees from Malaya and Java to hospitals in India.

In April 1946 he returned to England to command the flying boat base in Pembrokeshire before taking charge of the Maritime Aircraft Experimental Establishment at Felixstowe. He was later in charge of administration at RAF Kinloss in Morayshire, one of the RAF's largest maritime air bases.

He left for Malta in January 1955 to command No. 38 Squadron equipped with Shackletons. For his services during the Suez crisis he was again mentioned in despatches.

After attending the Joint Services Staff College and a tour on the plans staff in the Air Ministry, Hawkins returned to the maritime world as the senior air staff officer at No. 19 (Maritime) Group in Plymouth. In 1964 he took command of RAF Tengah, the RAF's largest operational base in the Far East – the station complement was some 15,000 people. His Strike Wing of Canberra, Hunter and Javelin squadrons were heavily involved during the Indonesian Confrontation campaign. At the end of his tour he was appointed CBE.

On promotion to air commodore in 1968 he commanded the RAF's large air transport base at Lyneham when he collected the RAF's last Hercules C-130K aircraft from the Lockheed factory in the USA.

As an air vice-marshal he was the senior air staff officer at HQ RAF Strike Command at a time when a new generation of combat aircraft were being introduced into service. He was appointed CB in June 1971.

Hawkins spent the last three years of his service before

retiring in July 1974 as the director general of Personnel Services (RAF) in the MoD. He then joined the Services Kinema Corporation as the deputy managing director, a post he held for six years.

He retired to Lymington in 1981 where he continued to enjoy his lifelong love of sailing. He was a committee member, captain of cruising, vice commodore and finally a trustee of the Royal Lymington Yacht Club.

A quietly confident but unpretentious and approachable man, Hawkins was liked and respected by his subordinates to whom he always showed great loyalty. One of his squadron commanders at Tengah commented: "Most of those serving under him at that time admit that it was one of their happiest tours."

Ted Hawkins married Joan Holford, an ex-WAAF officer, in 1947 who was widowed in 1942. She died in 2015. They had a son who pre-deceased him.

GROUP CAPTAIN JOHNNIE FOSTER

Group Captain Johnnie Foster (who died on October 30, 2017 aged 95) spent the majority of his long service in the RAF as a fighter pilot and earned a DFC for his support of operations off the Norwegian coast.

In late 1944 Coastal Command's strike wings of Mosquitos and Beaufighters based on the Moray Firth made concentrated attacks against enemy convoys carrying Swedish iron-ore to Germany and shipped from Norwegian ports. The Luftwaffe's fighter squadrons based in Norway and Denmark posed a serious threat to these operations, so it was decided to escort the strikes with long-range fighters. Foster was the flight commander of No. 65 Squadron when it was transferred to Peterhead with US-built Mustangs to fulfil this role.

When shipping was identified off the Norwegian coast, formations of up to 36 strike aircraft were launched, with Foster and his pilots providing an escort. The Luftwaffe countered with fighters and on February 9, 1945, forever known as 'Black Friday', they intercepted the large force as the strike wings attempted to attack shipping in the narrow Førde Fjord. Despite the intervention of Foster and his pilots, nine Beaufighters and a Mustang were lost. The Mustangs shot down four enemy fighters.

During another fierce engagement on March 25, the CO of No. 65, Squadron Leader Grahame Stewart, was shot down and Foster was promoted to take command of the squadron. Operations intensified and towards the end of April and in early May, U-boats attempting to escape from the Skagerrak were attacked. He led 12 of his Mustangs escorting the strike wings on May 2 when U-2359 was sunk on the east coast of Denmark and two days later they protected the strike wings on their last operation of the war. A week later, Foster was awarded the DFC.

The son of a doctor, John Watson Foster was born in Belfast on August 1, 1922 and attended Campbell College before entering Queen's University to study Medicine. After one year he volunteered to be a pilot in the RAF.

After training in Canada, he returned to the UK to convert to the Spitfire before joining No. 19 Squadron in April 1942, based in the south of England. Over the next few months he flew many sweeps over northern France in support of formations of light bombers attacking targets in the region.

The squadron was heavily engaged during Operation

Jubilee, the raid on Dieppe on August 19, 1942. During one sortie, Foster's aircraft was hit by anti-aircraft fire when he was wounded in the leg but he managed to return safely.

Throughout 1943 Foster was in constant action and had amassed over 600 hours flying time on Spitfires when he was rested to be a flying instructor. In April 1944 he converted to the Mustang long-range fighter. In September, he was posted as a flight commander to No. 65 Squadron, flying from air-fields in Norfolk, escorting bomber formations, before it was sent to Peterhead in north Scotland.

In late May 1945 the squadron returned to Norfolk for peacetime operations. By the time Foster left a year later he had accumulated 600 hours flying the Mustang having also been mentioned in despatches.

One week after he was married in September 1946, he left for the Far East to join the British Commonwealth Occupa-tion Force in Japan as an intelligence officer. He returned in June 1948 to fly Spitfires and Hornets before converting to the Meteor jet fighter. In July 1949 he took command of No. 263 Squadron at an airfield near Norwich.

At the time, the RAF did not have a permanently estab-lished aerobatic team and Fighter Command squadrons com-peted annually to represent the RAF. Foster built a team and it was selected for the 1950 season when it performed at many air shows including Farnborough. The first display he led was in front of King George VI and Princess Elizabeth. A year later he took command of No. 257 Squadron, also flying the Me-teor. He held the post for two years and in June 1952 he was awarded the AFC.

After two years at HQ Fighter Command, Foster left for Egypt to command the flying wing at Abu Sueir in November 1955. With the breakdown of relations between the UK and Egypt, RAF forces redeployed to Cyprus with Abu Sueir being the last RAF base to close in April 1956. The squadrons moved to Nicosia, where Foster assumed command of the flying wing. For his services during the Suez crisis (Operation Musketeer) in November 1956 he was mentioned in despatches.

In 1959 Foster served in the operations department of the Air Ministry before joining the staff of the Joint Warfare Establishment. For three years he served on the air staff of the Allied Air Forces Central Europe as a group captain and in June 1969 he was appointed to command RAF Church Fenton near York, the home of one of the RAF's main pilot training schools, where he took every opportunity to fly.

He spent three years as the air attaché in Rome before retiring from the RAF in September 1975.

He was a single handicap golfer who played well into his 80s.

Johnnie Foster's wife Mary died in 2016, just five months short of their 70th wedding anniversary.

JOY LOFTHOUSE

Joy Lofthouse (who died on November 15, 2017 aged 94) was one of the last two surviving 'Spitfire Girls' who flew the great Second World War fighter whilst serving with the Air Transport Auxiliary (ATA).

The ATA was established in 1939, responsible for delivering aircraft from factories to RAF units. Over the course of the war it delivered 309,000 of 147 different types, ranging from light training aircraft to heavy four-engine bombers. Pilots flew each type after a short briefing using a basic checklist and without any radio aids. Weather was their worst enemy.

In the summer of 1943, the sports-mad 20-year-old Joy and her elder sister Yvonne, whose bomber pilot husband had recently been killed over Berlin, answered an advert for pilots to join the ATA. The two applied with 2,000 others and just 17 were accepted, including the sisters. Neither had any flying experience and Joy had never driven a car.

Living in Cirencester, she had been drawn to aviation because the town was close to numerous airfields and she had met many young pilots. In later life she recalled: "I wanted to keep up, know more about what the boys in uniform talked

about. That's why I started reading *Aeroplane* magazine. You couldn't just stand there, useless, dumb, when the boys were talking about planes."

The sisters were amongst the first *ab initio* pilots to be trained by the ATA's own flying school at Thame near Oxford. Joy flew solo after 12 hours of dual instruction and, after completing her training, remained at Thame to ferry light aircraft such as the Tiger Moth and Magister from factories to

RAF flying schools. She then joined the all-female ferry pool at Hamble near Southampton, close to various aircraft manufacturers, including the Supermarine factory where Spitfires were built.

Over the next two years she flew 18 different types of aircraft, the majority single-engined aircraft. She delivered naval fighters to airfields in Scotland and during the run up to D-Day she was busy taking Typhoons, Tempests and Spitfires to squadrons on the south coast. Her favourite was the Spitfire, and she delivered more than 50 of them. She described it as "an iconic plane", and sitting in it was "like wearing a well-fitting dress". By the end of the war, Joy had converted to flying light twin-engine aircraft.

The two young women were the only sisters to fly with the ATA and were amongst the 164 female pilots who flew with the organisation. They were the forgotten women who broke through the barriers of male domination to fly fighters. Decades later their example would inspire many women to join the RAF and fly combat aircraft.

Joyce Gough, always known as Joy, was born in Cirencester on February 14, 1923 and educated at Cirencester Grammar School, after which she worked as a cashier in the local Lloyd's Bank until she saw the advert in *Aeroplane* and joined the ATA.

She left the ATA in September 1945 and never flew as a pilot again. She became a schoolteacher and brought up her family.

Throughout her life she remained in contact with her ATA friends and attended reunions. With seven of her wartime friends she was invited to the RAF's Officer and Aircrew Selection Centre at Biggin Hill in May 1990 to meet the first female candidates aspiring to become RAF pilots. She later wrote to the commandant: "Our visit to Biggin Hill brought back many happy memories – we were all made to feel young again for a short while."

Joy Lofthouse was a vivacious, adventurous and eloquent lady who was in demand as a guest on radio, at air shows and other events. In 2010 her sister visited from the USA and they were guests at the Kemble Air Day near Cirencester when the two were reunited with a Spitfire, the first time they had been together with the fighter since the war.

In 2015, at the age of 92, Joy took to the air again in a Spitfire, the first time she had flown in the aircraft for 70 years. Flying from Goodwood in a dual-control version of the fighter she professed to be "not as confident as I was when I used to fly them alone when I was young". After the flight she said: "It was lovely. It was perfect." The video of her flight became an internet sensation.

In July 2016 she was invited to take a seat in the Royal Box of Wimbledon's Centre Court together with other celebrities, and when she was introduced to the crowd she received a prolonged ovation.

Her role in the ATA and that of her fellow 'Spitfire Girls' was largely overlooked until in 2008 the prime minister, Gordon Brown, was persuaded to honour them with a commemorative badge. She told friends with a whimsical smile on her face: "For 60 years nobody asked me about my wartime job, but for the past 10 I've been dining out on it."

Joy Lofthouse married Jiri Hartman, a Czech fighter pilot, in 1945 and the marriage ended in divorce. In 1971 she married Squadron Leader Charles Lofthouse, a former Pathfinder Lancaster pilot, who died in 2002. She had a son and a daughter from her first marriage. Her other son from her second marriage predeceased her.

DUNCAN SIMPSON

Duncan Simpson (who died on December 5, 2017 aged 89) was one of the country's most distinguished test pilots. He played key roles in the development of the Hunter fighter, the Harrier vertical and short take-off and landing (V/STOL) ground-attack aircraft and the Hawk advanced trainer flown by the RAF's Red Arrows.

Simpson's long association with the Harrier began on August 25, 1962 when he made his first flight in the fourth prototype of the Hawker P.1127, the forerunner to the iconic V/STOL fighter. In an attempt to secure a collaborative agreement with the USA and Germany to finance the project, a British-American-German Tripartite Evaluation Squadron was formed at RAF West Raynham in Norfolk.

As a former RAF fighter pilot who had served at the Air Fighting Development Unit, Simpson was chosen to conduct the training of the 10 members of the squadron whose task was to perfect tactics and capabilities of the revolutionary jet, now given the name Kestrel.

Over the next few years Simpson conducted many test flights on the Kestrel, which was named Harrier by the RAF. He flew the first production Harrier GR 1 on December 27, 1967. In January 1969, by now Hawker Siddeley's deputy chief test pilot, he was responsible for training the first four RAF pilots to fly the Harrier.

Based at the company's Dunsfold airfield, the conversion course to the vertical take-off and landing aircraft had to be conducted without the use of a dual-control version. The four pilots practised hovering in a helicopter before making their first flight in a Harrier. Simpson passed instructions from the control tower and after eight sorties each, the four pilots left for their base at RAF Wittering to start converting the pilots of No. 1 Squadron.

The company developed a two-seat trainer version of the

Harrier and Simpson made the first flight of the prototype on April 24, 1969. Six weeks later, on June 4, the Pegasus engine of the aircraft failed at 3,000 feet. Simpson made numerous attempts to relight it as he headed for Boscombe Down, but all attempts failed and he turned towards the open country at Larkhill military range. At 100 ft he was forced to eject landing close to the burning wreckage, having been severely injured. He was taken by helicopter to Tidworth Hospital, where it was discovered that he had broken his neck as the ejector seat burst through the aircraft's canopy.

Simpson needed a bone graft and the surgeons had to carry out the challenging procedure by entering via his throat. For the rest of his life he spoke with a gravel-like tone and returned to test-flying nine months later. For his attempts to save the prototype he was awarded a Queen's Commendation for Valuable Service in the Air.

Duncan Menzies Souter Simpson was born on December 23, 1927 in Edinburgh and educated at Merchiston School. His enthusiasm for flying was fired when he saw Alan Cobham's Flying Circus and by his uncle who was a test pilot for Fairey Aviation.

After leaving school in 1945, with no demand for new RAF pilots, he began studies at the de Havilland Technical School at Hatfield, where he went from the training workshops into the experimental department working on the development of the early jet fighters and the prototype Comet airliner. He graduated in 1949 when he joined the RAF and trained as a pilot.

He flew Meteor fighters with No. 222 Squadron and in 1953 joined the Day Fighter Development Unit at the RAF's Central Fighter Establishment conducting trials on the latest fighters to enter RAF service including the Hawker Hunter. In 1954 Hawker's chief test pilot, Neville Duke, invited him to join the company. Simpson left the RAF and began his long association with the Kingston-based company.

He began as a production test pilot, mainly on the Hunter, before becoming more involved in development work when he made a significant contribution to the great success of the aircraft. This was followed by his close involvement in the revolutionary V/STOL programme, which culminated in the Harrier.

Once he returned to flying after his serious accident, he became the company's chief test pilot. He monitored the Hawk training aircraft from the drawing board to its first flight, which he made on August 21, 1974, just 10 days before demonstrating it at the Farnborough Air Show. He delivered the first Hawk to the RAF in 1976 where it has served as an advanced trainer and with the Red Arrows for over 40 years.

He was particularly proud of the Hawk, which started as a private company enterprise and was to be Hawker Siddeley's last project at Kingston. The performance of the advanced trainer exceeded expectations and was delivered on time and on cost. He had doubts that this could have been achieved had it been a collaborative programme.

In 1978 he retired from test-flying but continued to make a major contribution to the aviation world. He remained with Hawker Siddeley and took charge of Harrier and Hawk service liaison until the late 1980s. For 15 years he was the deputy director of the Society of British Aerospace Companies (SBAC) with responsibility for all exhibitions, including the world-renowned Farnborough Air Show.

For many years he flew and displayed some of Hawker's most famous fighters including the Hart bi-plane, the Hurricane and the Sea Fury. Acutely conscious of flight safety at air shows, he was a co-founder of the Historic Aircraft Association, which monitored safety and he was a strong supporter of the aviation museums at Brooklands and at Tangmere.

Simpson received many honours for his work as a test pilot. He was appointed OBE in 1973. In 2011 the Guild of Air Pilots and Air Navigators (GAPAN) awarded him the Guild Award of Honour in recognition of his "outstanding lifetime contribution to aviation". He had already received the Guild's Derry Richard Medal and the Alston Medal of the Royal Aeronautical Society, of which he was a Fellow. He was also a

Fellow of the Society of Experimental Test Pilots and of the Institute of Mechanical Engineers. In 2002 he was Master of GAPAN. A great enthusiast for all flying issues, he was stimulating company and in regular demand for speaking engagements and attendance at aviation events.

Duncan Simpson married Pat Jones in June 1958 with whom he had two sons and a daughter.

AIR CHIEF MARSHAL SIR PETER TERRY

Air Chief Marshal Sir Peter Terry (who died on December 19, 2017 aged 91) was the governor of Gibraltar when he authorised a security operation that resulted in the shooting of three members of the Irish Republican Army (IRA); in September 1990, he survived a revenge attack on his life.

After a long and distinguished career in the RAF, Terry was appointed as the governor and commander-in-chief in Gibraltar in November 1985. In late 1987 British intelligence detected that the IRA were planning an attack in Gibraltar, most probably at the changing of the guard ceremony outside the governor's residence.

Three IRA members were tracked to Malaga in Spain and in early March 1988 they crossed into Gibraltar with a car mistakenly thought to contain a bomb. On March 6 Terry authorised the local police and a team of SAS personnel to pursue and arrest them as part of Operation Flavius. In the event, the three terrorists were shot and killed.

On September 18, 1990 Terry was reading in a downstairs room in his house in Staffordshire. The curtains were partly open when a gunman fired some 20 shots through the window. Nine bullets hit him shattering his jaw and with two lodged in his skull close to his brain. He was also wounded in his side and left leg. His wife Betty suffered an eye injury, which later affected her sight. Their daughter, who was also at home, was uninjured but deeply shocked.

Prime Minister Margaret Thatcher said she was "utterly appalled and deeply grieved". Interviewed by the *Daily Telegraph* while her husband was recovering, Lady Terry spoke about the "wonderful" floral tributes and letters the family received, many from Ireland.

Terry spent many months recovering from his injuries and later led a very private life before moving to a new home in Buckinghamshire.

Peter David George Terry was born on October 18, 1926 at Ramsgate and was educated at Chatham House Grammar School. He enlisted into the RAF in late 1944 but was not called up until September 1945. Initially he served as an airman before being commissioned into the RAF Regiment.

In December 1948 he joined one of the Regiment's Light Anti-Aircraft Artillery squadrons in Germany providing air defence for RAF airfields. After three years he became the personal staff officer to the commandant general of the RAF Regiment.

In June 1953 Terry started training as a pilot and two years later joined No. 79 Squadron flying the Swift in the tactical reconnaissance and ground-attack role from airfields in Germany. He was soon identified as able to take more responsibility and was sent to complete the pilot attack instructor's (PAI) course, in which he came top, being awarded the Leconfield Trophy, a rare achievement for such an inexperienced pilot and in such a demanding role. This was soon followed by his appointment as a flight commander. At the end of his tour he was awarded a Queen's Commendation for Valuable Service in the Air (QCVSA).

He attended the Central Flying School and trained as a flying instructor before taking command of a jet training squadron at the RAF College Cranwell. After two years he was awarded a second QCVSA.

His attendance at RAF Staff College was followed by almost three years in the plans division of the RAF's Far East Air Force based in Singapore. During a busy tour, he was heavily involved in developing plans to support operations during the period of Indonesian Confrontation.

On his return to the UK in 1966 he assumed command of No. 51 Squadron equipped with Canberra and Comet aircraft specially adapted for gathering electronic and signals intelligence, operations described in those days as "long-range calibration" sorties. At the end of his tour he was awarded the AFC.

On promotion to group captain he was sent to command the large staging post and airfield at El Adem in Libya. RAF squadrons were also detached to the base for training on the local bombing and gunnery ranges. After the *coup d'état*, led by Colonel Muammar Gaddafi on September 1, 1969, Terry began plans to withdraw the RAF from El Adem. At a ceremony on March 28, 1970 he handed back the base and associated ranges to the Libyan authorities, bringing to an end the British military occupation of airfields on the North African littoral, which dated from the days of the Royal Flying Corps.

Terry's return from Libya signalled the beginning of a series of high-profile appointments in MoD, overseas and in NATO. Following a period as director of Forward Plans (RAF) he became assistant chief of staff (Plans and Policy) at Supreme Headquarters Allied Powers Europe (SHAPE), an appointment filled by the RAF's most capable officers and those destined for senior posts in the service.

On his return to the UK in 1977 he became the vice-chief of the air staff responsible for the operational and planning aspects of the RAF at a time when the service was adjusting to some heavy cuts and dealing with problems on service pay. These coincided with the introduction of the strike version of the Tornado, the purchase of Chinook helicopters and the development of the ill-fated Nimrod airborne early warning aircraft.

In April 1979, Terry returned to Europe when he was appointed the commander-in-chief RAF Germany and commander Second Allied Tactical Air Force. His RAF and Allied squadrons were in the midst of a major aircraft re-equipment programme and there was great emphasis on his airbases' ability to survive any pre-emptive attack. This included the construction of hardened aircraft and operations facilities and enhanced air- and ground-defence capabilities.

After a brief period as the deputy commander-in-chief at HQ Allied Forces Central Europe, Terry was expected by some of his contemporaries to be in line for the RAF's top appointment as chief of the air staff. One of them commented: "He was the best CAS we never had." However, with his wide experience, NATO had need of him and he became the deputy supreme allied commander Europe, a post he held for three years. He left the RAF in October 1984 and a year later became the governor of Gibraltar, retiring four years later.

He was appointed GCB (1983), KCB (1978) and CB (1975). In May 2006, after a wait of almost a quarter of a century, Terry was one of seven of Britain's most distinguished military officers who were finally installed before the Queen at Westminster Abbey as Knights Grand Cross of the Most Honourable Order of the Bath. Although they had been granted their knighthoods (GCB) in the 1980s, the longevity of previous holders of the honour had made the waiting list for one of the coveted 34 stalls set aside for the most senior knights unusually long.

Terry possessed a great intellect but was a private, unassuming and modest man. A colleague said of him, "his tact, manner and diplomacy were unrivalled". Throughout his long public life, Terry received great support from his wife Betty, none more so than during the long months of recovery following the attempt on his life.

He was a stalwart of his local church and played golf until late in his life when the effects from his leg wound began to limit his mobility.

Peter Terry married Betty Thompson in 1946 and they had two sons and a daughter. Their elder son predeceased him.

INDEX OF PERSONALITIES
(Italics denotes main entry)

NOTES

NOTES

NOTES

NOTES

NOTES